Losing Ground

Losing Ground

Reading Ruth in the Pacific

Jione Havea

scm press

© Jione Havea 2021

Published in 2021 by SCM Press
Editorial office
3rd Floor, Invicta House,
108–114 Golden Lane,
London EC1Y 0TG, UK
www.scmpress.co.uk

SCM Press is an imprint of Hymns Ancient & Modern Ltd
(a registered charity)

Hymns Ancient & Modern® is a registered trademark of
Hymns Ancient & Modern Ltd
13A Hellesdon Park Road, Norwich,
Norfolk NR6 5DR, UK

British Library Cataloguing in Publication data

A catalogue record for this book is available
from the British Library

ISBN 978-0-334-05983-7

Typeset by Regent Typesetting
Printed and bound by
CPI Group (UK) Ltd

Contents

Acknowledgement

Work on this book was supported by the Council for World Mission through its Dare (discernment and radical engagement) programme

Preface

The Ruth narrative opens with a biblical version of climate crisis – there was a famine in Judah's storehouse (Bethlehem, house of bread), to which a family responded by migrating, seeking asylum. This family would have crossed both land and water as many refugees do today in seeking asylum – because Moab was on the other side of the Dead Sea, and the Jordan and Arnon rivers were on the way.

In the unfolding of the narrative, some of the topics of critical concern to climate refugees (despite international law not recognizing 'climate' as a category among refugees) are addressed – for example, security in terms of food, home, land and inheritance. Around those topics, this book offers a collection of bible studies on the Ruth narrative in and from Pasifika (the Pacific Islands, Oceania) that interweave climate change with climate trauma, climate grief, climate resilience and climate injustice.

Flow of the book

This book flows over three clusters of chapters. It begins with a welcome in Part 1, offers native insights in Part 2, and closes with invitations in Part 3.

Part 1: Welcoming Ruth. The first two chapters situate this work in the contexts of key concerns in the studies of Ruth (Chapter 1), and in the culture and spirit of *talanoa* (Chapter 2). Talanoa is a word used in several (but not all) Pasifika islands to name three *oral(izing) events* – story, telling (of stories), and conversation (or weaving of stories and tellings).

These events are interdependent: a story comes alive in its telling(s) and the conversation(s) it sparks; a telling has content when it has a story, and both the story and the telling grow when conversation ensues; and a conversation makes sense when it involves both story and telling(s), and erupts into more stories, more tellings and more conversations. Story (talanoa), telling (talanoa) and conversation (talanoa) are like veins in the oral(izing) cultures of native Pasifika – they keep Pasifika ticking. And ticking.

Part 2: Pasifika Bible Studies. Chapters 3 to 9 present readings of the Ruth narrative over 20 bible studies. The bible studies are clusters of stories, tellings, conversations and invitations for further talanoa. These studies keep the 'big talanoa' (see Chapter 2) of Ruth ticking. And ticking.

Part 3: Interpretation Prolongs. With the spirit of talanoa and the wisdom of native people, the book closes with two chapters that look back over the tasks of interpretation. Chapter 10 invites readers to read with humility, and Chapter 11 encourages acclimatization. In the end, this book is also about attitudes. Perspectives help readers see (or not see), and feelings help readers sense (or not sense) (see Black and Koosed, 2019); this work adds attitudes and personalities to the concoction that helps readers tick (or not tick).

Pasifika bible studies

The insights that shaped this work were gleaned from bible studies on Ruth – referred to as Pasifika bible studies (PBS) in the following chapters – that i[1] conducted at Pasifika communities in 2019–20: Solomon Islands (Munda, Simbo, Gizo), Fiji (Suva), Nauru (Boe), Ma'ohi Nui French Polynesia (Tahiti, Raiatea, Tahaa, Bora Bora), Tonga (Tongatapu, 'Eua), Aotearoa New Zealand (Auckland, Gisborne), Australia (Adelaide, South Australia; Portarlington, Victoria; Parklea and Bankstown, New South Wales). To members of these communities, *vinaka vakalevu* (many thanks) for your wisdom, hospitality and generosity. The work on this book was supported by the Dare

(Discernment and radical engagement) programme of the Council for World Mission, thanks to the courage and kindness of Sudipta Singh.

The bible studies are drawn from and intended for *normal readers* – by which i mean those who may not have undertaken western, formal or theological education, but are critical thinkers who open up the interpretive limits. This work is for normal readers who have the courage – to borrow the responses of two participants to the question 'How far did Ruth go?' – to see Ruth going 'up way, down way, around way and even all the way' (Rosa Manueli) because 'it is not fun to go halfway' (Fuata Varea-Singh). With and for normal readers, this collection of bible studies invites going *all the way* in terms of ideologies and efforts.

While the PBS gatherings were initiated and framed by climate change, the participants read the Ruth narrative in other ways as well. Normal readers will find other interests that are woven into this work. And, obviously, the book *does not* represent all the diverse views of people in Pasifika. I did not glean information from all the islands and cultures in the region, but this collection offers a feel for how *islander criticism* unfolds in Pasifika.

As a process for engaging with the PBS bible studies, i invite readers (preferably in a bible study setting) to:

- read the text twice (a preferred translation, and my translation provided)
- reflect on the PBS bible studies, and be free to push back with alternative readings
- reflect on the 'Takeaway' questions (endorsing a Pasifika joke, about people who attend events to take away leftovers for later consumption – a modern form of gleaning)
- explore the 'Prompts for further talanoa', and
- most importantly, allow time and the reflections to flow.

Note

1 I use the lowercase for the first-person when 'i' am the subject, because i also use the lower case for 'you', 'she', 'he', 'they', 'it', 'we' and 'others'. The privileging (by capitalization) of the first-person singular is foreign to Pasifika native worldviews.

Glossary

(The Pasifika terms are italicized at their first occurrence, or when an emphasis or a pun is intended.)

ali'i nui	high chief
'eiki	noble
'ele'ele	land, blood
enga	yellowish-brown (colour of dead leaves)
fakafolau	punishment: person put in a canoe, taken to the open sea where holes are punched into the canoe and then set adrift
fale	house
falesi'i	little house, outhouse
faletua	backhouse, outhouse, wife of minister
fiepālagi	wannabe white, European (*also*: fiepālangi)
fie'eiki	wannabe noble
fākafoa	weep, shatter, fracture
fanua	land, people, culture, tradition, earth
fenua	*see* fanua
fonua	*see* fanua
gogo	black noddy birds
hapu	clan
hiku	tail end
kāimumu'a	know-it-all, speak out of turn
kainga	land, relation, relative (iKiribati)
kaupapa	communal purposes, practices, ways
lagi	sky (*also*: langi)
lei	garland
lolofonua	underworld (*also*: lalotai)
loto	inside, soul, heart
mana	power, magic, energy

marae	gathering ground, ceremonial site
mata	green (colour); eyes, face
moana	sea, ocean
moulu	gentle
nuu	village
pākehā	pālagi
pālagi	white, European (*also*: pālangi)
paopao	canoe
pikopiko iku mai	going round and around, and back to where it was
polopolo	harvest
pulotu	home of native deities
siolalo	shun, look down upon
sola	outsider
taari	sea, brother, sister (iKiribati)
talanoa	story, telling, conversation
tapu	sacred, whole, complete, taboo (*also*: tabu)
tāpuni	close
tekeroi	lift the ban
tepu	spur, spark
tui	head of clan, king
tuku'uta	field, backward, uncivilized
toktok	conversation
tolotolo	creep (in)
toutu'u	community plantation
'ulu	head
'Uluenga	hottest month (between November and December) in the Tongan calendar
vā	relationship
vanua	*see* fanua
ve'e tonu	luck, talented
wantok(s)	one-talk, people of one language, one family
whakapapa	ancestry lineage, family tree (*pronounced*: fakapapa)
whānau	family, relatives (*pronounced*: fānau)
whenua	*see* fanua (*pronounced*: fenua)

PART I

Welcoming Ruth

Ruth in contexts

[That the book of Ruth opens by] returning to the days of the judges dramatizes that the past is not a 'permanent landmark' set in stone; rather, it is a place that can be revisited, reconstructed, reimagined. If the past can be reimagined, then so can the present and the future. (Fewell, 2017, p. 27)

Ruth (narrative, book) has been lifted, homed and chased (away and after) from and for many contexts for a very long time. Almost, if not all, approaches to biblical criticism have been witnessed and redeemed on this narrative, and their harvests have been poured into the line(age)s of biblical scholarship as well as (through readers and their readings) into the lines, and into the gaps in-between the lines, of the Bible. Generations of readers have come out to glean for their own times and contexts, and to thresh and trade the insights and privileges of the dead. And still, this narrative has survived to (re)migrate and spawn among the living. Ruth (character, narrative, book) is not married off to the patriarchal project, nor carried under the wings of stealthy and threshing readers. Ruth (re)turns. Still.

Ruth (character) is not pronounced dead in a narrative that is alert to the interests of the dead. A narrative that seeks to keep some of the dead characters present, at least in name, did not at the end bury Ruth. Ruth survived the narrator's closing *whakapapa* (Māori for lineage) to find refuge in other fields and floors, other gates and towns, other witnesses and neighbours, other whakapapa and alternative communal purposes (Māori *kaupapa*).[1] In that afterlife, i wonder if Ruth could have wandered back to Moab. The gate of the town was not shut, and nothing was stopping Ruth from returning. To her whakapapa and her preferred kaupapa. At Moab. And. She. Found. Orpah. And so, how might one return to this narrative in the arms of Orpah?

My question looks in both directions, towards Ruth as well as towards Orpah. How might they welcome each other? And how might they, and we as readers, welcome characters whom the narrative and other readers have written off? Moreover, how might we welcome characters, within but also beyond the narrative, who are *losing ground*?

My questions fail the tests of historical and literary criticisms, but they draw attention to the politics of exegesis. Where and with whom one reads influence who and what one sees and hears in the text, as well as who and what one misses. Orpah and other minoritized characters are not seen because most exegetes read for the main characters and for events that sacred traditions endorse. Those readers assume that they are thereby faithful to the narrator (Amit, 2001, pp. 1–10) who must have been clear, sincere, reliable and straight. However, the eyes, presuppositions and orientations of those readers, like every other reader, are shaped by their own experiences, commitments and contexts. Those readers too are shaped by their whakapapa and kaupapa. At the same time, coming from the other direction, the experiences, commitments and contexts of readers can also blind and desensitize them. In other words, whakapapa and kaupapa also render readers blind.

The foregoing musings weave into a simple assertion: context matters in the reading of biblical texts. In the following sections, i circle around three contextual matters that shaped the readings presented in the bible studies in the following chapters: (1) Ruth in the canons; (2) Ruth among readers; (3) Ruth from contexts.

Ruth in the canons

The book of Ruth is included in two canons, but it is placed at different locations in those two Bibles. The two Bibles were canonized at different times for different communities and for different purposes, the historical and redactional analyses of which, and their implications, are outside of the drives of this work (on the narrative flow from Judges to 1 Samuel, which Ruth interrupts or transitions, see Jobling, 1998, pp. 28–37). Placed side by side, the two canons unmoor Ruth – so the story is not anchored to only one canonical context. That is to say that, in the canons, Ruth is not stuck with one agenda, one purpose, one duty, one people, one whakapapa, one kaupapa, or other ideas of one-ness.

Hebrew Bible

In the Hebrew Bible, Ruth is one of the five scrolls that make up the Megilloth (part of the Kethuvim, Writings) where it is located between Song of Songs and Lamentations. When i read Ruth after reading the poetic and erotic texts in the Song of Songs which express delight with the body and sexuality, i am incited to sex up my reading. But this incitement is more about flirting (with rhetoric) than permeating (with force). The tension between the deep longing of the lover (Song 2.10–17) and the out-of-reach-ness of the beloved (Song 3.1–3) invites flirting with, without succumbing to the temptation to control, the Ruth narrative.

In the Megilloth, Lamentations follows Ruth, grieving against an extreme example of control. Babylon has carried Jerusalem's leaders into exile, the neighbours stood by and offered no help, and readers of Ruth are turned back to wonder – could Ruth's 'return' to Bethlehem be an exile of some sort? Followed by the grief and despair expressed in Lamentations as a result of the destruction of Jerusalem (Lam. 1.1–6), the Hebrew Bible placement of Ruth invites me to take the matters of land and inheritance seriously. This coincides with my own activist leanings, and advocacy for lands and inheritances that have been unjustly taken. From ancient Canaan to modern Palestine and the bloody bootsteps of the Doctrine of Discovery, stampeding across Africa and America and all the way to Asia and Pasifika, i am attentive to the grabbing of (is)lands and the confiscation of native wealth and inheritance. I foreground these commitments in my reading of Ruth. But this does not mean that i stop sexing up the narrative, to the jingles of Song of Songs. Land and sex are complementing realities, and they do not have to be anchored upon the bodies of women. In other words, when land is gendered, as some languages require, it does not have to be female only.

In Pasifika the land is gendered (in our languages and perspectives) as both female and male. Like other indigenous cultures, natives of Pasifika relate to the land as our mother. She homes, nourishes and teaches us. As mother, the land is the primary carer of us. We also relate to the land as father because it homes and makes our ancestors (male and female) present. As father, the land connects us to those who have passed, to one another, to those who are to come, and to the circles of life around us. The land does not stop being mother in order for it to be father; in caring for us, the land teaches us how to care for others – past, present, and future – for our ancestors, for all our neighbours (and not just the human kind), and for the descendants of tomorrow. It is unfair to divide the functions that the land plays for us between mother and father, between female and male, because caring, raising, connecting and teaching interweave in one body – the land.

Our native rituals and links to the past run through the land. Without the land (or access to it), which extends into *moana* (the sea), we have no connection with our ancestors. It is therefore inadequate to only feminize the land; it is necessary also to name and acknowledge that the land is masculine as well. This bi-gender view interrogates the assumption that if the land is gendered then it can either be male or female. In Pasifika the land is gendered, and it is both male and female.[2] This bi-gender native view will be reflected in the following bible studies, in which matters that are usually taken to be only feminine or only masculine will be troubled.

The patriarchal project, which has been carried around the world in the arms of colonial and religious (including Christian) missions, feminizes the land to license its land- and blood-thirst. Patriarchal men and women take women and think that they have the right to also take the land; patriarchal men and women rape the land and think that they can also rape the women. The patriarchal project is driven by an agenda that is land and gender based – coloniality. To thwart the patriarchal agenda requires one to intervene at the intersection of land and gender. It is not enough to protest only against the taking of land without also protesting against the taking of women, and vice versa.

In the context of Pasifika, land is not a commodity to be taken and raped. To echo the cries of the indigenous Australian group Yothu Yindi, the land is not 40,000 dollars or more but 40,000 years of culture and more (Yothu Yindi, 'Gone is the land', 2000). Against the colonization of Australia, Yothu Yindi is adamant in 'Treaty' (1991) that the land was never ceded, and never sold and bought. And, most critically,

> The planting of the Union Jack
> Never changed our law at all.

Protest against coloniality is alive and strong in the so-called secular society of Australia. The ongoing struggles of indigenous Australians are shared by other native Pasifika groups whose (is)lands and minds are still under occupation by the foreign governments of the USA, France, Chile and Indonesia. I rage against these injustices in my daily life, and my rage manifests in the following chapters in the interrogation of the patriarchal agenda in the Ruth narrative. Put another way, not much is objective and/or innocent about the bible studies in this book.

The difference between the longings and the flirts in the Song of Songs, in comparison to the befallen and stricken temperaments in Lamentations, invites readings that negotiate between moods of 'not yet' and 'been there'. In its location in the Hebrew Bible, i am encouraged to be playful and sensual in my reading of Ruth as well as be stern and vigilant on such matters as land, inheritance and redemption. These drives are complementary, and i see and hear them in male and female characters. Reading Ruth in between Song of Songs and Lamentations pulls me away from the patriarchal agenda and gives

7

me a placard of decoloniality to carry to the gates of biblical criticism (see Chapters 10 and 11).

Christian Bible

In the Old Testament of the Christian Bible,[3] which inherited the structure of the Septuagint, Ruth is located between Judges and 1 Samuel. At this location, Ruth is made to function as a point of transition from judgeship to kingship (Linafelt, 1999, pp. xviii–xx). The leadership of the judges has proven to be ineffective, with the famine announced at Ruth 1.1 as another nail on the head of judgeship; and at the end of the Ruth narrative, the monarchy is anticipated in David's whakapapa (Ruth 4.18–22). This shift comes as no surprise given one of the refrains in the book of Judges – 'in those days there was no king in Israel; everyone did what was right in his own eyes' (Judges 17.6, 18.1, 21.25). There was no common system and the only thing that seemed consistent was that the judges could not keep the children of Israel on YHWH's good side: they fall into trouble; they cry to YHWH; YHWH sends a judge to deliver them; when that judge passes on, the people get into trouble with YHWH and the cycle starts again. *Everyone*, including judges, did his or her (Deborah was a prophetess and judge) own thing, and the book of Judges invites readers to look forward to the day when there will be a king over Israel. When that day comes, things are expected to be better.

Ruth signals that an appropriate king for Israel is coming (cf. Block, 2015, p. 29) and invites readers to anticipate the patriarchal canon to peak with David and his narrative (and the narrative of his household in 1 Samuel to 2 Kings). David is coming and he will be appropriate because he will rise from the whakapapa of Judah. In its location in the Christian Bible, the Ruth narrative serves a political function – to locate, announce and authorize David. The Old Testament co-opts the Ruth narrative in the name of David.

The Ruth narrative serves a second political function in that the whakapapa ignores Samuel (the king maker) and Saul, the first king of Israel, even before he is chosen and anointed. To mark a place for David, Ruth unmoors Saul – who was of the tribe of Benjamin, and who came from Gibeah (the tribe and the hometown are both outside of the southern and Judean orientations of the patriarchal canon). When one reads Ruth in between Judges and 1 Samuel, one would be prepared, if not eager, to pass over the narrative of Saul. To fast forward to David would be the yearning of readers who are attentive to the function of Ruth in the flow from Judges to 1 Samuel. The fate of king Saul (cf. Gunn, 1980) is already anticipated in Ruth.

David will become a king over Israel, but the flow and structure of the Hebrew Bible (as a whole) does not privilege the Davidic line nor the monarchical system. The narrative that i implied above to be at the heart of the patriarchal canon (1 Samuel to 2 Kings) closes with the upper-class Judean people in exile, and so does the Hebrew Bible as a whole (concluding with 1 and 2 Chronicles). At the conclusion of both corpus – the patriarchal canon and the Hebrew Bible as a whole – the kingship system fails, the divided nations of Judah and Israel fall, and the privileged elected people end up in diaspora: these are the lost grounds at the centre of the grief of Lamentations. In these regards, the political functions that Ruth plays in the Deuteronomistic history are not faithful to the overall drive of the Hebrew Bible. On the other hand, Ruth is an interruption to the extended narrative of the judges (see Jobling, 1998, p. 71). If one reads straight from Judges into 1 Samuel but ignores Ruth, then one would find the leadership of Saul and David, and of all the other kings after them, to also be examples of 'everyone doing what was right in his own eyes'.

How does (re)locating Ruth in between Judges and 1 Samuel make it a Christian project? The obvious answer for me, as a Christian reader, is simple: the Christian fathers canonized the Christian Bible to authorize David so that when the days of Jesus come (in the narrative), he could easily be received and endorsed as the 'son of David' – as he is introduced in the opening verse of the New Testament: 'An account of the genealogy of Jesus the Messiah, the son of David, the son of Abraham'

(Matt. 1.1). This is also the primary reason for reordering the books of the Old Testament, moving the books of The Twelve (Minor Prophets) to the end of the collection where Malachi is the final messenger before the narratives of Jesus. Malachi 4 closes with anticipation of the day of the Lord and Matthew 1 opens with the whakapapa of Jesus, in which Ruth 4.18–22 plays an essential role. In the Christian Bible, the books of the Hebrew Bible are borrowed and shuffled to make the Old Testament; and this Old Testament becomes the foundation for the New Testament. In this Christian project, Ruth plays a significant role – in anticipation of Jesus, with David as *tepu* (Tongan for a spur, or a spark). In this Christian project also, the fellowship that canonized the Christian Bible did what was right in their own eyes.

Put differently, Christians (and the Christian Bible) need David more than the adherents of Judaism (and the Hebrew Bible) do. Christians need David so that Jesus may be accepted as an appropriate king. Ironically, many Christian readers have spilled a lot of ink arguing that Jesus was a different kind of king. Moreover, mainly out of respect to interreligious relations and guilt for the legacies of the Holocaust, Christians hesitate to point out how David also did the right thing in his own eyes. Christians put David on history's pedestal and masked the Christian project by referring to the Old Testament as the Hebrew Bible – to give the impression that the Christian project was endorsed by Judaism. And lest we forget, the Ruth narrative plays a key role in this Christian project.

Two streams

The bible studies in the following chapters reflect the double placements of Ruth in the canons. That this short narrative is located at two different contexts, in two different canons, testifies to its utility, on the one hand, and slyness, at the same time. Ruth (narrative) is both nifty and stealthy. It invites readings that are both right and left, top and bottom, for and against, side and side.

These bible studies present the Ruth narrative as if it's a raft that drifts in two streams. Where the two streams cross, the narrative gets tossed and turned. At the points of crossing, the bible studies strain the tensions between pleasure and grief in the Hebrew Bible as well as problematize the political functions that Ruth is made to play in the Christian Bible. The character of Ruth embodies the confluence of two streams – Ruth is a widow who 'holds the title' to Judean land and inheritance, and a Moabite daughter-in-law who becomes great-grandmother to a significant Judean. The unmooring of Ruth in the narrative is countered by the transient and drifting flow of the readings in the bible studies that follow.

Ruth among readers

> No one work can account for every aspect of Ruth scholarship sufficiently, and some important areas of critical inquiry are better covered in other commentaries or by other genres of scholarship. (Schipper, 2016, p. xi)

The book of Ruth has been studied by many scholars. All commentary series have harvested Ruth at least once, and there are specialized studies around the characters (Fewell and Gunn, 1990), the reading perspectives (van Wolde, 1997), the structure (Korpel, 2001), the ethics (Lau, 2010), the afterlives (Koosed, 2011), the intersection of survival with comedy (Fentress-Williams, 2012), the performances (Giles and Doan, 2016), the theologies (Lau and Goswell, 2016), the impact of the later history of Israel (Jones III, 2016; Fewell, 2017), the matter of desire (Powell, 2018), the voice of earth (Sinnott, 2020), among other matters for scholarly threshing. It is no surprise that feminists have taken a liking to Ruth with two volumes in the Feminist Companion to the Bible series (Brenner, 1993; Brenner, 1999) and one volume in the Wisdom Commentary, a commentary series aimed to provide feminist interpretations of every book in the Bible (Laffey and Leonard-Fleckman, 2017). Furthermore, some women have authored volumes in traditional commentary series (e.g. Sakenfeld, 1999, for *Ruth: Interpretation: A Bible Commentary for Teaching and Preaching*; Eskenazi and Frymer-Kensky, 2011, for *The JPS Bible Commentary: Ruth*) and a collective of contemporary Jewish women have tried to 'reclaim' Ruth (Kates and Reimer, 1994).

It would require several volumes to introduce and map the many scholarly threshing floors where scholars have spread their wings over Ruth, and then covered her with the shawls of academic excellence, intellectual objectivism, hermeneutical explorations, and suchlike. However, in order to locate this work, i identify some of the energies that shape the following bible studies. In doing so i 'out' my interests and biases – or, to use an image from Ruth, i show my hermeneutical sandals – in relation to the ways that others read the book. Though i am a native islander, i do not read alone or in isolation – two unfair expectations upon my kind. I too read in company, and with interests. In presenting the bible studies in the following chapters, i am intentionally showcasing the commitment to minoritized subjects, the embodiment of the call to queer, the affirmation of dirt in the fabrics of life, and the courage to protest for tomorrow people.

Minoritization

In the company of activists, i read *for* minoritized subjects and *against* cultures of minoritization in Scripture, in society and in biblical scholarship. Liberation and feminist critics have made significant contributions in these regards, drawing attention to the intersections of the matters of gender, race and class.

Location makes a difference in biblical scholarship as well, and black scholars have been vocal in demanding the removal of the sandals (see Ruth 4.7) from the feet of traditional and mainline biblical scholarship. I use 'black' intentionally here, in reference to scholars who expose and subvert the whiteness of traditional and mainline biblical scholarship. Black is a political positioning rather than a reference to skin colour or to

African heritage. When 'black' is limited to the sons and daughters of Africa, as Michael Jagessar explained to me in several conversations, whiteness wins by dividing those who resist and protest against whiteness into blacks and non-blacks, African blacks and African non-blacks, African blacks and non-African blacks, from the global south or from the global north. I do not deny these differences, but i resist letting whiteness win.

The bible studies in the following chapters are offered with black spirits that welcome and home minoritized subjects. In the case of the Ruth narrative, some minoritized subjects have over time received more attention than others. Some women receive attention as racialized (e.g. Ruth the Moabite) and *classified* (e.g. Naomi the mother-in-law) characters but many remain undiscovered (e.g. the older women in the neighbourhood), in part because readers are not always willing to make the Bible talk (as encouraged by Callahan, 2006). The few readers who have the courage to make the Bible talk hear some of the hidden subjects and read their hidden transcripts. Orpah is among the hidden subjects that have been heard and it takes certain orientations – for example, to read with native (Donaldson, 1999) and black (Dube, 1999) interests – to find her in and in-between the letters of the narrative. The bible studies that follow shuffle these orientations, by both looking for hidden subjects as well as reading for hidden transcripts in the Ruth narrative, and in partnering narratives.

Reading texts in juxtaposition, the relish of intertextual and contrapuntal readers (see Fewell and Gunn, 1990), encourages hidden subjects to come out and speak up. At times, the juxtaposed texts carry remnants or reminders of one another that *talk across* textual limits. At other times, the remnants are like thorns that make the juxtaposed texts *talk back* at one another. And on yet other occasions, the juxtaposed texts even transgress one another.

Of course, the interests of readers influence how the juxtaposed texts intersect and interject. The bible studies are also not free of my interests, which show up in the juxtaposition of the Ruth narrative with written and oral texts, and with close attention to minoritizing moves.

Queer

Some critics latch on to the cleaving of Ruth to Naomi as something of a coming out event. On the road to Judah, the word that the narrator used to describe Ruth's cleaving (דבק; *davka*) to Naomi (Ruth 1.14) is the same word used in Genesis 2.24 to describe the cleaving of a man to a woman in marriage (West, 2006), and Ruth's cleaving words to Naomi (Ruth 1.16–17) have been repeated or echoed in many heterosexual marriage vows. The two women had known each other for some time, but in an in-law relationship. On the road, they were on the way to a different location with an opportunity for different relations. On the road, this queer line of reading suggests, the two women came out – from Moab, from their previous situations, and from other closets.

Boaz joined the two women later in Judah, and together they formed what Mona West calls a 'family of choice' (West, 2020). The crucial issue with a family of choice is not the possibility of their being homo- or bi-sexual but, like many modern LGBTQIX families, that they form their family outside of the norms. In breaking through heteronormative limits to entertain an alternative family structure, the next step in West's reading is also queer. I draw this conclusion on the basis of Stephen Moore's understanding of 'queer' as

> a supple cipher both for what *stands over against* the normal and the natural to oppose, and thereby define, them, and what *inheres within* the normal and the natural to subvert, and indeed pervert, them – this opposition and subversion privileging, but by no means being confined to, the mercurial sphere of the sexual. (Moore, 2001, p. 18, italicized in the original; cf. Stone, 2001, p. 117; Althaus-Reid and Isherwood, 2007)

In the following bible studies, *supple ciphers* are found everywhere in Ruth and the *mercurial sphere of the sexual* overruns with the spheres of death, politics, community and more. And because reading (like theology, according to Althaus-Reid,

2005, p. 11) is a sexual act, the following bible studies befriend, seduce, wed and even birth alternative and queer meanings.

Dirt

The agency, perspectives and voices of Earth and of Earth creatures (who are many more in kind and number than the human kind) in the Ruth narrative have recently received sustained attention (see Sinnott, 2020). This recent turn in biblical scholarship encourages one to step back from the default anthropocentric starting points by which one reads, with human interests, instances in the narrative relating to famine, harvest, inheritance and (the redemption of) land. One is thus free to ponder, for instance, if a famine (while it certainly devastates human lives) could be seen differently by Earth and by other Earth creatures? Does a famine benefit or impoverish Earth and Earth creatures?[4]

The opening verse of the Ruth narrative kicks up dirt and dust. A famine brings to mind dry and barren(ed) land (see Figure 1.1), and a family of four that set out seeking refuge in a foreign land would have travelled a dirt road (Ruth 1.1). Dirt comes back to mind six verses later,[5] when Naomi and Ruth travelled in the opposite direction. And upon their arrival, dirt is everywhere in Judah – in the harvest field of Boaz (Ruth 2), on the threshing floor (Ruth 3), and at the gate on that auspicious 'morning after' (Ruth 4). The Ruth narrative throws up dust and dirt in front of readers, and the following bible studies call attention to the various forms of 'dirt' in the narrative.

In the company of Upolu Vaai, i see dirt in a positive light (Vaai, 2021a). Pasifika natives, like other indigenous people, are familiar with dirt. We are people of the dirt, and a God of the dirt makes more sense to us compared to a clean and (white)washed God. Vaai's affirmation of dirt and dirtification of God echo the imagination of the Yahwist narrator, for whom the human kind were made from dirt (Gen. 2.7). From the same 'ground' (האדמה) that the humans (האדם) were made, YHWH also made the plants (Gen. 2.9) and the animals (Gen.

Figure 1.1: D. S. Yatawara, 'Mother land'.
Courtesy of Monica J. Melanchthon.

2.19).[6] And at the end of their lives, all kinds of Earth creatures
will return to dust and to dirt (Gen. 3.19). For the Yahwist,
there is interconnection between life and dirt.

Similarly, there is interconnection between the human body
and land in D. S. Yatawara's 'mother land' (Figure 1.1). Yatawara, a Sri Lankan street artist, explained that 'mother land'
is his depiction of Sri Lanka, referring to both his homeland
and his people – both of which are dry. More appropriately,
his homeland and his people have been dried up. Parched.
Cracked. Bared. Naked. Vulnerable. Yet, embracing. Shielding.
Surviving. Yatawara's homeland has drunk the spilled blood
of its people and cuddled the fallen bodies (represented by the

child) of its animals and plants, as a consequence of colonial abuse, persisting poverty, civil war, religious violence, social and political instabilities. In the arms of his 'mother land' is a clinging child, who appears to have been dismembered. The child represents the 'heart' of the 'mother land' which, for Yatawara, is alive and, suggested by the exposed breast, could be nourished into life. Such a hope rises through the cracked skin of the land (Sri Lanka), upon the dirt that is pushed around under the narrative (Ruth), and in the following bible studies.

Tomorrow mothers

Yatawara's 'mother land' has nothing to do with Ruth, but it invites attention to the child that Ruth gave birth to at the end of the narrative (Ruth 4.13). The women of the neighbourhood took the child from Ruth and gave him to Naomi (Ruth 4.14–16), and then to David (Ruth 4.17); the whakapapa provided by the narrator indicates that the women succeeded in dragging the narrative to David (Ruth 4.18–22). The women thereby served the patriarchal agenda. Nationalism prevailed.

As far as the narrative is concerned, David would qualify as one whom reggae artists call 'tomorrow people'. He will become tomorrow's national(ist) leader, and the narrator would have expected readers to approve and assent: Long live the king.

Yatawara's 'mother land' holds me back from going all the way with the women and the narrative. How did Ruth the birth mother react to her child being taken (read: dismembered, as suggested in Yatawara's work) and used as a hinge in someone else's whakapapa? How might Ruth queer the collaboration between the women of the neighbourhood with the narrator, in the interest of the patriarchal agenda? What would Ruth say to 'tomorrow mothers' from whom children are taken, or for whom minoritization and dirt are their daily food? These questions murmur behind the bible studies here.

Ruth from contexts

The conversations around the conviction that *all* interpretations
are shaped by 'contexts' (of the text, of the processes of transmission of the text, of the various stages in the afterlife of the
text, and of the reader) have been taking place in different
forums. In my journey in biblical studies, the chorus of *Voices
from the Margin* (appealing to multi-volume works edited
by R. S. Sugirtharajah, since 1991) along with *Reading from
this Place* (appealing to the works co-edited by Fernando F.
Segovia and Mary Ann Tolbert, since 1995) encouraged contextual interpretation as well as opening up the conversation
for alternative directions. The opportunities in contextuality
and the problematics of it continue to be tossed and turned,
and i take those stints and swings on the horizons of contextuality for granted in this work.

What counts as 'context' are many types: some contexts are
physical and visible, some contexts are ideological and sublime,
with smidgeons of the popular and faked here and there. Context is more than geography and location; ideas and biases are
contexts as well, and so are the networks of media, global-
ization, capitalism, pandemics and endemics. We always read
from many places and the places from which we read are not
fixed or stable. Sometimes the margin becomes the centre, and
sometimes personalities from the centre take over the 'voices'
of the margin. No matter the kind, contexts shape how we
interpret texts, how some texts are *not interpreted*, and why
some texts are *not even read*.

The spirits of several leaders in contextual interpretation
hover over these pages. I name a few of those leaders here
because they are kept outside of the mainline enterprises of
biblical scholarship in general, and contextual biblical interpretation in particular: from Asia, Shoki Coe (Taiwan) and
Ahn Byung-Mu (Korea) were among the frontrunners in contextual interpretation, and R. S. Sugirtharajah (Sri Lanka) and
Kwok Pui Lan (Hong Kong) promoted the turn to postcolonial
criticism. From Latin America, Leonardo Boff (Brazil) and
Gustavo Gutiérrez (Peru) obliged readers to 'the preferential

option for the poor', and Marcella Althaus-Reid (Argentina) brought body and queer theories to the table. Black theologians have added their contextual tweaks from Europe (e.g. Mukti Barton, Anthony G. Reddie), the Americas (e.g. James Cone, Katie G. Cannon, Emilie Townes) and Africa (e.g. Mercy Amba Oduyoye, Tinyiko Maluleke). From the Arab world, Naim S. Ateek and Nur Masalha (Palestine) have kept the hope for liberation alive, with Athalya Brenner-Idan providing leadership in feminist criticism. Native and indigenous critics (e.g. Jenny Te Paa Daniel of Aotearoa and Pasifika, Laura Donaldson and Vine Deloria Jnr of the Americas) have been critical of the mainline enterprise, but they have not always been heard in the halls of theology and biblical scholarship.

There are many other leaders from each of these places, and they share the conviction that contexts matter in biblical interpretation. The bible studies in the following chapters echo the drives of these leaders *from the margin*, and their comrades, from *many places*.

Climate as context

Adding to the conversation on the politics of contextuality, this work takes the climate crisis as context (see Elvey, 2020) for interpreting the Ruth narrative. In the old-fashioned mindset, climate (change) is *not* context because it is not a physical space nor a set of ideas and biases, obvious or otherwise. But climate (trauma, grief) shapes mindsets and behaviours whose impacts spread over bodies of land and water. Like media (Havea, 2021b) and the Covid pandemic (Havea, 2021a), the climate crisis is part of the contexts that we in the 2020s and beyond read biblical texts rather than something that is within it. This work invites such a contextual turn.

Climate (change, trauma, grief, crisis, injustice) is a global reality (rather than a phenomenon or an issue), despite the denial by some world and academic leaders. And it is not new. We in Pasifika have experienced the impacts of climate change for generations – especially in the rainy and sunny months, in the hurricane seasons, and in the harvests (or lack of) from the land and the waters – but we did not call it 'climate change'. Climate change as a concept is new, but climate change as reality has always been part of our island lifestyle.

We have Pasifika terms and teachings about the fluctuations of life. In Tonga, for instance, the driest and hottest period of the year is November and December, the name for which in our native calendar is *'Uluenga* – meaning that the head (*'ulu*) of the (is)land is yellowish-brown (*enga*). Tongans expect this time of the year to be difficult. The food from the previous harvest would by now be low, and may even be gone, and the island will be *enga* (yellowish-brown, as if it has died) rather than green (*mata*, as when it is alive). Associated with this condition is a saying: *ka ai ha 'ofa pea tali ki 'Uluenga* (if you have any pity or love, save it for 'Uluenga). That is the time when islanders need to share what they have stored with their less fortunate neighbours.

As a young person, however, i regularly heard those of my parents' generation saying that they were struggling even before 'Uluenga started. What they harvested from the land was not enough to feed their families for the whole year, and the dry and hot period extended into January and February (when they expect rain for the new crops). 'Uluenga, for my parents' generation, stretched from two to four months. Moreover, in my generation, the hurricane season has become longer – it used to be March and April, but we now have cyclones as early as December and as late as September. We recently learned that these realities are impacts of climate change, but such realities have always been with my parents' generation and they are getting worse in my generation.

From Pasifika, i have seen the politics of climate change (e.g. using islands as poster-images of climate trauma; see Havea, 2010) and realize that climate risk is severe in other lands (e.g. Bangladesh, Kenya, the Amazon, Canada, Germany and other first world nations). This is not to say that climate change is worse in some places compared to others, but to affirm that it is a global reality.

Hence the invitation of this work: to read Ruth from the

context of the climate (in its complexity). Sadly, doing so will not slow or reduce carbon emission, lower the temperature of Earth or calm the rising seas. But reading from the interweaving context of the climate can shape mindsets, and that is one of the challenges that this book offers.

Bible study as context

> There are various kinds of commentaries. They differ between a pious paraphrase for the pulpit (taking every story to have really happened) and the well-wrought works of academics (pondering on versions, sources, and redactions, claiming that only a core of the text could be original). (Becking, 2021, p. 1)

In this work, pushing back at the distinction that Bob Becking makes, i affirm 'bible study' as a context in which critical biblical interpretation takes place. There are two controversies in this affirmation: first, my affirmation problematizes the expectation that bible study is always uncritical and conservative, which is encouraged by the divide presumed to segregate bible study (done in community or church settings) from biblical study (done in scholarly or academic circles). This divide gives the impression that, in Pasifika for instance, bible study is the context in which readers engage with local, native and contextual wisdoms while biblical study draws upon western, enlightened insights. Having experienced this bifurcation in other regions, i invite readers on both sides of the divide to recognize that there is much to learn from the 'other side'. More directly, with this work i beg scholars and academics to not look down upon readers and readings in community and church settings. And similarly, i beg readers in community and church circles to not eulogize or be intimidated by scholars and academics. Both of these leanings, along with the divide between the two sides, testify to the same project: coloniality. Without shifting on both sides, coloniality prevails.

The readings in the following chapters were gleaned from a series of 'Pasifika Bible Study' (PBS) in and with communities of 'normal people' in Fiji, Solomon Islands, Nauru, Mā'ohi Nui (French Polynesia), Aotearoa New Zealand, Australia and Tonga. I use the terms 'normal people' and 'normal readers' in contrast to 'experts' on the scholarly and academic fronts.[7] In light of the divide noted above, normal readers are those who interpret in the context of bible study while experts interpret in the context of biblical study. They carry out the same task – interpret – but in different contexts. Caveat emptor: many experts sit within the circles of normal readers, but they remain experts.

The second controversy is that i refuse to let conservative and fundamentalist people of faith own 'bible study' as a practice. Bible study can be creative and critical, appealing to the intellect and to the will, and is not just an excuse for making altar calls and passing round the collection plate. The majority of normal people who inspired the bible studies offered in the following chapters were not trained in theology or biblical studies, nor ventured beyond the shores of their home(is)lands. But their insights are creative and critical and, in my humble opinion, better than normal.

Because i was trained in the ways of traditional and mainline biblical scholarship, then dunked in poststructuralism and its ripples, i value the harvests from those enterprises. I shared some of those insights at the PBS sessions but i did not use the 'expert' cloud to overtake the *voices from the margins* of Pasifika. I did not even out myself as one who earlier published and edited works on Ruth. I made that conscious decision not because i value objectivity, but because this work emerges from different contexts with different concerns and politics. Put another way, while we read from many contexts, our contexts shift, change and accumulate, so should our reading.

Pasifika as context

Perhaps greatest of all the debts I owe to Jione Havea was the cleansing of my mind from any lingering vestiges of ideas of racial superiority. There were others; but daily contact with

Jione Havea made any notions of white superiority absurd. (Ernest Edgar Vyvyan Collocott, *Pacific Islands Monthly*, 17 April 1942, p. 8)

The islands and waters of Pasifika were discovered, crossed and settled by natives over several waves of migration. Each island has legends of discovery, myths of belonging, and explanations for why its first human inhabitants left their ancestral homelands. The obvious should be stressed here: *all islands were first discovered by sea, land and air creatures before natives arrived.* This requires another qualification: Pasifika myths of origin praise natives as sons and daughters of *navigators*, which both affirms that our ancestors came from somewhere else as well as explains why our ancestors were able to cross and endure the moana (sea, deep ocean). These affirmations are not for the purpose of hammering home the fact that natives were the *first* discoverers and settlers of Pasifika, the obsession of historians and ethnographers, but in order to highlight the fact that natives have memories and histories that are among the 'hidden transcripts'.

The first wave of visitors to Pasifika came from neighbouring islands that have nowadays been regionalized as Asia – especially the groups of islands that are known as Taiwan and Indonesia, before those islands faced cultural whitewash from the north and the west. The similarity and borrowings between our native languages are reminders of the inter-island relations that were built early in our (oral) history. The ancestors of the indigenous people of Taiwan and Indonesia were navigators also.

Years later, European explorers, cartographers, traders, botanists and convicts also came in waves. Abel Tasman of the Dutch East India Company is historicized as the first European explorer to arrive (twice) in the 1640s, with James Cook of the British Royal Navy credited for leading three explorations to the region in the 1770s. (Cook was murdered in Hawai'i in 1779, in response to his attempt to kidnap the *ali'i nui* (high chief) of the island – the natives fought back and prevailed.) With the landing of European missionaries, Pasifika became a mission field, divided up between mission bodies who baptized our people, (is)lands and waters for the colonial governments to grab – and the British took the lion's share. Nowadays, the British have left, but coloniality continues in Pasifika.

Two avatars of coloniality in Pasifika cannot be ignored. First, colonization continues through the ongoing occupation of Pasifika (is)lands and waters. At the time of writing, the USA has the lion's share, with France, Chile and Indonesia as fellow occupiers. The USA still occupies Hawai'i, Tutuila (Samoa), Guam, Mariana (CNMI), Palau, Micronesia (FSM) and the Marshalls (RMI); France still occupies Kanaky (New Caledonia) and Māʻohi Nui (French Polynesia); Chile still occupies Rapa Nui (Easter Island); and Indonesia still occupies West Papua. In Pasifika, colonialism has not reached the 'post' – Pasifika is not yet post-colonial.

Second, the reincarnations of the myths of whiteness in Pasifika are evidence of the backing by Christianity of the colonial project. Many natives in the modern times preach the superiority of whiteness because they regard the trinity of Christianity, Civilization and Development as gifts that the *pālangi* (White, European; the term 'pālangi' refers to people who 'touch or pierce the sky') brought for the benefit of our islands. The pale-skin pālangi brought light and life, and we are expected to respond, 'thank God for the pālangi who have come to save us'. The pālangi are thus deified (as the term suggests), and white supremacy is consequently licensed and taken as normal, if not local. White supremacy still wins.

Today we have taken a step backwards from the critical awareness and firm standing reached by the generation of my grandfather (whose name i was given). In the epigraph at the beginning of this section, Ernest E. V. Collocott (1886–1970), a pālangi and former principal of Tupou College, paid tribute to my grandfather upon his death in 1942: my grandfather cleansed his 'mind from any lingering vestiges of ideas of racial superiority ... daily contact with Jione Havea [1869–1942] made any notions of white superiority absurd'. This book comes in my grandfather's spirit, seeking to make 'any notions of white superiority absurd'.

There is nothing 'pacific' about this work. This work seeks to shift the appreciation of Pasifika, from being a cluster of islands to be discovered and settled, harvested and marketed, and from being a region to be Christianized, saved and whitened. Pasifika is more than a 'sea of islands' (as the late 'Epeli Hau'ofa preached). Pasifika is also a sea of memories, sea of wisdoms, sea of stories, sea of theologies, and sea of much more, to be engaged.

Multi-plying contexts

The foregoing brings me to two interweaving conclusions: No one reads from only one context, and everyone reads from several fluid contexts.

Prompts for further talanoa

1 The Bible Project, 'Overview: Ruth', www.youtube.com/ watch?v=oh1eoBeR4Jk, accessed 5.5.21.
2 Jione Havea and Peter H. W. Lau (eds), *Reading Ruth in Asia*, Atlanta: SBL, 2015; www.sbl-site.org/assets/pdfs/pubs/978 0884141006_OA.pdf, accessed 5.5.21.

Notes

1 To avoid the cluttering of italics, native terms are italicized in their first occurrence and when they need to be emphasized.

2 In Kiribati, the term for land is *kainga* which literally means 'relative' (female and male); similarly, the term for sea is *taari*, which means both 'sister' and 'brother'. Land and sea are gendered, as both female and male.

3 I break from the convention of using 'Christian Bible' as reference only to the New Testament. While the books of the Old Testament are taken from the Hebrew Bible (scripture of Judaism), the books are arranged differently. The same content arranged differently makes a different book, to serve a different function. Because the Old Testament is a Christian project, both the Old Testament and the New Testament make up the Christian Bible.

4 These questions apply also to the processes of planting and harvesting, and to the assumption of ownership or transference of land as property (inheritance). And in the context of Covid, in what ways does a pandemic benefit or impoverish Earth, and organisms and creatures beyond the human kind?

5 The deaths of Elimelek (1.3), Mahlon and Chilion (1.5) also bring dirt to mind. They are mortals, whom death returned to dust and dirt.

6 The priestly narrative is a little more complex, because Earth (Gen. 1.11) as well as the waters have creative energies (Gen. 1.9, 20).

7 In light of Stephen Moore's definition (cited above) of 'queer' – as something within 'the normal and the natural' that subverts, perverts and stands over against 'the normal and the natural' – the 'normal' in my construction is 'queer'.

2

Ruth at talanoa

Like Ruth going out to glean in the field of Bethlehem, i went to the Pasifika bible studies (PBS) communities to (re)search and gather, and to (re)learn. I went to (re)learn what Pasifika natives hear and feel when they make the book talk (cf. Callahan, 2006), and this collection of bible studies contains some of the seeds and grains (and some husks and stalks) that i found and carried away. Instead of reading (as i would do in the comfort of a library or study) and repeating what others have published about the book of Ruth, which are in colonial languages and available to those who have resources and opportunities, i engaged the PBS participants in a native-style learning process that i associate with talanoa.

For most of the PBS sessions, i took only a Bible, a pen and a notebook[1] (plus snacks for the children and grandchildren who also came along). And for at least two sessions in all of the PBS communities, i did not even take a Bible – so that the participants would teach me how parts of the narrative 'talk' in their vernacular bibles. I was familiar with some but not all of the native languages, and the echoes and borrowings across the island tongues testify (somewhat like the elders who witnessed for Boaz at the gate) to our voyaging ancestors. Natives of Pasifika are people of the moana (sea, ocean): moana shapes who we are, what we do and how, what we see, value and remember. But also, moana shapes most of what we do *not* become, see, do, value or remember. Moana is in and behind us, and moana is more than each of us.

Talanoa is (re)searching

> A story is meant to be told and so we tell the story to people who will hear. And you will hear different things from the same story. (Champion, 2014, p. 21)

The term talanoa, used in some but not all Pasifika languages, carries three meanings – *story*, *telling* (of stories), and *conversation* (concerning issues around stories and tellings). A story (which is usually a combination of stories) is lost and forgotten if no one tells it and if a group does not gather to talk about and around it; a telling is dry if it has no story, and it turns into scolding or lecturing without a conversation; and a conversation withers without story and telling. As an event (of storytelling/conversation), talanoa involves (re)gathering and (re)purposing. Talanoa is ongoing, and it furthers. It extends beyond its own event. In these regards, talanoa is (re)searching Pasifika-style.[2]

Indigenous Australians understand and value talanoa in a similar way because, as Denise Champion puts it, a story 'is meant to be told' to 'people who will hear'. The willingness of listeners to hear is vital. And depending on the interests of listeners, and the event and situation in which the story is told, different listeners 'will hear different things from the same story' (Champion, 2014). What people hear is incited but not controlled by the story, provoked but not limited by the one who tells the story. The story is a spark and a platform for something more.

Normal people (see Chapter 1) favour talanoa, but some schedule-driven experts and time-tight native academics see it as a waste of time. There is justification for this view, because the 'noa' in tala*noa* also means 'nothing', hence the term may be defined as the telling of nothing. Nonetheless, talanoa keeps Pasifika breathing and i borrow it as a stimulus for research and reading, for several reasons:

1 Talanoa takes oral texts seriously – to be 'read' as one does with written scriptures. Talanoa scripturalizes oral texts.

2 Talanoa stretches the scopes of orality. Orality is not just about stories and *toktok* (Pidgin for talk-talk, telling and conversation). Rather, orality touches all aspects of living – orality forms what we do and how we live, think, hope, love, trick, lie and die – and it is preserved in many forms including poetry, artwork, handicraft, dance, ritual, ceremony, etc. Orality is more than the uttering of words; orality is also about the embodying of memories, thoughts and longings.

3 Talanoa – to borrow a postmodern image – allows the authors to die. Texts (scripted and oral) from the past are remembered and retold, and those who *toktok* around those 'rememberings' decide whether and how to pass those to future generations. Talanoa is the event that lets the authors rest but awakens future generations to receive stories, tellings and conversations.

4 Talanoa encourages the weaving of orality with oratory. Talanoa energizes orators to bring the past, the dead, the forgotten, together with the present and the future, into remembering, and into life. Talanoa awakens orators to send forth their stories, tellings and conversations.

5 Talanoa embraces poly- or many-ness. The drive for one-ness (e.g. one truth, one way, one leader, and other one-deals) does not suit the ways that Pasifika natives think, read and theologize (Vaai, 2021b). We need talanoa because we are many, and we consequently protect talanoa to be many.

6 Talanoa is an opportunity to break social barriers. Experts, academics and executives may humbly sit and talanoa with normal people, to co-learn and inter-enlighten.

Talanoa is neither philosophy nor methodology (in the western sense), but native event-and-practice that is rooted deeply in Pasifika.[3] Pasifika breathes (because of) talanoa. Without talanoa, meanings hide and relations sag. This collection of bible studies is a product of, and an invitation to, talanoa.

Caveat emptor: there are two qualifications that i need to make (for now) around the connections between talanoa with space and time.

Routes and roots: space

The first caveat relates to talanoa as an event that makes room for the overlay of roots with routes. Talanoa situates (roots) as well as moves (routes).

Prior to the invasions by (misconstrued as 'contacts with') western powers and their forms of government, which introduced and took advantage of the unifying of people (it is easier to claim rule over subjects if they are perceived to be unified), native Pasifika societies were divided into clans who related to one another through duties and responsibilities. In Tonga, for example, the clans were assigned duties that situate them in relation to one of the four domains of island life – sea, land, sky, underworld. The wellbeing of the ancient society depended on all of the clans fulfilling their duties and responsibilities to one another.

The clans were scattered across the islands (divided in terms of space), to carry out different duties and responsibilities (divided in terms of functions). In a village situation, one clan will be in charge of fishing and other tasks related to the sea; another clan will be in charge of funeral and (underworld) ancestral duties; and other clans will take care of duties related to land (e.g. gardening) and sky (e.g. navigation). A village functions well when its clans perform their duties and share the instructions and harvests from the four domains of the island.

Each clan had a head(s), who led them in carrying out their duties and in the check-and-balance scuffles[4] when another clan(s) fails in its responsibilities. In this way, native Pasifika societies were customarily divided – but effectively organized and functional – before the unification project of European powers (read: colonization, missionization).

The head of clans was known in several of the native languages as *tui*, a term that the Europeans used to translate 'king' in the vernacular Bibles. Prior to European colonization, each island group had many tui – Tonga had three, Samoa had four, and the larger island groups had more. But with the establishment of European-style governments to rule over island affairs, on behalf of *the* sovereign (king, queen), the cohorts of native tui were subjected under a governor (in the name of the foreign sovereign) and the clans were dismantled. As a consequence, the duties and responsibilities of the clans were ritualized and the natives began to lose touch with the *mana* (power, magic, energy) and *tapu* (sacred, wholeness) of the four domains: *moana* (sea), *vanua* (land), *lagi* (sky), and *lolofonua* (underworld).

The colonial project confiscated more than (is)lands and resources; it also took (read: whitewashed) native minds, ways and practices. The colonial project spread at different times and strengths across Pasifika, but the whitening of native societies had similar effects. Put another way, *losing ground* took place at two interconnected platforms: at the material and physical world (read: we lost our roots), and at the intellectual and spiritual level (read: we lost our routes). And the colonial project is ongoing.

The talanoa event advocated herein works against the colonial project of unification and one-ness. In my talanoa above, i briefly revisited the period prior to colonization in order to highlight that divisions under many leaders (or many-ness, as Vaai puts it) were customarily, orderly and functional, and such leanings are present and influential in talanoa. I went back not because i am a traditionalist, but because talanoa reflects the divisions and many-ness of native Pasifika societies prior to European colonization. To repeat an often used play on words, i went back (re)searching for our *roots* in order that i could see our *routes*. The brief (re)gathering above is an example of how the overlay of roots and routes takes place in the event of talanoa. Put another way, talanoa is (at) both our roots and routes.

More importantly, talanoa can break the hold of coloniality and its 'onefication' project. For example, the most popular Māori legend about the discovery of Aotearoa New Zealand names Kupe as the ancestral navigator who discovered and named the island group. This legend became the orthodox myth of discovery thanks to white (*pākehā*) New Zealand historians and ethnographers who aimed to discredit claims that this group of islands was discovered by white European explorers

(Tasman, Cook, and others). Their intention was noble, but their obsession with historicity shut down Māori tangents to which talanoa can give energy and receive inspiration in return. Two Māori tangents are relevant here: first, Kupe is not the only Māori discoverer of Aotearoa. Maui, Māku, Toi and Whatonga are other discoverers remembered by different *hapu* (clans) at different *marae*. Second, there were several Kupe (taken as a title versus a proper name) who came at different times to different parts of Aotearoa. One Kupe came up north and another came down south; other Kupe arrived at other shores of the island group. To borrow Champion's words, Māori hear different discoverers from the same title – Kupe.

All of the above versions and tangents are orthodox at different hapu and marae, and talanoa can advocate for each and all of them. With talanoa, there is room for many orthodoxies. Talanoa routes and roots native legends. Similarly, in the bible studies in the following chapters, talanoa routes and roots the Ruth narrative.

On and on: time

The second caveat that i raise here relates to the ongoing nature of talanoa. Talanoa does not end with story, with telling, or with conversation. Talanoa does not freeze and stop. I found a recent example of this conundrum in a text by an American anthropologist, Matt Tomlinson, with an appealing (or insulting, for different reasons, depending on how one looks at it) title: *God is Samoan*. At the end of his conclusion come three asterisks, which suggest that the paragraph that follows is an afterword or even an afterthought, but clearly a significant thought for Tomlinson:

> Whenever I think of my original fieldwork in Kadavu, Fiji, one moment always returns to me as an especially resonant and uplifting one. It took place at a kava session, which might not be surprising because so many things take place at kava sessions and kava sessions take place every day. But

this moment was at the end of a session. At such times, all of the people seated near the bowl, including the mixer and cup-bearer, clap together in a five-pulse rhythm. In Fiji, you clap with your hands cupped crosswise, producing a deep and resonant sound. And if you have spent decades farming and fishing as many Kadavuans have, you can produce an especially impressive clap. This was a night like any other, but for some reason, this is the instant [sic] I will always remember, with bodies sitting cross-legged on the mat, all of us together in the late hours in a small house whose corrugated iron walls added extra resonance to handclaps that took on the weight of cannon shots. Five claps and finished: *the kava was empty, the night was over, and we were all together in a way that could borrow a page from social theory but was turned toward something bigger* – human, divine – in a moment that had everything to do with both culture and ultimacy. (Tomlinson, 2020, p. 108; my italics)

At the moment when things are supposed to be over, and the gathering is ready to be dispersed, something bigger erupts. Talanoa does not end when the gathering ends. Where the gathering ends, talanoa prompts. It opens up. When that happens, when the event becomes sacred, one drifts into the confluence of *mana* and *tapu* that talanoa makes possible.

Knots

Because there is generous space for overlaying and fluid time for gyrating, strands (of stories, tellings and conversations) often end up in knots in, during and through talanoa. This is not a failure or a bad thing. The knots that tie up because of talanoa reflect reality. Put simply, talanoa (event) shows that reality and life are in knots.

Ruth is talanoa

Ruth (narrative, book) becomes talanoa when the three – story, telling, conversation – interflow. Intermix. And interrupt. Interruptions blow talanoa into life (aflame) and, in the context of bible and biblical studies, bring life to the text under study. In the PBS events that inspired the bible studies in the following chapters, the interruptions enabled the participants to make Ruth talk in their own senses and bodies, and in their telling(s) and conversations.

As i figuratively dragged Ruth across Pasifika and encouraged native communities to spread their wings over Ruth, the text talked more and more. Excited, but also nervous. Troubled. Covid-19 curtailed my roaming and saved other Pasifika communities from my disruptive PBS itinerary, but the bible studies presented here testify to the many lives and meanings that Ruth accumulated upon the waters of Pasifika.

Big talanoa

The accumulation of additional story, telling and conversation transforms any talanoa into 'big talanoa'.[5] With that awareness, the Ruth narrative is presented in the following chapters as a big talanoa composed of seven clusters of shorter talanoa. The flow of the big talanoa is straightforward: a family migrated, fell apart, and one survivor returned; the sole survivor brought back a companion who helped her resettle, reconnect, reclaim and re-establish what and where her family had left behind:

Ruth 1.1–5: Migration and asylum
Ruth 1.6–19a: Remigration and rejection
Ruth 1.19b—2.7: Resettlement and (re)connecting
Ruth 2.8–23: Food and comfort
Ruth 3.1–15: Home and belonging
Ruth 3.16—4.11a: Resolution and inheritance
Ruth 4.11b–22: Roots and lineage

The clusters of talanoa are explained and interwoven in the following chapters and i will only add two structural observations here. First, there is a positive, affirming and transforming feel to the flow of the big story. The problems at the beginning (famine, asylum seeking, death) are resolved by the end (harvest, redemption, birth). Second, there is also a positive, gender transforming turn in the flow of the big story. The men of the family died off in diaspora (Moab), and the men and women of Bethlehem came (at the field, at the gate, and in the town) to the aid of the woman survivor and her foreign helper. Structurally, the big talanoa holds together its narrative resolutions with its gender transformations, or transgressions – depending on where one sits at the gender-gate, and how one reads the flow of the big talanoa.

Nonetheless, undercurrents push and pull the big talanoa in several ways, and in several directions – into the arms of other memories and anticipations in biblical literature, which together show that the talanoa is not confined to the limits of the text. In its so-called final form, the text reaches beyond itself. And on the wings of talanoa the PBS groups helped the text reach further and further, as far as Pasifika, and tie up several knots on the way. Put in relation to Callahan's (2006) project, the PBS groups made the biblical narrative of Ruth talk into and out of Pasifika. Talanoa enables reading the same narrative in two ways: into the world of natives (where missionaries stopped) and out of the world of natives (to where Callahan is most welcomed).

Clusters of talanoa

In Chapters 3–9, 20 bible studies are presented across the seven clusters of talanoa. The decision on the textual limits for each bible study was done with and across the PBS groups. We started divvying up the narrative at the earlier PBS events, and the latter ones shifted and reconfigured the earlier efforts into the following:

Ruth 1.1–5: Migration and asylum
   (1) Ruth 1.1–2: Bethlehem family seeks asylum in Moab
   (2) Ruth 1.3–5: Death visits Moab
Ruth 1.6–19a: Remigration and rejection
   (3) Ruth 1.6–7: Widows leave Moab
   (4) Ruth 1.8–14a: Naomi pushes her daughters-in-law
     back
   (5) Ruth 1.14b–19a: Orpah obliges, Ruth cleaves
Ruth 1.19b—2.7: Resettlement and (re)connecting
   (6) Ruth 1.19b–22: City buzzes over marred Naomi
   (7) Ruth 2.1–3: Ruth discovers Boaz's plot
   (8) Ruth 2.4–7: Boaz discovers Ruth
Ruth 2.8–23: Food and comfort
   (9) Ruth 2.8–13: Boaz comforts Ruth
   (10) Ruth 2.14–18a: Boaz heaps Ruth
   (11) Ruth 2.18b–23: Ruth feeds Naomi
Ruth 3.1–15: Home and (in)security
   (12) Ruth 3.1–5: Naomi pimps Ruth
   (13) Ruth 3.6–9: Ruth uncovers Boaz
   (14) Ruth 3.10–15: Boaz (re)covers Ruth
Ruth 3.16—4.11a: Resolution and inheritance
   (15) Ruth 3.16–18: Naomi and Ruth unsettle Boaz
   (16) Ruth 4.1–6: Boaz unsettles the redeemer
   (17) Ruth 4.7–11a: Boaz un-sandals the redeemer
Ruth 4.11b–22: Roots and lineage
   (18) Ruth 4.11b–13: YHWH gives Ruth a son
   (19) Ruth 4.14–17: The women give Naomi a son
   (20) Ruth 4.18–22: Tradition gives David a heritage

The interflow between, and the knots in, the pericopes are presented in the bible studies. At this juncture, i acknowledge that, at the end, the limits of the pericopes were determined so that the bible studies convey the feel of talanoa in two ways. First, so that the space and time dimensions of each pericope are stressed (pun intended). What might easily be read as roots is also read as routes, and vice versa. For instance, Ruth 4.11 is split between two pericopes so that the redeemer is credited for knowing the sandal tradition (in 4.7–11a) and YHWH is credited for making Ruth conceive (in 4.11b–13). Moreover, the pace of the narrative is interrogated in the bible studies. The swift turns and shifts of the narrative are slowed down in the bible studies, to give opportunities for the on-and-on feel of talanoa. The upshot, as indicated above, is that the big talanoa ties up into knots at several places in the PBS bible studies.

Second, the pericopes were determined so that the bible studies interweave the narrative resolutions with the ideological transformations and/or transgressions (especially in terms of gender, race, class, labour) in and of the big talanoa. For instance, the 'return' on the road (Ruth 1.6–19a), which is traditionally read to privilege Ruth's vow, is divided into three pericopes that raise ideological questions such as: Did Naomi use her daughter-in-law to cover up her escape (1.6–7)? Why did Naomi reject her daughters-in-law (1.8–14a)? How did Orpah feel (1.14b–19a)? Put simply, the bible studies let the authors die and enable the scriptural text to breathe and talk, into and out of Pasifika.

Invitation for more talanoa

One of the critical observations made with the PBS groups relates to the genealogy, a list of names, that closes the big talanoa (Ruth 4.18–22). In terms of genre, the list feels like an attempt to stop, to plug, to stuff, the flow of the narrative. But in the world of talanoa, the list is also inviting. The list of names invites readers to do more than simply fill in the gaps. It also invites readers to add more talanoa, in order to make sense of what the names represent. This list of names is an example of an interruption that allows readers to enter and make the text talk, further and further. When readers add more talanoa, the list of names become whakapapa. The catch, however, is that the list comes at the end. It therefore opens the narrative at and from its end.

The PBS observation and invitation are reflected in the tone of the following bible studies, in which Ruth (as narrative) reaches beyond itself – into other biblical texts, and even

beyond scriptural limits. No kidding: Ruth (character) disappeared from the biblical narrative after she delivered a redeemer
– who could be Boaz and/or Obed – for Naomi (4.14), and she
popped up in Pasifika with the PBS communities. In general, in
the end, each bible study prompts and invites further talanoa.
When readers bring more talanoa, Ruth accumulates more
lives and meanings, and becomes a bigger and bigger talanoa.

Going native

This work is part of a personal mission to celebrate 'native'
as a marker also for those of us whose roots/routes flow from
and for Pasifika. As a marker, 'native' was used by European
anthropologists and missionaries in the early days of western
invasion to downgrade our people – they stigmatized the natives
as people who were uncivilized, unlearned, pagans and savages.
This experience of being downgraded was shared across the
'new world': the 'discoverers' were white, and the natives were
red, black, brown, tan, and a host of other colours and shades.

I grew up troubled by the favouring of white and European
ways in the Tongan society, by *fiepālagi* (wannabe white)
natives, and the shame and shun (*siolalo*) that many in my generation felt towards our local and native ways. I soon learned,
when our family moved to Fiji (i was younger then), where
i was exposed to other native Pasifika people and cultures,
that the fiepālagi-and-siolalo complex was shared across our
waters. Against the fiepālagi-and-siolalo complex, this work
celebrates our native ways of being and native ways of knowing. This work is a witness to the wisdom of the native people
of Pasifika.

I prefer 'native' over against the other problematic markers
'indigenous' and 'aboriginal', which were also given by pālagi
(white, European) scholars. The 'native' marker accommodates
the navigational heritage of our people. *Our ancestors were
navigators* is a mantra that we celebrate, and in native ears it
affirms that our ancestors came from somewhere else to make
Pasifika their home. The 'native' marker affirms the courage

and wisdom of our ancestors, without my having to prove that they were the 'first people' (connotations of the terms 'indigenous' and 'aboriginal') of Pasifika. The 'native' marker is more about belonging than about being first or sovereign, which are pālagi concerns.

My going native is not an attempt to raise the flag for nativism, the arrogance that only natives know and should speak about native things. That is not my mission here. Rather, my drive in this work is to invite and enable native *and* pālagi interpreters to also read Ruth (at least) with and through native Pasifika eyes.[6] One of the dangers with this kind of mission is the lure to romanticize, in order to appropriate, native views and values. I had to learn to see this over and over again with each PBS community. My most memorable learning – to not romanticize the natives – was at the Solomon Islands, prompted by a participant thinking of the widow at Zarephath (1 Kings 17.7–16).

Widow of Zarephath

It was during a session in which i emphasized that Naomi was not the only widow in the narrative. Ruth too was a widow, and she took care of Naomi. She went to glean at the field, and from the threshing floor, in order to find food and security for Naomi. To that, an older woman, herself a widow, brought the widow at Zarephath into our talanoa. In the story of Ruth taking care of Naomi, she could also hear the widow at Zarephath taking care of Elijah. Her interjection became an opportunity to divert to 1 Kings 17, and the points of connection and disconnection between the two widows began to flow into our talanoa.

To cut a long story short, another participant interrupted with a humbling claim – that he saw me in the same way that he saw Elijah. I froze, and then began to explain that i was not a prophet and that i have no healing powers. In response, he corrected me: i was like Elijah in the way that i asked too many questions and made too many demands. His reading was sharp and unapologetic: Elijah should have seen that the widow was collecting sticks (1 Kings 17.10) and realized that she was in need. Instead of helping her collect sticks, Elijah asked her for a drink (17.10). There was no water around where they were, so she had to go and get the drink from somewhere else. And before she could do this, he asked her to also bring a piece of bread (17.11). And even after she explained that she was preparing for their final meal before they die (17.12), Elijah put himself ahead of the widow and her son: 'But *first make a small loaf of bread for me* from what you have and bring it to me, and *then make something for yourself and your son*' (17.13b NIV, my italics). The conclusions reached by this interrupting Solomon Islander were obvious: Elijah was very insensitive and being a prophet does not excuse him from his self-centredness. Those were the characteristics that he also saw in me.

The widow at Zarephath came back again with the Ma'ohi PBS. I was better prepared then, and they spared me the embarrassment of being likened to the prophet Elijah. Several of the Ma'ohi participants were involved in the September 1995 anti-nuclear and pro-independence riot that resulted in the burning of parts of the airport and Papeete, and their reading was fiery: Elijah was thick, and a narcissist.

Both times that the Zarephath widow was dragged into the talanoa of Ruth, the PBS groups refused to pacify their views. Both times, the participants charged me to not tone down nor romanticize their views. They are natives, but not naive. This reminder applies both to the reading of scripture as well as to the struggles in the contemporary society, two subjects – scripture and society – that intermix and interrupt in talanoa.

Climate knots

Adding to the knots in this work are the dimensions of climate change that are woven into the bible studies. These dimensions are engaged with native Pasifika interests and terms, but they play out in the larger global context.

Climate change is one of the modern struggles in which native views have been romanticized and coopted (see Havea, 2010). It is no secret that we in Pasifika struggle with the effects of climate change; but drowning in despair is not the final word for us. Some of our people have drowned, some have moved away, and some have come back to join those who (like the agricultural community that stayed behind in Bethlehem, when the family of Naomi and Elimelek fled to Moab) continue to survive in the face of climate trauma. Our vulnerability and resilience shape the native views that are presented in the bible studies in the following chapters.

(alter)Natives

I set out to (re)search and (re)learn with PBS groups, and i discovered that Pasifika natives are also interested in making the text talk about normal and alternative subjects. 'Interesting' but 'irrelevant' were two popular keywords in their responses to many of the historical and literary observations that i associated with biblical scholarship, while 'really?' and 'what if?' were the responses to observations inspired by local experiences. At the beginning, i took the affirmation of local realities as evidence that the PBS groups were contextual thinkers. But by the end of my PBS journey, i came to understand that the natives were also interested in freeing the text (see also Boer, 2007) so that it talks more than experts tend to allow.

Natives of Pasifika can indeed speak (cf. Spivak, 1988) and make the Bible talk (cf. Callahan, 2006) alternatively. On and on (see Chapter 10) …

Prompts for further talanoa

1 Jione Havea, 'Reading Ruth with Native Islander Eyes', www.youtube.com/watch?v=1EAplzpK3zw&t=17s, accessed 5.5.21.

2 Tagata Pasifika (TVNZ), '2009 Samoa Tsunami: Ten Years On', www.youtube.com/watch?v=eJrTCWFtxJo, accessed 5.5.21.

3 'A Participatory Video made by Chivoko Village, Solomon Islands', www.youtube.com/watch?v=zgTqt4qbLhg, accessed 5.5.21.

Notes

1 But i did not always take notes, because that practice interrupts the flows of talanoa and clips the wings of imagination (not to mention that taking notes is more for the benefit of the learner than out of respect to the educators).

2 Talanoa has been employed in regional peacebuilding (in the Solomon Islands, following civil unrest) and reconciliation (in Fiji, following political coups) exercises, in hermeneutical and theological exercises, and recently appropriated by the United Nations to inspire and mobilize dialogue on climate change. The ripples and rhythms of talanoa are reaching beyond the edges of Pasifika.

3 Other native people have similar cultures and practices, so the event that we call talanoa is not unique to Pasifika. But for this work, my attention is on Pasifika. For this reason also, i resist translating talanoa as 'storytelling' – a term that has connotations in the academic and theological English-speaking worlds that oversimplify, and thus pacify, the Pasifika event-and-practice.

4 Historiographers often describe these scuffles as tribal or civil wars, and thereby give the impression that they were primarily territorial. What historiographers fail to see is that the scuffles were about customary duties (e.g. not give appropriately from the harvest) and relations (e.g. take someone else's partner).

5 The Samoan practice of 'big telling' (*talalasi*) encourages the accumulation and transformation of talanoa (see Ma'ilo, 2018).

6 Alas, the term 'Pasifika' (for Pacific) is also problematic. There are less-problematic markers, like Oceania and Moana, but Pasifika is the better known of these markers.

PART 2

Pasifika Bible Studies

3

Ruth 1.1–5
Migration and asylum

All creatures migrate. However, the bible studies in this chapter have a limited focus: the migration of humans from situations of crisis.[1] Crisis makes people migrate, seeking asylum (refuge, security) in other places within (internal displacement) and outside (into foreign lands) of national borders.[2] While the bible studies focus on the Ruth narrative, migration and asylum seeking continue into the modern age and crises are caused by many dynamics – such as war, persecution, famine, cyclones and other ecological crises that have been induced and hastened by climate change.

Migration involves crossing borders, and borders rise and stand in many forms. For this opening reflection, i limit myself to two forms of borders that relate to the bible studies that follow: physical borders that are visible, and cultural borders that are hidden but manifest in the interactions (noticeable when there are differences and tensions) between migrants and locals. Though different in form, these borders impact both the migrants and the locals as well as those people who dwell at the borderlands (most of whom are poor; see, further, Anzaldúa, 1987).

Among the physical forms are ecological (or natural) borders such as valleys, cliffs, rivers and reefs, formed by the energies and the movements of the land, the ocean, the sky and the deep (or underworld). Some of these natural borders have been bridged, filled or levelled to ease human travel (and tally up the logbooks of tourists and capitalists), but at a cost to the ecology.[3] When land- and sea-scapes are disturbed and altered,

living creatures are displaced and some species get extermin-
ated. With respect to human migration, crossing borders is
one thing, bending and blending borders are different things
altogether; but all of these border activities privilege human
interests over against the wider *circle of life*. At the borderlands are living creatures who are treaded upon and many are
endangered when humans cross, block or convert the borders.

Some physical borders are constructed by humans – like
the walls and fences that nations build to divide, separate and
segregate peoples and their cultures. The towering southern
border of the USA (which is quite imposing in comparison
to its northern border) and the so-called security walls of the
modern State of Israel[4] are examples of such borders. A less-
impressive and lesser-known border – but erected for the same
reasons and guarded with the same ruthlessness – is the barbed
fence that Indonesia enforces between Papua New Guinea
(PNG) and West Papua. The indigenous people of West Papua
and PNG are 'one people, one culture' on the largest island in
Pasifika, but Indonesia occupies the western side of the island
more ferociously than previous colonialist regimes did.[5] The
Indonesian border prevents West Papua and PNG from also
being 'one (is)land, one destiny'. These examples of constructed
physical borders from the modern age serve national interests,
and people who wish to cross those borders need permits in
order to pass through port authorities.

There are also economic motivations for the erection and
defence of national borders, as in the cases of the rich natural
resources that Indonesia (in collaboration with companies
based in the USA and Australia) are mining from the land of
West Papua and the bottom-line of the UK's Brexit strategies
(see Reddie, 2019). The proverbial elephant in the room of
these cases is racism (see De La Torre, 2021), which lies deep
within the foundation of those national erections.

Second, there are cultural borders (many of which have religious sanctions) that are not often noticed. When one migrates
across the borders between distant nations[6] – for example,
between the Netherlands and Papua – one crosses between sig-
nificantly different cultures and it would be easy for migrants

from one nation to insult the locals in their new location. Cultural borders are enforced by protocols that infuse customs and ideologies that vary between settlements (villages, towns, districts) in larger nations, and figuring out the appropriate thing to do or say in the new location is complicated by the different languages used by the migrants (e.g. the Dutch) versus the locals (e.g. Papuans). The language border is further complicated in the case of lands where locals speak multiple languages, as on the island of Papua where there are around 700 living languages. Which local language to use? This is a critical question not just because using the wrong local language can insult the local people but also because language shapes the way that locals think, read and perceive. The barrier of language is very raw for people in minority cultures, whether they are at home (locals) or away from home (migrants). The language and cultural barriers between the Dutch and the Papuans would have been experienced by Moabites and Judeans, in the background of the Ruth narrative.

A critical Pasifika example of the difference that language and translation make is the 1840 Waitangi Treaty in Aotearoa New Zealand. The treaty was written in English then translated into Māori (*Te Tiriti*). According to the English version, the Māori leaders gave the Queen 'all the rights and powers of sovereignty' over their land (Article 1). In the Māori version, which the majority of Māori signatories signed, they gave the Queen *Te kawanatanga katoa* (total governance) over the land. The word *kawanatanga* is a transliteration of the English term 'government', so in the eyes of the local Māori they were signing over the care of (governance over) the land to the British crown rather than relinquishing their sovereignty over the land. There is a Māori equivalent for sovereignty – *Te tino rangatiratanga* – which is used in Article 2. The writers and translators were aware of the Māori understanding of Te tino rangatiratanga, and they took advantage of the language border to give advantage to the British empire to sell the land of the Māori, and its subjects to buy it.

It is sometimes easier to cross national (physical) borders than to cross cultural (unseen) borders, especially when the factors of religion, ideologies and language are taken into account. And it makes a difference if the migrant is from a minoritized culture – they are more noticeable because of their colour and accent as compared to migrants from dominant and white cultures. In Aotearoa New Zealand and Australia, for instance, migrants from neighbouring Pasifika islands who overstay their visas are raided and deported, but the majority of those who outstay their visas in both nations hold British passports and immigration officers do not see them as overstayers. The British overstayers pass because they blend in with the powerholders in both nations, and they also speak English. They speak with strong accents, but they have the accepted skin colour – white. Overstayers from dominant white societies escape being seen as illegal immigrants, but the brown and black bodies get picked on even though their appearances are closer to those of the native local people. Why? White supremacy, period.

Migration is a complex experience that should not be romanticized. On top of the matter of borders are the reasons why people migrate. In the following bible studies, two reasons are pertinent: people migrate/return seeking asylum (refugees), and people migrate/return in response to ecological crises. These two reasons intersect at the plights of 'climate refugees', even though this status is not recognized in international law. Climate displacement is not included among the forms of displacement that produce legal refugees. Those who migrate because they have been displaced by war, political violence and hunger are recognized by international law as refugees, whereas those who migrate because of climate disasters are not recognized to have any legal status as refugees.

International law is stipulated on lands where people could evacuate in the face of ecological disasters and then return to rebuild their homes and survive on reserves and investments, but Pasifika island states like Tuvalu and Kiribati are in danger of 'sinking' in the rising sea-level of climate change and hence 'return' is not an option. One of the recent projections is that these islands will disappear by 2050, at which time the natives will not have a home island and they will be stateless wherever they end up. While the debate on climate change circles around the issue of responsibility – are humans responsible for the acceleration of global warming, bearing in mind that people with power and promise are good at shifting the blame (see Fewell and Gunn, 1992, pp. 22–38) – the natives of low-lying island states are in danger of (political) statelessness and (existential) lifelessness.

In light of the foregoing reflection, the following bible studies examine Ruth 1.1–5 (in two sections, Ruth 1.1–2 and Ruth 1.3–5) through the joys and stresses of migration, taking the famine that caused the family's migration as an ecological disaster. I do not need to claim that this famine was caused by climate change, but in the following bible studies i hold in mind famines today that result from climate change (among other causes). Famine is real nowadays, as it was in biblical times.

(1) Ruth 1.1-2: Bethlehem family seeks asylum in Moab[7]

[1] { } When judges were judging
{ } a famine was in the country
so ( ) a man from Bethlehem Judah went to be a stranger in the field of Moab, he and his wife and his two sons
[2] ( ) The name of the man, Elimelek
( ) the name of his wife, Naomi
( ) the name of his two sons, Mahlon and Chilion
Ephrathites of Bethlehem Judah
They came to the field of Moab
( ) they were there

The narrative unfolds with the assumption that when the family of Elimelek and Naomi migrated from Bethlehem to Moab, they crossed physical borders. The account does not chart their route, but readers and hearers of this talanoa would imagine crooked terrains and bodies of water (including the Dead Sea) between Judah and Moab that had not been levelled or bridged. There would have been people and creatures on their way, at the borderlands as well, but the narrative does not show any interest in them either.

Flight

The narrative moves quickly from the family's departure (Ruth 1.1b) to their arrival (1.2b), stepping over many gaps that caught the attention of the Pasifika Bible Study (PBS) participants. First, there are gaps with regard to the matter of time, which tends to be fluid for most islanders. In the world of talanoa, a story takes time to unfold through its telling(s) and the conversation(s) that it inspires.

The Ruth narrative does not state how long it took for the family to decide (and whose idea it was) to migrate, nor how long it took them to cross from Bethlehem to Moab. They did not jump into a desert vehicle or flying boat to evacuate. It must have taken them a long time to cross over, and the narrator's haste curbs readers' chance to imagine and see the physical space and borders that the narrative crosses over. The narrator's *flight* gives the impression that the wide and impressive ecological border that the family crossed was empty, thus bringing to mind another event of migration – that of colonialists and settlers who claimed that 'the new world' they had 'discovered' was *terra nullius* (empty land), and thereby gave themselves permission to claim it for their crown (see Brett, 2018). In holding back from the narrator's flight i intersect the matter of time with the matter of space and draw attention to how human migration events, including the spread of religious missions, have colonialist potentials.

I call attention to the matter of time in part because the family of Naomi and Elimelek did not have to rush. A famine is not like a cyclone, which arrives in a matter of days. There must have been signs of the famine in Judah unfolding over weeks and months, which would have given people enough time to prepare to face the famine or to evacuate. The signs may be in the form of a drought, a poor harvest in the previous season – so that seedlings for the next crop were 'no good'

– a decrease in the labour force, frequent and more intense desert storms, heatwaves and a host of other signs. The narrator rushes through the family's preparation and experience of border crossing, but readers do not have to hustle along at the same pace.

Furthermore, the narrative does not situate the family's departure in relation to how long the famine had been in the country. This missing piece of information makes me wonder about the kind of family this was. It appears to be a significant family in the eyes of the narrator because he named all four of them – Elimelek, Naomi, Mahlon and Chilion – but whether they departed in the first week or the tenth month of the famine makes a difference for the PBS participants. If they departed in the early days of the famine, that was a sign that they were not 'people of the land', who would have found means to face and survive the famine. The people of the land have ways of surviving with, and over, the ailments of the land. Many people stayed behind and faced the predicaments of the famine, and some of them were there when Naomi returned (over ten years later) with Ruth at her side.

Also related to the matter of time, it is not clear how long the family had intended to stay in Moab. They went 'to be stranger(s)' (לגור) in the field of Moab (1.1b), and the contrast between 1.1b (they went to be strangers or sojourners) and 1.2b (they continued to be there) suggests that initially the family planned to be in Moab for a short stay (until the famine passes) and they ended up staying longer than planned. The intended length of their sojourn in Moab will give one a better feel for whether they intended to return to their inheritance – herein is the difference between the family abandoning their inheritance and leaving it in the care of someone else – and whether they were prepared for the strains of migration.

Herein is the second gap in the narrator's account that caught the attention of the PBS participants: crossing of borders requires sustenance. Did the family carry food for the journey? Even for a short journey, a family of four would carry more than 'some bread and a skin of water' (Gen. 17.14) which were not even enough for Hagar and her one son, Ishmael.

I suspect that if the narrator was a mother, a minoritized migrant, asylum seeker or a native Pasifika islander, she would have paid attention to matters that would sustain the family as they crossed the border between Judah and Moab. Across the wilderness, water to drink and some apparatus to give shade are essentials that the narrator ignored in his haste.

Did the family carry a lot of baggage? Did they have helpers?[8] In relation to other significant biblical migrants, i wonder if this was a wealthy family that could afford to pay helpers or acquire slaves to assist them in their migration. Abram was a wealthy slave owner when he migrated from Haran to Canaan (Gen. 12.5), so there would have been a decent-size travel party at his disposal. His wealth was willed to his son Isaac (Gen. 25.5), but his grandson Jacob was so enterprising that by the time he re-migrated from Haran to Canaan he had acquired two wives with their maidservants, ten sons (Benjamin was born in Canaan) and one daughter Dinah (see Gen. 34), as well as a lot of wealth, cattle, and male and female slaves (Gen. 32.6). When Jacob later migrated from Canaan to Egypt because of the famine, his family numbered 66 people not counting the wives of his sons (Gen. 46.26) and his travel party included slaves, flocks and herds (Gen. 47.1). These migrant families were wealthy, including when there was a famine. The PBS participants thus wondered if the family of Elimelek and Naomi took some of their wealth with them, and whether they had assistance as they crossed the border from Judah to Moab. Or did they leave everything behind in Judah because their flight was meant to be temporary? The narrator is not interested in this line of questioning,[9] but it is the kind of query that islanders, migrants and refugees, bring to this talanoa.

Famine

Although the cause of the famine is not described, many readers conclude that this narrative was a critique of the chieftains or judges (1.1a). The famine is evidence that they were bad leaders (a point that is repeated in the book of Judges), and this was justification for both the *shift of leadership* (from judges to kings in 1 Samuel) and for the *shift of location* of the book of Ruth (from between Songs and Lamentations in the Hebrew Bible to between Judges and 1 Samuel in the Christian Bible). I discussed these shifts in Chapter 1, in relation to the political functions that Ruth plays in them, and i turn here to the traumas of the famine.

The narrator passes over the famine as if it was not critical.[10] On the other hand, famine is a straining reality in the eyes of refugees and in the context of climate change. Famine and poverty push hungry people into the paths and camps of refugees, and hunger is not just an African or Latin American reality[11] for there are poor and hungry people at all corners of the globe. In the hostile context of climate-affected (is)lands, traditional crops no longer grow, so the local people are forced to change their diet and learn to depend on imported processed food, which are not healthy nor cheap. In Pasifika, the change of diet contributes to the high number of cases of diabetes and obesity and keeps the local people poorer than they would be if they did not have to spend so much money on meals (and we eat a lot). In human eyes, famine combined with poverty (and other struggles such as poor leadership and lack of foresights) cause trauma.

Resisting the narrator's swift turn from the famine (Ruth 1.1a) to the asylum-seeking family (Ruth 1.1b—2a), i linger on the famine because it also causes trauma to 'the land'. In human eyes, a famine is when there are not enough 'fruits of the land' for human consumption, human progress and human prosperity. Human eyes, however, do not always see the trauma of the land. In this connection, one has a better chance of seeing the trauma of the land when one thinks from, and reads through, the context of climate change. At the underside of this proposal is a reminder that climate trauma is not just about the benefits for humans, but the welfare of the land as well. How might climate trauma shed some light on the hidden subject of the land in the situation of famine in Ruth 1.1? This question invites a return, back to the extended garden story in Genesis 2.4b—4.16.[12] For this return, i focus on the subject of the land (unseen in the Ruth narrative) which, in Pasifika, always already intersects with the sea, the sky and the underworld.[13]

In the extended garden story, the land gave from its own wetness a mist to water the whole face of the ground (Gen. 2.6), and the land also provided the dry dust (read: dirt) that the Lord needed to create a person (*'adam*, Gen. 2.7). The land enabled trees of all kinds to grow (Gen. 2.9) and when the Lord decided to create a helper for the earthly person, the first set of helpers were animals and birds that also came from 'the ground' of the same land (Gen. 2.18–19). In the extended garden story, the earthly person, the trees and the animals shared the same compositions – they all were 'fruits of the land'.

Then the story of the land turned sour. The earthly person named but was not satisfied with the first set of helpers that it was provided with, so the Lord formed a human-woman and as a consequence the earthly person became a human-man (Gen. 2.23). Then a serpent, who was the wisest of the fruits of the land, comes into the story to correct the misinformation between the Lord and the human creatures (Gen. 3.1–7). To cut a long story short, the serpent was correct, and the Lord was upset and cursed the serpent (Gen. 3.14) and the woman (Gen. 3.16) individually and as a pair together with their off-spring (Gen. 3.15), as well as cursed the land on account of the man (Gen. 3.17). The Lord cursed the land to bear thorns and thistles (Gen. 3.18). On account of the Lord's curse, therefore, famine became a possibility.

But the curse of the land is broken when Cain 'brought from the fruit of the ground an offering to the Lord' (Gen. 4.3). Abel, his brother, also brought an offering from his flock, which the Lord favoured over against Cain's offering (Gen. 4.4–5). That the Lord did not favour Cain's offering (Gen. 4.6), which brings to mind an earlier event when Cain's father did not favour the first set of helpers that the Lord presented to him, embarrassed Cain. I can understand Cain's embarrass-ment, for he was the firstborn and the first to bring an offering to the Lord. But i cannot condone what unfolded as a conse-quence: Cain rose up against Abel and killed him when they were in the field (Gen. 4.8). In response, the Lord cursed Cain 'from the ground, which opened its mouth to receive the blood' of his brother Abel (Gen. 4.11). The land is cursed further – to not 'yield its strength' to Cain – and Cain is destined to be a fugitive and wanderer for the rest of his life (Gen. 4.12).

The connections between Abel and the land are disclosed at three places: first, in his offering which, in light of Genesis 2.18–19 and the reading proposed above, was also 'fruit of the land';[14] second, in his blood crying 'from the ground'; and third, in the banishment of Cain to be a restless wanderer (read: exiled) 'in the earth'. Whereas the first suggests that Abel too broke the 'curse of the land' given in Genesis 3, the second and third offer new twists to the curse of the land. The land has drunk blood and expected *to see* the wandering of exiled people seeking asylum. This reading accounts for two native Pasifika views:

• First, the name for the spokesperson for a chief or community in Fiji is known as the *mata-ni-vanua* which translates as 'eyes-of-the land'. In this construction, the land can see.
• Second, one of the Samoan words that translates as 'soil' (or dirt) is *'ele'ele*, a word that also translates as 'blood'. In the Samoan understanding of 'ele'ele, land (soil) and life (blood) are one, and thus one expects one to be in solidarity with the other.

In these connections, the land can see the plight of Cain (as a figure for refugees) as well as identify with his burden (Gen. 4.13–14).

There are mixed views concerning the land in the extended garden story. On the one hand, the land has creative strength to give and sustain life. Even after it was cursed the first time, the land still 'bore fruits' for Cain and Abel. On the other hand, the land was cursed first to bear thorns and thistles (in Gen. 3) and then to not bear any fruits at all (in Gen. 4). Famine became a possibility in Genesis 3, and a punishment in Genesis 4. With this reading in hand, i return to the famine in Ruth 1.1.

In his haste, the narrator belittled the crises of the famine and masked the trauma of and to the land. To the contrary, by giving attention to the subject of the land the reading proposed herein unapologetically goes against the drive of the narrator. This reading is encouraged by my drive to read biblical texts in the context of climate change. In other words, this form of contextual interpretation invites one to go beyond the limits and blind spots of Ruth 1.1. To appropriate the words of Amos, this reading wandered from sea to sea seeking to hear the story of the land (see Amos 8.11–12). That story was ignored by the narrator but, with the help of PBS groups, i have drawn it out from the extended garden story (somewhat like drawing a bone out of a body). This reading is a first step in the drive to give attention to other minoritized and overlooked characters in Ruth 1.1–2.

Moab

Twice the narrator mentioned 'the field of Moab' (Ruth 1.1b and 1.2b) but he did not fix the exact location where the family came to sojourn or any of the nearby towns. In simply using 'field' (sadeh) the narrator connects Moab to the land.[15] This 'field' was not godforsaken, but it was a land that survived the curses in the extended garden story and the shame that the incest in Lot's family casted over the land and people of Moab (Gen. 19.30–38). In Ruth 1.1–2, the field of Moab was fertile, and it was open to refugees.

The word 'field' has a village[16] and countryside feel, and this stands out in contrast to the precision with which the migrant family is located at Ephrathah, Bethlehem, Judah. The field is somewhere in Moab, but the family came from a specific and named location. The narrator thus ambiguates (read: disfavours) the Moabite location, and the irony here is that it was at the field of Moab that the Judahite family found asylum. There was a famine at Bethlehem (literally, 'house of food', like a storehouse) and they found refuge at the field of Moab. Unnamed and ambiguated, the field of Moab is presented as if it were a refugee camp.

In the Tongan bible, 'field' is rendered as tuku'uta, a term that connotes country or bush (as compared to town). There is a derogatory tone in the Tongan rendering because tuku'uta folks are assumed to be unlearned – like 'savages', as missionaries and anthropologists saw our people – as compared to townspeople. This derogatory tone exhibits missionary influence, propagated by two assumptions: first, the missionaries assumed that the ways and wisdom of our people were tuku'uta (read: backward, uncivilized) and second, they assumed that real 'enlightened' wisdom comes from the west and is taught by white teachers in classrooms in towns. These assumptions are part of the myth of whiteness that continue to plague native minds even in the age of post-independence.[17] Nonetheless, tuku'uta has another connotation: it is the Tongan equivalent of the English 'breadbasket' and so it is an appropriate translation for 'beth-lehem' (storehouse of food). In this twist, the tuku'uta (field) of Moab is better at being a beth-lehem than the Bethlehem of Judah. Both nuances of tuku'uta provide meaningful twists to Ruth 1.1–2.

Staying with the richness of Pasifika languages, another appropriate translation for 'field' is the Mā'ohi Nui term *marae* (also in Māori and Rarotongan). A marae is a gathering place for celebration, mourning, instruction, worship, asylum and other rites and passages of life. In Polynesian legends, one of the central marae is Taputapuātea on the island of Raiātea ('faraway sky'). The ancient name for Raiātea was Hāvai'i (Hāwaiki in some legends) and it is considered to be the homeland of our ancestors. It was at the Taputapuātea marae that Tupaia (1724?–70) was trained as a native priest and educated with indigenous wisdom; Tupaia was the native who navigated the *Endeavour* through the waters of Mā'ohi Nui and mapped the islands of Pasifika for James Cook. His wisdom was learnt at a marae, and the Mā'ohi rendering invites seeing the field of Moab in a similar light.

This reflection finds positive affirmations of the field of Moab and, by extension, the land of Moab overall. There is no reason on the basis of Ruth 1.1–2 to discriminate against Moab, or against Moabite people. Like Egypt for the family of Joseph, Moab was a place of refuge for the family of Naomi and Elimelek. But the field of Moab was more than a storehouse and a refugee camp. Like a marae, the field of Moab was also a place for learning, for worship, and for dreaming.

Neighbours

In the relational cultures of Pasifika, life orients towards kin and community. One keeps and nurtures relationships (*vā*) that unfold and play out in lived time and public space (see Vaai and Casimira, 2017). Vā are not issues or concepts, but events that are lived, that are affected, and that are formative in the ways that islanders behave, work, worship, think and read. Put another way, it is difficult for islanders to live in isolation (see Vaai, 2021b). Islanders exist in and because of vā, and neighbours have a place in the intersections of island space with island time. Kin and community are at the foreground of the vā framework, and neighbours are at the background shaping (on a daily basis) one's praxis and principles. Kin and community are the occasional vā partners (in community and public gatherings), while neighbours are the daily and regular partners.

For the PBS participants, the absence of a reference to neighbours in Ruth 1.1–2 is an invitation to fill in the gap (cf. Gunn and Fewell, 1993, pp. 163–6). As far as the story-world is concerned, they expected that the migrating family of Naomi and Elimelek had neighbours at Bethlehem as well as neighbours when they settled in the field of Moab. Without neighbours, the story-world is disconnected if not empty. As such, what did the Judean neighbours think about the family's departure? And what did the neighbours at Moab think about these refugees, with their foreign customs and language, coming into their field? These questions are outside of the narrator's interest, but they are critical in the island context where neighbours watch closely and gossip freely. Neighbours see things that one might not want to be seen, and say things that may disturb. In island settings, 'neighbour watch' is surveillance with an attitude!

On the other side of the coin, did the family of Elimelek and Naomi say anything to their neighbours at Bethlehem and at the field of Moab? Anyone who has done anything with refugees knows that they have many stories to tell, and that they would tell their stories if they had the chance and, in some cases, if they feel safe enough to speak up. They might be homeless and stateless, but not speechless. And definitely not talanoa-less! The family of four would have said many things but the narrator was not interested in how they thought or felt about their situation. In this connection, many of the PBS participants find the narrator to be very insensitive. Their resolution was simple: the narrator may not have cared, but that should not stop readers from asking about neighbours.

I ask about neighbours in order to give this narrative an islander feel and a sense of reality. In the world of talanoa, Ruth 1.1–2 is a dead story – the narrative flutters over the tick-tocks of time, and it sterilizes the spaces that it narrates as it zips across them. Outside of locating the famine in relation to the judges (which is such a long stretch of time, over many generations, that it reads as a broad brushstroke that problematizes the veracity of the narrative), the story does not exhibit awareness of the flows of time. Nor a sense of space as lived, which could have been done for example by 'neighbouring' (giving vā to) the family of Naomi and Elimelek and by populating Bethlehem and Moab.

The query concerning neighbours puts Elimelek and his family under the shadows of Rahab and her family who were spared (Josh. 6.17, 22–23) because of her strength and negotiation skills (Josh. 2), but their neighbours were decimated by the invading Israelites. Rahab and her family did not strip their neighbours as the Israelites did when they left Egypt (Exod. 12.35–36), or murder their neighbours as Esther and Mordecai negotiated for the Jews (Esth. 7–9), but they might as well have done. This reflection is thus not just about who was neighbour to the family of Naomi and Elimelek (see also Luke 10.25–37), but also whether this Bethlehem family was neighbourly to their neighbours.

So what?

This bible study looked at and through some of the details in Ruth 1.1–2, as well as details that are important to refugees and islanders but ignored by the narrator. In the context of climate change, neighbours at both (inter)personal and (inter) national levels are important. Bringing the drive of this bible study on Ruth 1.1–2 to the question of who the neighbours for climate affected (is)lands are, the answer is simple: they are the ones who collaborate for climate justice.

Pasifikation

This bible study engaged with, but was not limited to, Ruth 1.1–2. It was not trapped by the narrative, and it did not give in to what were assumed to be the intentions of the narrator. On the other hand, the bible study reflected the courage of the PBS groups to doubt, and to see the blind spots in, the biblical text.

There is a world of difference – much more complicated than the differences between Dutch and Papuan cultures – between scriptural and talanoa cultures. If the PBS participants were the narrators of Ruth 1.1–2, the narrative would have been much longer, more detailed and entwining. But the PBS participants have blind spots also, and so this bible study is an invitation to reconsider one's reading of these two opening verses.

Takeaway

1 What might the neighbours have thought about the family's decision to move?
2 In whose care might Elimelek and Naomi have left their home and inheritance?
3 How do refugee stories in your context reflect, or not reflect, Ruth 1.1–2?

(2) Ruth 1.3–5: Death visits Moab

³ ( ) He died, Elimelek husband of Naomi
[but] she remained, with her two sons
⁴ ( ) they lifted for themselves wives, from the Moabites
  the name of the first, Orpah
  the name of the second, Ruth
( ) they dwelled there for about ten years
    ⁵ (then) they died also, both of them, Mahlon and Chilion
(but) the woman remained, from her two children and from
her husband

Death

Refugee camps are not exempt from the visitation of death, but
the death of refugees hardly get noticed outside of the immediate family (if they are there) and close associates. Refugees
are stateless people and at death they are quickly buried. The
case of Elimelek is different. He was the first in the immediate
family to die, and his death is noticed and remembered (Ruth
1.3a). His family found refuge in the field of Moab, but they
did not find refuge from death. In terms of the story-world,
they brought death to the field of Moab.

With the visitation of death, roles change. Whereas members
of the family are identified in relation to Elimelek in 1.2a (Naomi
was 'his wife' and Mahlon and Chilion were 'his sons'), at death
Elimelek is identified as 'husband of Naomi'. This might have
been the convention, but the fact that there was an alternative for the narrator to use makes this a *telling* (in the sense
of talanoa) announcement. The patriarchal biases of biblical
scriptures would have made identifying Elimelek as 'father of
Mahlon and Chilion' appropriate if not normal, so identifying
him in relation to his widow is quite telling.

Naomi is now, if not earlier as well, the head of the household. Naomi was not a tag-along kind of wife, and she may
have even contributed to the decision to move to Moab. As a
mother, i imagine that she would have been very concerned for

the survival of her family and could have initiated the decision to move to Moab. She may not even have any attachment to Judah as her husband did, through his inheritance (see Chapter 6). Her heritage is concealed from readers, and the etymology of her name is not certain, so nothing in the story-world prevents her from hailing from a land outside of Judah. Was she, like Rahab, the daughter of a foreigner? Or was she, like Bathsheba, the granddaughter of a privileged neighbour to figures of power (2 Sam. 11)? These questions invite locating Naomi in the shadows of women characters who had power and courage.

When Elimelek died, 'Naomi remained with her two sons' (1.3a). Here also, the narrative is fudgy with respect to time. The narrative does not state how long the family was in the land before Elimelek died, nor how long it was after his death when the sons were married to daughters of Moab (see next section). After marriage, Naomi and her sons 'dwelled there for about ten years then they died also, both of them, Mahlon and Chilion' (1.4b–5a). Ten years is a long time, so the death of Naomi's sons cannot be blamed on their Moabite wives as if they cursed the family in the way that Judah blamed Tamar, mother of Perez and Zerah, for the death of Onan (Gen. 38.11b).

Shifting to the platform of gender, the deaths of Elimelek and his two sons mark the exit (read: death) of patriarchy from the narrative world. The narrative rids its male members (in other words, the narrative literarily kills the men), and leaves only female characters at the field of Moab. In this connection, the story is more than a critique of judges; it is a 'sign of the time' for burying patriarchy.

Turning to the context of climate change, the foregoing reading invites attention to the death of the (is)land itself. Across borders, (is)lands are struggling to stay alive. The more frequent and stronger cyclones, the higher global temperatures, the quickened melting of glaciers, the ongoing droughts, the bleaching of coral life systems, the upheavals caused by mining (on land and at the seabed), are making the approach of death to (is)lands quicker than expected. Death is on the horizon.

But death does not have the final word in Ruth 1.3–5. The death of the father was an opportunity for the sons to be married, and the death of his sons was an opportunity for the surviving widows to bury patriarchy, to decide for themselves, and to push back at one another (see Chapter 3). If there is to be a final word for Ruth 1.3–5, it should reflect the confirmation that 'she/the woman remained' after the death of her husband (1.3a) and the death of her sons (1.5b). She remained (שאר). Strong. Steadfast. The men in her life perished, but she persisted. She was steadfast (cf. Judg. 7.3) through both of the visits of death (or, through both death accounts).

Marriage

After the death of Elimelek, Naomi oversaw the marriage of her two sons to local Moabite women. She might have even initiated and directed the choice of partners for her sons, as Hagar did for Ishmael (Gen. 21.21) and Rebekah did for Jacob (Gen. 27.46). It was important for Hagar and Rebekah that their sons were married to women from their own homelands, and in that light i wonder if the marriage of Naomi's sons was a signal to her heritage. Might Naomi have been from Moabite roots?

The sons' contribution to the selection of their wives is also telling, in the way that it is phrased – 'they lifted for themselves wives' (1.4a). The verb 'to lift' (נשא) may simply mean that each son *picked* the woman to marry, and it also suggests that each son *carried away* (cf. Ezra 5.15) the woman to become his wife. Force is implied in the second connotation of the term despite the sons' voicelessness.[18]

The marriage of Hebrew males to non-Hebrew females is condemned in biblical Israel (see Num. 25, Ezra 10.1–44; Neh. 13.23–31; cf. Venter, 2018) but nevertheless practised even by its royalties (see 1 Kings 11.1–5). In Ruth 1.3–5, marriage to foreign wives does not appear to be an issue at all. There is no anxiety in the narrative with the crossing of cultural borders, and this gives the story an unreal feel. There must have been some tensions, starting with the solemnizing of the marriages (another detail that the narrator passes over). That the wives were picked from the field of Moab (a biblical version of a refugee camp) should not be taken to mean that their parents would let them get married (or lifted) without a celebration. Even the poorest of poor people in slums and refugee camps today go to great lengths, often far beyond their means, to have a 'proper ceremony' for their children's (especially daughters') weddings. I imagine the same for the parents of Orpah and Ruth (who could have been sisters, like Leah and Rachel) – the parents would have expected a proper ceremony, as Laban did for Leah (who, according to the protocols of their place, had to be married first; see Genesis 29.21–26).[19]

Joeli Ducivaki, a Fijian Methodist pastor who participated in one of my classes at Trinity Methodist Theological College (Auckland, Aotearoa New Zealand), insisted that a cultural ritual must have been conducted to solemnize the weddings at Moab. As a rite of passage, the ritual would have symbolized the tying of the knots and the exchange of agreement between the couple (and their families, in the case of arranged marriages). Such a ritual would be important for cross-cultural couples. This leads to a critical question: Why can't the cultural rituals be taken as religious events? Behind this question is the interest in 'lifting the ban' (in Kiribati, this ritual is known as *tekeroi*) from the perception of Moab. Moab must have had customs and protocols according to which the parents of Orpah and Ruth would have wanted the weddings to be properly conducted. My concern here is not to determine what the Moabite rituals involve (see Chapter 3), but to challenge naïve and negative perceptions of Moab. My challenge is straightforward: Moab was not an irreligious land. The Hebrew narrator was not interested in seeing this side of Moab, but readers could 'talk back' to the scriptural narrative on matters of cultural border crossing such as this.

In Pasifika during the white missionary era, the cultural rituals of our ancestors were banished because the missionaries saw those as the practices of darkness and paganism. Our cultural protocols were demonized and many of those are now forgotten. The few protocols that survive have been whitewashed and appropriated into Christian ceremonies. With respect to the marriages of Orpah and Ruth, the cultural protocols of Moab are forgotten by the memorializing verses of both Hebrew and Christian scriptures. Or have they? Could the Moab rituals be the source for Ruth's committing words on the road, later in the narrative (see Chapter 3)?

On the one hand this narrative affirms the fruitfulness of Moab, but on the other hand it deters readers from finding anything good or religious coming out of the field of Moab. In the marriage of Naomi's sons, for instance, the narrative encourages the impression that the boys from Bethlehem were the privileged parties to the relationship. They 'lifted' their wives, they must have brought something needful (e.g. wealth and legacy) to the Moabite families, and they would therefore have had the upper hand in the relationship with their Moabite in-laws. This is a Judean view.

The condition of the marriage suggests otherwise. The boys were fatherless and possibly landless (unless Naomi had an inheritance in Moab), and their marriage was not to other migrants in the field but to daughters of the land. Orpah and Ruth were natives of Moab, and their selection was most likely because they had something to offer Naomi's family (e.g. land and plantation). The marriage of Naomi's sons could therefore have been for survival and economic reasons, intersecting the (private) needs and affairs of home with the (public) politics of tying family knots across cultural borders. In the eyes of the PBS participants, the daughters of natives *lifted* the sons of migrants.

The narrative names the wives and husbands but does not identify who married whom. The brothers are named in the same order in Ruth 1.2 and 1.5, Mahlon and then Chilion, as if to suggest that Mahlon was older than Chilion. In the naming of the brides, Orpah is the first to be named and then Ruth (Ruth 1.4). Since Ruth was the widow of Mahlon (Ruth 4.10), the order in which they are named at marriage suggests age – Orpah was older than Ruth so she was married first, but to the younger brother. How age and birthplace shape their thinking and undertaking will become clearer as the narrative unfolds. At this point, with islander eyes, the PBS participants see age and birthplace (for husbands and wives) as having to do with respect and inheritance. Naomi approved the marriage of her sons to Orpah and Ruth because they had respect and inheritance that would benefit her migrant family – they would help secure refuge and settle them down in the field of Moab. In this reading, marriage was an indication that they were in Moab to stay. In this reading also, marriage was more complicated than the narrative implied as it unfolded.

Widows

Death ended three marriages and shifted three women in the story-world of Ruth 1.1–5 into the state of widowhood. But they were not disempowered as a consequence. The narrative focuses on Naomi as if she was the only 'woman who remained' (1.5) but Orpah and Ruth became widows after the death of their (first?) husbands, and they too remained speechless and faceless.

Orpah and Ruth were wives for around ten years, and the narrative does not report if they had any offspring. Ten years is a long time so they would have had many chances (assuming that they were not sexless couples) to bear children – sons (the pride of patriarchy) and daughters – in the fertile field of Moab. If they did, the narrator was not interested in them and readers should not be surprised for he has a habit of fast forwarding the story and writing over (read: ignoring) significant details.

Widows also have a special place in the charity box of the Bible alongside orphans, foreigners and the poor (Exod. 22.22; Deut. 10.18; Job 29.12). Nonetheless, there are some biblical widows who lack wealth but are rich in generosity (1 Kings 17.7–16) and devotion (Mark 12.41–44; Luke 21.1–4). There are strong widows also in the biblical narrative including Bathsheba (who, after the murder of her husband Uriah, moved into the palace of David and masterminded the instalment of her son Solomon to the throne of Israel; see 2 Samuel 11.14–17 and 1 Kings 1.5–31), and Herodias (who authorized the killing of John the Baptist, who was so critical of her marriage to Herod, brother of her husband Philip; see Mark 6.17–28). And there are widows who are seen as wicked and nasty. At the top of the nasty list is Jezebel, who concocted the plan to kill Naboth for his ancestral land and vineyard (1 Kings 21.1–16) and she is blamed for bringing Ba'al worship into the house of Ahab. She became a widow (but not many readers see her as one) after the death of Ahab (1 Kings 22.37–38) and later died a violent death (2 Kings 9.30–37; cf. Melanchthon, 2021). In other words, there are widows and there are widows in the Bible[20] and one of the challenges for readers is to allow the three widows in Ruth 1.1–5 to differ, one from the other. Naomi, Orpah and Ruth were all widows, but they did not have to be the same kind of widow.

Naomi held the attention of the narrator maybe because she was the widow who lost the most – a husband and two sons – but in ignoring the loss to Orpah and Ruth the narrator literally sidelines both of them. They were not as important *as* Naomi, the survivor with the highest rank in Elimelek's family. Orpah and Ruth may not have been of any significance *to* Naomi (an issue to revisit as the narrative unfolds) but at this juncture it is clear that Naomi is the survivor with entitlements over Elimelek's inheritance. The heirs are dead without any sons, and Naomi is the next in line. Unless. Unless the widows of Mahlon and Chilion challenge Naomi for the right to inherit (see Chapter 3). If Elimelek's inheritance was of any interest to Naomi, the narrative helped by sidelining Orpah and Ruth.

Elimelek's inheritance was back in Judah, and if Naomi was interested in it, she would have to return to Judah. If Naomi opts to return, she will have access to something that many climate refugees no longer have – home and security (see Chapter 5). Following this shift, the story of Naomi may be read as and through the experiences of climate refugees who decide to return to their home(is)land.

So what?

Widowhood does not have the final word in Ruth 1.3–5. Death took their husbands, but the women remain in the narrative and draw readers to follow their stories.

The two bible studies in this chapter encourage the imagination of readers to migrate beyond the limits of the text and the interests of the narrator. The PBS insights that inspired these bible studies are in clear violation of the favoured practices of exegesis in biblical studies, which confine readers within the borders of textuality. In one way, these PBS bible studies sidetrack from the proper ceremonies of biblical studies. And in another way, metaphorically speaking, these bible studies followed the migration of the narrative focus from Bethlehem and Judah (pride lands of biblical studies) to the fertile (is)lands of Moab and called attention to 'fruits of the land' that are hidden from the narrator's account.

Pasifikation

In Pasifika, the (is)lands are dying. The two images below show the death of the (is)lands at two critical places of transition: at places of birth (see Figure 3.1) and at places of burial (see Figure 3.2).

Figure 3.1 shows the maternity ward at Betio, a town in North Tarawa, Kiribati. The highest point on this island is around 3 metres above sea-level. During the king tide (which usually lasts for four to five days each month), seawater calmly rises up and comes through and on to the (is)land. The photo shows how high the waves come on to the grounds of the Betio maternity ward, the main one on the island; at high tide, the waves are higher than the shoreline. Also, the photo shows how calm the sea is behind the wave. One wonders how high the waves get when the sea is rough, and the wind picks up?

In Figure 3.1, children come out to play in the crashing wave at the maternity ward; but this is a common sight on other shores of this island. This is the context where most of the

Figure 3.1: Maternity ward at Betio, Kiribati.
Courtesy of Maria Timon.

Figure 3.2: Burial ground at Togoru, Fiji.
Photo courtesy of Marcelo Schneider.

children of North Tarawa, and Kiribati as a group, are born. The 'today mothers' of Kiribati give birth to 'tomorrow people' in parts of the (is)land that drowns several times a month.

And at the other end of life, as can be seen in the burial ground (on the left of Figure 3.2) at the village of Togoru on Fiji's largest island, Viti Levu, there is no rest at the 'land of the dead'. These tombstones did not walk into the sea. The graves used to be on the island, with an ocean-view, but the sea has gnawed the (is)land and the burial ground is now in the sea, looking back on to the (is)land. One wonders, how do the sons, daughters, grandsons and granddaughters of those who were buried in these graves breathe upon seeing their drowning parents or grandparents?

The tombstones mark the graves of the wealthier people, most of whom were Europeans (missionaries and business-people) and a few locals from chiefly families. The normal people did not have tombstones, and there is no certainty if their remains are still there, where they were buried.

Seawater has crossed the borders of Pasifika (is)lands and brought death to lands into which natives are born (in Kiribati) and buried (in Fiji). The death of the land is an unavoidable reality in Pasifika.

These drowning and dying (is)lands invite a return to the dead characters in Ruth 1.3–5. What else does their death say? Because of their names, it somewhat makes sense that Mahlon ('sickness') and Chilion ('destruction') died. In light of the Betio situation, they were born into sickly and destructive conditions – famine, migration, asylum-seeking. But why did Elimelek ('my God is king') die so soon in narrative time? Elimelek's name 'signifies not simply theological devotion but political resistance in an imperial world' (Fewell, 2017, p. 27), on the one hand, but his death, in light of the situations in Betio and Togoru, also signifies the possibility that God is no longer king.

Takeaway

1 What might have been other reason(s) for the sons marrying Moabite women?
2 What events, stories or movies does Ruth 1.3–5 bring to mind?
3 How might you rewrite Ruth 1.3–5?

Prompts for further talanoa

1 Tod Linafelt, 'Ruth', *Bible Odyssey*, www.bibleodyssey.org/people/main-articles/ruth, accessed 5.5.21.
2 Bruce Routledge, 'Moab', *Bible Odyssey*, www.bibleodyssey.org/places/main-articles/moab, accessed 5.5.21.
3 Daniel L. Smith-Christopher, 'Immigrants and Foreigners in the Bible', *Bible Odyssey*, www.bibleodyssey.org/people/related-articles/immigrants-and-foreigners-in-the-bible, accessed 5.5.21.

Notes

1 Two qualifications are necessary here: first, other living (and some dead) creatures also migrate; second, there are other reasons why creatures migrate (e.g. for comfort, advancement, mating, giving birth, dying).

2 On the other side of the coin, crisis also makes some people migrate to deliver aid, service and charity (see Storie, 2020).

3 In Pasifika, for instance, the causeways that link nearby islands redirect the waves and currents to other parts of the islands where they gnaw and wash shores and land away.

4 I distinguish between the Israel of history, the Israel of biblical historiography and the modern State of Israel that was established post-World War Two. They all share the same name, but they are not to be confused.

5 The Dutch occupied West Papua together with Indonesia (while Germany occupied PNG). In 1945 Indonesia received independence from the Dutch government, and in 1962 the Dutch relinquished West Papua only to be invaded and occupied by Indonesia from 1963 to the present (see, further, McLeod, 2015).

6 On the other hand, some cultures are divided by national borders as in the case of Somalis, across Somalia and Kenya; the Luo people across Uganda, Kenya and Tanzania; the Maasai across Kenya and Tanzania; and the Kisu across Kenya and Uganda (see Kamaara, 2020).

7 In these translations, the curly braces { } represent the Hebrew ויהי (and it was, then it happened). I leave it for readers to decide how ויהי might be translated – whether the event described coincides with or comes later as a consequence of the-moment-of-ויהי.

The round brackets ( ) represent the Hebrew ו-conjunction (and, but, so, then). I propose how the (ו) might be rendered in some places, and invite readers to imagine other possibilities.

8 These questions would also give an idea regarding, as raised above, how long they planned on being away.

9 This is the kind of prodding that mainline biblical scholars call 'eisegesis' (when a reader inserts meaning into the text) as compared to 'exegesis' (when a reader takes meanings out of the text). It is of course difficult to make a hard distinction between these two modes of reading – exegesis without eisegesis is an illusion, and effective eisegesis involves some exegesis.

10 Compare with the detailed accounts of the crises and traumas in the flood in Genesis 6—9, the famine in Genesis 41.53—47.26, and the plagues of Egypt in Exodus 7.14—12.36.

11 Instilled in the minds of children when parents try to convince them to eat their food – 'think of all those hungry people in Africa or Latin America'.

12 The controversy in this claim is that i read the Cain story as part of the garden story rather than a separate 'east of Eden' story.

13 I intersect three names in the Hebrew Bible for the subject of the land – earth (ha'eretz, Gen. 2.5a), ground (ha'adamah, Gen. 2.5b) and field (sadeh, Gen. 1.19; the same word is used in reference to Moab in Ruth 1.1–2 and is discussed in the next section).

14 I use 'fruit' figuratively, as one finds in 'fruit of the womb' (Ps. 127.3) and in the underwear brand 'fruit of the loom'.

15 This suggestion is supported by the use of terms usually translated as land in the Māori (whenua) and Fijian (vanua) translations.

16 This is the sense of the term nuu used in the Samoan translation; nuu is popularly understood to mean village but it could also be used for town or city.

17 Bearing in mind that Pasifika islands are not all independent: Hawai'i, Tutuila and the Federated State of Micronesia are colonies of the USA; Kanaky and Mā'ohi Nui are colonies of France; Rapa Nui is a colony of Chile; and West Papua is a colony of Indonesia.

18 In Ruth 1.1–5, the men died speechless – a condition against which sings Princess Jasmine of Agrabah in the movie Aladdin.

19 One may also argue that it was in the interests of a proper ceremony that Jesus provided good wine at the wedding at Cana (John 2.1–12).

20 Notwithstanding, with respect to whom a priest should not marry – all widows are the same (together with divorced women, defiled women, prostitutes; see Lev. 21.24).

4

Ruth 1.6–19a
Remigration and rejection

Albert Wendt's novel *Sons for the Return Home* (1973) tackles the realities and struggles that migrants and remigrants (migrants who return home) face, and the difference that race, class, gender, generation, ethnic and cultural backgrounds make for them. The protagonist is a Samoan student in Aotearoa New Zealand who got a pālagi student pregnant and both were sent back to their homelands: he to Samoa, she to the UK.

To cut a long story short: when the two characters returned, they both struggled in their home(land)s but for different reasons. He did not feel at home in Samoa, nor she in the UK, and the novel ends with the protagonist boarding a flight back to Wellington (Aotearoa New Zealand). Home was not homely. Homecoming was not as expected.

There is more to Wendt's rich autobiographical novel (see also Ma'ilo, 2018),[1] but for the purpose of this chapter *Sons of the Return Home* helps make the point that rejection is a common experience for (re)migrants no matter whether they are privileged children in the shades of empires or struggling second-generation FOBS (fresh off the boat) under coconut and breadfruit trees in Pasifika. The burden for both migrants and remigrants is that the homeland is not as accommodating as they had hoped, and ideas about 'home' are thus problematized.

Climate change has added a new twist to the notions of 'home' in the case of Pasifika natives. For natives living on (is)lands (previously) under occupation, and this applies to most Pasifika islands, 'home' has become more foreign than native: What does 'home' mean on islands administered according to western Christian principles and rules of law, where most things were 'made in China'? For natives living in diaspora, their struggle is with being caught between two homes – the home(land) of their parents, and the foreign home where they now live – so their angst relates to where and which *is* home: What does 'home' mean for second-generation natives in diaspora, whose parents insist that they look, eat and talk as if they were back in the islands? Can 'home' be in two or more places?

In the face of climate change, the angst is about what home means when the home(is)land has been washed away by the rising seas: for example, what will 'home' mean for Tuvaluans after the islands of Tuvalu disappear (projections vary, but this could be as soon as the 2050s)? For the majority of Pasifika natives, two or three of these angsts apply. I imagine similar angsts in the thinking of Naomi, Ruth and Orpah, as they set out on to the road from Moab to Judah.

The burdens of remigration and rejection, together with the angsts about home, play out in the three bible studies offered in this chapter. Instead of rushing in order to get to Ruth's commitment (Ruth 1.16–17), reflected in many marriage vows and read as the highlight of Ruth 1.6–19a, or rushing in order to condemn Orpah for turning away from Naomi (1.14b) in comparison to Ruth the loyal daughter-in-law, the following bible studies slow down the transition over 1.6–19a in order to imagine the motivations for departure and feel the emotions that come with departure (1.6–7), and the mixed emotions that arise on the road (1.8–14a). The following bible studies thus delay arrival (1.19a) because the journey is also interesting. In other words, again against the 'flight' of the narrator (see Chapter 2), the pace is slowed down in order to smell the roses as well as feel the thorns on the paths of (re)migration. The journey of these widows is not too different from other (re)migration journeys, but the journey was experienced differently because of their different motivations and statuses – Naomi as a remigrant with Ruth and Orpah as possibly first-time (virgin) migrants.

(3) Ruth 1.6–7: Widows leave Moab

⁶ ( ) She arose with her daughters-in-law
    ( ) She returned from the field of Moab
    For she heard in the field of Moab
    that YHWH has visited his people, to give them food
⁷ ( ) She went forth out of the place where she had been
    ( ) her two daughters-in-law with her
    ( ) they went on the way, to return to the land of Judah

The eyes of the narrative are on Naomi. She arose, together with her daughters-in-law (who are not named in this pericope), to leave the field of Moab. There is no hint of secrecy about their departure. They did not sneak away or leave under the cover of darkness. Their travel log is different from that of Abraham, who set out 'early the next morning' (Gen. 22.3) with his son Isaac and two other lads, as if they were trying to sneak away from the rest of the family.[2] I get the impression that Abraham prepared for the journey (packed provisions for the three days' journey, and cut enough wood for the burnt offering) in the dark, as the people of Israel did one Passover night in Egypt (Exod. 12.1–30) many, many generations later. The exodus led by Moses departed in the middle of the night.

Once again, there is no indication of time in the case of Naomi with her widowed daughters-in-law, and there is no hint of their voices. I see them in the narrative, but they make no fuss and no noise. They arose silently. And there is no hurry, no discussion, no worries, and no secrecy about their destination. They departed with the assumption that they were all going all the way. Judah or bust. They departed as a group of three, but Naomi is the primary subject and suspect in the narrative. This is her journey. Her return. Judah for good, the narrative suggests. Judah for ever.

They must have carried womanly belongings like oils, perfumes and jewellery that they inherited or acquired over their lives, as well as some provisions for the journey – bread and water (cf. Gen. 21.14) at the very least – and maybe one or two changes of clothes. If they were like native islanders, who

take a mat to lie on and something to cover themselves with
during boat journeys, i expect the three widows to also carry
something to rest on when they need to take a break on the
road (cf. Mark 2.11). The widows may have travelled light,
but their departure – three women, together, with baggage
(and maybe a helper) – would have been noticed by the neighbours. Since the death of Naomi's husband, i imagine that the
neighbours (as expected in a patriarchal setting) would have
expected Naomi to return to Judah. No one would have found
her departure shocking, even if the neighbours did not come
out to farewell them when they departed.[3]

The protocols that make me expect Naomi to return to
Judah also make me expect Ruth and Orpah to return to their
own homes. 'Until death do us part' ends with the death of
the husband, so widows are free to return to their parents and
family (or somewhere else) if their departed husbands did not
leave them a home and support system. In the case of Naomi,
that home would be back in Judah; and that home would be
tied up with the homes for Ruth and Orpah. Judah was home
for Naomi, and at the end of this 'return' journey it will become
home for Ruth and Orpah as well.

Land

YHWH visited 'his people' to give them food, but there is no
indication what the situation was like in Moab. In all likeli-
hood, with respect to cultivation and harvest, the situation in
Moab had not changed. Death visited the field of Moab, but
the gods of Moab did not leave their people, so food would
still have been abundant there. What changed was Naomi's
preference. The narrative gives the impression that she was
going back for 'home food' (the longing of most migrants).[4]
Could there be other motivations for Naomi's decision to
return to Judah?

Unlike other times when YHWH visited (פקד) with plagues
and punishment (e.g. Exod. 20.5–6 and 34.6–7), this time
YHWH visited with seeds and fruits. It is curious that YHWH

is said to have visited the 'people' (Ruth 1.6), but Naomi's journey was to the 'land' (1.7). While land and people are connected in the eyes of native Pasifika, this distinction gives the impression that Naomi's interest was not only with food but also about the land that has become fertile again. She was going back to a land that she had the right to occupy, since the death of her husband and sons. She did not have daughters who could claim her dead husband's land, as the daughters of Zelophehad did (Num. 27.1–11; Num. 36), but as a widow Naomi is first in line to (be packaged with) the land and heritage of her husband. After Naomi come the widows of her sons. However, these contenders do not get a welcoming depiction in this pericope. They are not even named. Rather, the narrative refers to them as 'daughters-in-law'; the narrative thereby subjected them to Naomi.

The land, as inheritance, is a reminder of Naomi's place in the levirate system. According to Deuteronomy 25.5–10, Naomi may be taken by her husband's brother in order to (re)build her dead husband's family. If this was what she wanted, but the brother (or next of kin, according to the levirate system) refuses, then she could go up to him in the presence of the elders, take one of his sandals off, spit in his face and say, 'This is what is done to the man who does not build his brother's line.' That man's line shall be known in Israel as The Unsandaled Family (Deut. 25.9b–10).

If Naomi did not want this opportunity, then why did she get up to go back to Judah? She could have 'stayed low' and maintained her freedom in Moab, for there was no obligation for her to return to her husband's land and face the patriarchal burdens of Judah.

If inheritance and access to levirate indulgence were what Naomi wanted, then why did she take her daughters-in-law along? They could have jeopardized her mission, for they too were eligible for what Naomi was seeking – more so, in fact. It does not seem wise to take along possible rivals who were most probably younger and more attractive (fitting the allure of foreign women), unless Naomi was not planning to take Ruth and Orpah all the way to Judah. In other words, unless Naomi was taking them simply as insurance to get her outside of the field of Moab and then ditch them on the way. This reading takes the gravity of Ruth 1.6–7 to fall on getting Naomi out of the field of Moab, and both references to her exit (1.6a and 1.7a; my italics below) are linked to her daughters-in-law as if she depended on their company:

⁶ ( ) She arose *with her daughters-in-law*
   ( ) She returned from the field of Moab

⁷ ( ) She went forth out of the place where she had been
   ( ) *her two daughters-in-law with her*

In both references, Naomi needed her daughters-in-law to enable her departure. They departed together, but Naomi did not plan on all three of them arriving together at Judah. In this reading, taking the daughters-in-law along was a tactic to give the neighbours the impression that all were well and as expected. Naomi was playing a trick, using her daughters-in-law to get her going.

Distance

'How far did they go?' was a question raised by several islanders in the PBS gatherings. Despite the narrowness of most islands, distance is a big concern for islanders; when one does not have a lot of space, one tends to be curious about how much space over which one could move. On the matter of space, islanders share similar anxieties with people in refugee camps, prisons and hospitals.

How far did Naomi need her daughters-in-law to come along? According to the reading proposed above, Naomi needed them to come far enough so that she is safely away from the eyes and ears in and of the field of Moab. In Pasifika settings, this means several miles because natives can see long distances (even in the dark) and hear the proverbial drop of a pin on the grapevines. I imagine that Naomi would have known those capacities, and thus needed her daughters-in-law to accompany her beyond the perceptions and gossips of villages and fields. That they went 'on the way, to return to the land of Judah' (1.7b) does not mean that it was intended for them to go the full distance. They were simply 'on the way', but there was no intention to go 'all the way'.

As far as the narrative was concerned, the daughters-in-law lost their subjectivity under the interests of Naomi. By twice labelling the journey as a 'return' – from the field of Moab (1.6), and to Judah (1.7) – the narrative submits Ruth and Orpah to Naomi's plot. It was all about Naomi. She was the only one returning, remigrating; *returning* did not apply to Ruth and Orpah. This was not about them; this might have been their first departure from the field of Moab. The mixture of joy, distress and trauma that comes to a first generation of migrants would also be upon them. Migration was new for them, but not the burdens of submission to their mother-in-law.

The narrative further submits Ruth and Orpah to Naomi by referring to them as 'daughters-in-law' instead of 'widows'. In the eyes of the narrator, Orpah and Ruth are pawns in their mother-in-law's board. And in the reading suggested earlier, that she wanted them to go with her until she is outside the field of Moab, Orpah and Ruth were pawns in Naomi's eyes as well. The matter of 'distance' thus raises a flag regarding the relationship between Naomi with Ruth and Orpah, an issue of critical concern for the PBS participants.

Pasifikation

There are around 75 kilometres between Moab and Bethlehem. That is a very long distance, for any land-based traveller. The question 'How far did they go?' was not because the PBS participants wanted to understand how long it would take to cross over, but because land and distance are critical in Pasifika. Five centimetres may not be significant in the eyes of many people, but 5 centimetres of land are a lot when those centimetres are being washed away from the shores of the narrower islands.

The widest part of Funafuti, the capital island of Tuvalu, is around 400 metres. For Tuvaluans, that 5 centimetres of land makes a big difference. The same goes for Betio and Togoru (see Chapter 2). The lesser-known island group of Tokelau is even smaller. Its largest atoll Nukunonu is about 4.7 square kilometres with the widest point of the island being around 200 metres. Like the Tuvaluans and iKiribatis, the Tokelauans try to protect every 5 centimetres of land by building and rebuilding seawalls. Unfortunately, the king tides do not respect seawalls and the islanders are losing the battle against the invasive powers of the sea.

King tides are also troubling higher islands. Nauru, for instance, is one of the high islands now affected by the king tides (at the north side of the island). The highest point of Nauru is around 65 metres, at the 'topside', but the higher grounds have been destroyed by phosphate mining and the natives are pushed to the coasts. Nauru is only 21 square kilometres, four-fifths of which have been made uninhabitable and uncultivatable by phosphate mining (which benefited the overseas miners more than the local people).

So these 5 centimetres may not come to mind when most people think of distance, but they mean a lot when islanders talanoa concerning land, and particularly on islands that are *losing ground*. From this frame of mind, it made good sense to the PBS participants that Naomi might have wanted to 'return' some 75 kilometres in order to be in a position where she could claim her late husband's inheritance; it made good sense, even if all that she was going to inherit was 5 centimetres of land.

Takeaway

1 What other motivations may have contributed to Naomi leaving Moab?
2 If you were Ruth or Orpah, how far would you walk away from home before you start wondering whether you should continue on Naomi's return journey?
3 How much joy, distress and trauma could you endure, when or if you migrate (on foot) to another land?

(4) Ruth 1.8–14a: Naomi pushes her daughters-in-law back

⁸ ( ) Naomi said to her daughters-in-law
'Go, return, each woman to her mother's house
May YHWH do kindness with you
As you did with the dead, and with me
⁹ May YHWH give to you, and you find rest
Each woman in the house of her husband'
( ) She kissed them
( ) They lifted their voice, and they wept
¹⁰ ( ) They said to her,
'For – with you we will return, to your people'
¹¹ ( ) Naomi said, 'Turn back, my daughters
Why go with me?
Are there still sons in my womb, to be husbands for you?
¹² Turn back my daughters, go
For I am old to have a husband
For if I should say, there is hope for me
Even if I had a husband tonight and even bear sons
¹³ Would you wait, until they had grown up
would you shut yourselves for them, never to be for a
   husband?
No, my daughters
For – a lot of bitterness is in me, from you
For – the hand of YHWH has gone forth over me.'
^{14a} ( ) They lifted their voice, and wept again

Silence breaks. Naomi speaks, firmly: 'Go, return, each woman to her mother's house' (Ruth 1.8a) followed with 'Turn back, my daughters' (1.11a). Naomi's desire is clear – she wants to stop the two women from coming along. Their participation in her exit was accomplished. Finished. They are not needed for the rest of Naomi's 'return'. Their 'return', on the other hand, was in the opposite direction: each to her mother's house.

Out of the eyes and ears of Moab, Naomi makes her move to cut free from her daughters-in-law. She does not want them, both of them, to come along. In the world of talanoa, the two occasions (1.8–9a and 1.11–13) amount to a two-part telling-off, a scolding. The message is clear. Go back. Go home. Go away. Finish.

Rebuke

The PBS participants rebuked Naomi, with the strongest rebuke coming from the Pasifika migrants in Aotearoa New Zealand and Australia. They were certain that Naomi took advantage of Ruth and Orpah, and they noticed that Naomi did not tell them to go back each to her 'mother' but, instead, each to her 'mother's house'. This distinction suggests that the house (home, family) could still be standing but the mother may have died. In native ears, Naomi's command also gives the impression that the father too could have died: they were to go back to their mother's house where they would be better welcomed as compared to their father's house. This reading reflects Pasifika cultures: we tend to feel more at home with our mother's family.

Naomi justified her command by claiming that she has nothing left, and that she has nothing coming, to give to her daughters-in-law. It is in their interests that they turn back. They have more opportunities at their mother's house.

For Pasifika migrants who have taken roots in the diaspora, the idea of 'returning' to their mother's house meant going back to a situation and lifestyle out of which their own mothers brought them. In their case, the 'mother's house' has moved (to where they were at that time). Naomi's command thus goes against the wisdom and courage of their own mothers, and so their rebuke of Naomi reflects their own situations: despite Naomi having lived for over ten years 'as a migrant' in Moab, she still failed to understand and account for the complex realities that migrants face. The location – Naomi tried to turn her daughters-in-law back while they were on the way, in between places – put Naomi in very bad island-light. To put it in an island setting: after the canoe cleared the reef,

Naomi told her daughters-in-law to jump off and swim back home.

Bitterness

What's in a name? In the double telling-off events, Naomi shifts from addressing Ruth and Orpah as 'each woman' (twice in 1.8–9) to 'my daughters' (thrice in 1.11–13). This shift reads, first, like a declaration of care if not intimacy: for Naomi, Ruth and Orpah are not *any* women, but her very own daughters. Naomi here acknowledges that she has oversight over them. On the other hand, the same shift may be read as evidence of 'power *over*': as daughters, Orpah and Ruth should listen and obey. How one reads the shift in Naomi's voice depends on how one imagines the relationship between them.

Herein is a paradox. The shift is open to the imagination of readers, but Naomi becomes more vicious with her words. Naomi is affectionate in the first scolding – she affirms their kindness, and she blesses them ('May YHWH give to you, and you find rest') – but not so in the second. Naomi actually blames them ('a lot of bitterness is in me, *from* you') along with YHWH ('the hand of YHWH has gone forth over me') for her *bitterness* (מר, *mar*). In this regard, Naomi was a bitter woman (*marah*) – already (cf. 1.20).

Before this point, the plot unfolded with the words of the narrator. Up to this point, Naomi has been voiceless. Then she opens her mouth, from outside of Moab and Judah, and bitter words pour forth.

Why did she open her mouth after all that time, and those movements? Did she finally feel safe enough, away from Moab, to speak? Did the location, being on the road, have something to do with her opening up? These questions bring to mind the talanoa of Miriam, the (older?) sister of Moses who sided with her older brother Aaron, while on the way from Egypt to Canaan. Miriam and Aaron challenged the authority of Moses: 'Has YHWH spoken only through Moses?' (Num. 12.2). Taking the wilderness as a place of transition, tests and trials (see Exod. 15.22—17.7), and for pushing back (see Exod. 32), Naomi's episodes fit snugly with established biblical traditions. Naomi opens up against her daughters-in-law because that kind of 'opening up' (outburst) happens on the road (a biblical version of a parent's response to 'are we there yet?').

Naomi is the first of the characters to speak up, and her bitterness seems to have built up for some time across the different stages of migration. Out of Judah. Into the field of Moab, for around ten years. She went, or may have been dragged, through a lot. And now on the road back to Judah, she bursts. She tells Ruth and Orpah (to go) off. And she kisses them off. I cannot tell if Naomi is inherently, by nature, a bitter woman. But given their location and situation, i can understand her bitterness. At this juncture, she is boiling. Hot.

Sex

Naomi makes the talanoa hot in another way. She brings the subject of sex on to the road, into the open. She tells Orpah and Ruth to return to their mother's house so that they might be taken into the house of a husband, where they may find 'rest' (1.9). In the ears of several PBS participants, Naomi's command may be heard in three ways: First, this may be a tongue-in-cheek critique. Naomi implies that Ruth and Orpah prefer to 'rest' where they are expected to do something, to work in the field of Moab, for and with their husbands. In this first option, looking back to their previous situation, Naomi may be heard as saying that Ruth and Orpah preferred to rest (read: they were lazy) while they were wives to her sons. Second, Naomi may also be affirming her sons: they were such good husbands that Ruth and Orpah were at rest when they were wives. Against expectations for a wife to be overworked and overused (cf. Prov. 31.10–31), Orpah and Ruth were restful housewives. And third, 'rest' may be taken as a metaphor for sex. This option is a stretch because the term מנחה (rest) occurs eight times in the Hebrew Bible, and it connotes taking a break. When i tried to explain this to the PBS participants, the same response came back from three different groups: 'and what do they do when they take a break?' In this regard, the wording can trick readers.[5]

The undercurrents to Naomi's outbursts ripple in the direction of sex. Which reading is closer to what Naomi had in mind i cannot determine, if not all of the above, but in alluding to husbands and rest Naomi brings sex into this talanoa. Opportunities for rest are available for Ruth and Orpah, back in Moab. That is why they should turn back. Naomi starts with her widowed companions, then she turns to herself. They may return for rest but she, on the other hand, will continue on the road of restlessness.

True, Naomi is old. But she did not rule out the possibility that she could have another husband, even that very night, and have more sons (1.12). She could still join the club of rested, but not retired, housewives. All of those ideas are within the realms of possibility. Naomi, however, ruled out two prospects in the case of Ruth and Orpah: first, Naomi doubts if Orpah and Ruth could endure the wait until her (imaginary) sons grow up and, second – which comes across as an accusation – if they were capable of fidelity (to 'shut' themselves from other husbands). Prejudices can easily convince readers: what else would you expect from these Moabite women? Social stigmas imagine Moabites as godforsaken people. Naomi's distrust, for Judean readers, was reasonable. Ruth and Orpah come from a people who, as several PBS participants put it, 'itch if they keep their legs shut for too long'.

Naomi experienced the kindness of Ruth and Orpah before (1.8), as a tributary from the kindness that they extended to 'the dead' men in her household. What their 'kindness' involved is open for query and queering. The issue here for me, and for many PBS participants, is why, if she liked their kindness, did she try to send her daughters-in-law back home? Why stop a good thing? Was Naomi looking ahead to receiving similar or better kindness when she arrives in Judah?

Good that Naomi had experienced the kindness of Ruth and Orpah, but 'no good' (a popular expression in Pasifika) that Naomi is unwilling to share with her daughters-in-law the kindness waiting for her in Judah. Naomi looks like some-one who likes to take but does not like to give. Her mercurial behaviour would not be appreciated in relational and reciprocal cultures (like those in Pasifika; see Vaai and Casimira, 2017), nor relished in the platforms of sex.

Weeping

After each telling-off, the daughters-in-law broke into weep-ing. Weeping is a response with which people who have been scolded are familiar – they break down into tears. This sense is conveyed in several of the Pasifika bibles. In the Tongan bible, for instance, the term *fākafoa* is used for 'weeping' – this term translates as 'to shatter' and 'to fracture'. The term invites Tongan readers to imagine Ruth and Orpah to be in pieces, as the outcome of being told off by Naomi.

After the first telling-off, the daughters-in-law wept as well as gave a verbal response: 'For – with you we will return, to your people' (1.10). The response is short, but straight to the point. *With you we will return* – they started the journey with Naomi, and they have joined her 'return' – *to your people*. According to their response, what is significant in Naomi's return is that she was going back to her *people* (rather than to the land). In the shadows of Yhwh's return visit to the people (1.6a), the daughters-in-law identify their 'return' to be destined for the same people. Naomi might be going for the land, but they are going for her people.

After the second telling-off, the daughters-in-law wept 'again'. They lifted their voice, but no words came out. Broken. They, only, wept. Grammatically, the text has space for Naomi too to weep because the subjects that wept in 1.9b and 1.14a are females (third person feminine plural). However, since the subject of the kiss in 1.9b sets Naomi apart from Ruth and Orpah – 'She kissed them ( ) They lifted their voice and wept' – i see Naomi as the kisser and this sets her apart from Ruth and

Orpah as the weepers.⁶ Orpah and Ruth wept; Naomi stood before them, but did not weep.

At this point, my focus is on the power and determination of Naomi. She told Ruth and Orpah off, and they wept loudly but with no words. Naomi's second scolding rendered Ruth and Orpah speechless. Orpah and Ruth wept, but did not say anything to Naomi; Naomi stood before them, but did not say anything in response.

Pause

The road is rarely empty. There might be robbers on the road, as well as priests and Levites, traders and profiteers, and other kinds of people and animals that travel between settlements – some of them may also carry viruses and other troubles. Since the days when white European explorers and colonialists brought scabies, smallpox, measles and cholera to the shores of Pasifika, and into other places in the 'New World', to the more recent outbreaks of H1N1 (swine flu, 2009–10) and Covid-19 (a strand of coronavirus that took root in 2020), the threats to the lives of travellers are both seen and unseen. Some of the travellers are wounded on the road, and some may be infected and thus carry diseases back to their homes, to their partners and loved ones. On the road, (re)migrants and refugees are vulnerable to dangers and challenges.

People and animals live on the roadside, and they see and wonder about travellers who pass by. So when the three women travellers stopped, in order for Naomi to try to turn Ruth and Orpah back to Moab, the residents on the roadside would have wondered why there was a pause in their journey. Whether they huddled in a circle or Naomi stood apart from Ruth and Orpah, in the middle or on the side of the 'road', would have said something about their pause even if one could not hear the words that were exchanged ... unless Naomi was loud in telling Orpah and Ruth off. Did she shout at them? What and how might the people of the road and the other travellers make of the weeping? With whom might they be sympathetic? The people and animals of and on the road are not visible through the biblical narrative, but they came alive with deep concerns for the two weeping women in the PBS sessions – Naomi must have said and done something terrible to make Ruth and Orpah weep. The PBS participants did not stay within the limits of the biblical narrative but journeyed further in the spirit of talanoa.

The road is a place in itself (cf. Anzaldúa, 1987). As a public place, what happens on the road is not limited to the telling (talanoa) of the biblical narrator but is open to the exchange (conversation, talanoa) with readers and listeners. In the world of talanoa, readers may have something to add to the narrator's version. In that light, one of the troubling questions for the PBS participants is how the road and the land might have viewed the pause in the journey of these three widows. In Pasifika, as reflected in the Rotuma saying *Pear ta Ma 'on Maf* ('the land has eyes and teeth, and it knows the truth'), the land can see and avenge wrongdoings (see Hereniko, 2004). The land bites those who abuse or twist 'the truth' (understood as the *tapu*) of the land.[7] In the eyes of the land, their weeping suggests that Ruth and Orpah have been wronged. On behalf of the land, therefore, the key challenge for PBS participants was to find justice for the weeping women.

The passage for this bible study pauses the journey on the road, and with weeping (1.14a). Before continuing, this bible study puts the cries of the widows to the 'eyes and teeth' – in Pasifika, we read with our eyes as well as with our teeth (we bite for nourishment, and in resistance) – of readers.

Pasifikation

'Bitterness' and 'weeping' are hot topics in climate-affected Pasifika islands – bitterness for having to bear the brunt of the consequences from humanity's shared global carbon civilization, and weeping over the trauma of losing ground. These traits, bitterness and weeping, are contrary to the stereotypical expectation that islanders are happy and carefree with no worries (or: *hakuna matata*, to borrow from *The Lion King*). In reality, there has always been bitterness and weeping in Pasifika islands despite the failure of our colonizers and baptizers to notice. Our bitterness and weeping are more pronounced in the current warming and changing climate, and our hope is for 'pause' to come soon.

In the rhythms of life, the opportunity for relief and rest increases when pause takes place. Pause means that one is not obsessed with the journey or the task at hand. Pause also means that one is concerned for the subjects that surround her or him. Pause also means that one is not a prisoner of time. Time is fluid, in Pasifika also.

What do these matters – bitterness, weeping, pause – have to do, if anything, with sex? In Pasifika, everything. And, back to the text for this bible study, more so because the exchange on the road in Ruth 1.6–14a was between widows. What other topic would make widows pause, weep and become bitter!

Takeaway

1 How might you feel if your mother-in-law (or employer, teacher, stepparent or significant other) tells you to go home because you no longer belong (or are needed)?

2 How do you usually react to seeing people weep painfully but do not say anything?

3 How might you draw the positioning and the postures of the bodies of Naomi, Ruth and Orpah as they paused on the road?

(5) Ruth 1.14b–19a: Orpah obliges, Ruth cleaves

^{14b} ( ) Orpah kissed her mother-in-law
( ) Ruth cleaved unto her.
¹⁵ ( ) And she said, 'Look, your sister-in-law returned to her
people and to her God(s)
( ) Return after your sister-in-law.'
¹⁶ ( ) Ruth said, 'Do not make me abandon you
To turn back from following after you
For – where you go, I will go
( ) where you will be, I will be
Your people, my people
( ) Your God, my god
¹⁷ Where you die, there will I die and be buried
Thus may YHWH do to me, and thus add more
For death to separate between me and you.'
¹⁸ [When] She saw that she was steadfast to go with her
( ) She eased off from speaking to her
^{19a} ( ) The two of them went on
Until they entered Bethlehem

There were, then, two travellers. After the second scolding, Orpah kissed Naomi then returned to her people and to her god(s) (1.15a). In silence. Ruth, on the other hand, refused to obey her mother-in-law. Ruth was set to 'go all the way' with Naomi.

The PBS participants, who are products of Pasifika patriarchal cultures (which basically means that women do not always speak up) that privilege the elderly (which basically means that older people, male and female, are usually not challenged), were quick to see and stress that Orpah and Ruth did 'push back' at Naomi. Ruth and Orpah did not bow out. Naomi did not get her way with them. They responded, pushed back at Naomi, but in different ways.

Orpah turns

Who abandoned whom? This question serves as a reminder that twice Naomi told Orpah and Ruth to go back home. It is therefore unfair to read here that Orpah abandoned, or even betrayed, Naomi. Naomi was actually the one who abandoned Orpah.

Orpah responded to Naomi's abandonment through action – she kissed Naomi, and she opted to remain silent. Orpah seized her moment and agency, to kiss rather than to be kissed, and she appropriated the power of silence.

In turning back to Moab, it may appear as if Orpah gave in to the wish of her mother-in-law. Ruth's vow to *not abandon* Naomi has unfortunately influenced many readers' opinions concerning Orpah, and this is reflected in works of art that depict Orpah walking away from Ruth and Naomi. When i showed images of artworks by notable Christian artists like William Blake (1757–1827),[8] Gustave Doré (1832–83)[9] and He Qi (1951–)[10] to PBS participants, they noticed how the artists tend to sideline Orpah. Naomi and Ruth are in the foreground of those works, facing those viewing the pictures; in the background, Orpah is shown walking away from Naomi and Ruth and so from the attention of those looking at the pictures. The PBS participants preferred that Orpah walked towards readers, so that she is not forgotten or abandoned. The two drawings (Figure 4.1 and Figure 4.2) discussed below indicate what the PBS participants had in mind.

Orpah's eyes

Like the land in the Rotuman proverb mentioned above, Orpah too has eyes and teeth, and she 'knows the truth'. She joined Naomi's journey, she was on the road, she was told off (twice), she wept, and when she turned back to Moab readers tend to forget her. The PBS participants, on the other hand, do not want to let her go away without 'taking a bite' at the talanoa. In this regard, the PBS participants read against the biblical narrator's plot.

Figure 4.1: In Orpah's eyes.

Figure 4.1 is from the PBS in Fiji. Naomi is at the centre of the image, turning her back on a chest of riches that represents Moab. Moab was not poor or desperate, as Bethlehem was at the beginning of the talanoa. Naomi, who looks European rather than Fijian, did not leave empty handed. She carries a bag of money in her left hand and pushes (someone, something) away with her right hand. Clinging to Naomi's right hand is the younger and smoother right hand of Ruth. At the bottom left corner of the drawing is the 'rugged left hand' of Orpah. This drawing puts viewers in the place of Orpah, and invites them to read the story through her eyes and teeth.

The left hand of Orpah is rugged, representing the hands of Fijian women who work in family gardens (for daily needs) and fields (for hire). The Fiji PBS participants thus add native twists to the narrator's plot: could Naomi have left workers and labourers behind in Moab, unpaid? Did Orpah go back to a household of debts?

Orpah eyes

Figure 4.2: Orpah's Burden.

Figure 4.2 is from the PBS in the Solomon Islands. Naomi and Ruth hold hands and walk away (to the east, and the next day), but Orpah walks towards the viewer with tears streaming down her face. She holds her hands behind her head, a sign of someone who was burdened and disappointed in the Solomon Islands. Was Orpah burdened by what might be waiting for her at Moab? Was she disappointed with Ruth and Naomi? And/or was she disappointed with readers?

Juxtaposing these drawings gives rise to two invitations: first, they invite readers to take Orpah's perspective into account – learn to read the story through the eyes and teeth of Orpah. This invitation shapes the bible studies presented in these pages. And second, the drawings invite readers to imagine that Orpah is looking at them, eyeing them and their readings. So it is not just about reading through Orpah's eyes, but reading as if *Orpah eyes* one's undertaking. These invitations indicate the depth of the PBS drawings, even though they are nowhere near to the artistic range of William Blake, Gustave Doré and He Qi.

Orpah did not say anything (as far as the text is concerned) when she turned back to Moab, but that does not mean that she did not have thoughts in her mind and spirit. In light of Ruth's long response (see 'Ruth responds' below), i imagine that Orpah must have had many thoughts in her heart when she kissed Naomi and returned to Moab. She turned, in silence, but with burdens.

Ruth responds

Against Naomi's attempt to abandon her, Ruth talked back to her mother-in-law. Ruth refused to be speechless. She will not be scolded, nor shut down. Refusing to give way to Naomi's third attempt to turn her back – 'return after your sister-in-law' (1.15b) – Ruth cleaved to Naomi with a seven-part commitment (1.16–17):

1   To not abandon Naomi.
2   To go with Naomi.
3   To be with Naomi.
4   To join Naomi's people.
5   To take Naomi's God.
6   To die and be buried with Naomi.
7   To be inseparable from Naomi.

There are seven parts, but they all go back to Naomi. Naomi was the culprit.

Over the centuries, Ruth's response has been studied by many readers and appropriated by countless couples. I will not repeat those readings and revisions here but present two native moves that were favoured by the PBS participants: first, the realization that Ruth was not as loyal as readers assume and, second, the suggestion that there is an 'ahh moment' in Ruth's response.

Garland of smooching

Moab was not godless, and Naomi affirmed this when she praised Orpah for returning to her people and to her god(s) (1.15a). Ruth and Orpah would have therefore received aid and advice from their people and, similar to what happens in Pasifika, family and community elders would have bombarded them with 'too much information'.

As suggested in Chapter 2, there must have been Moabite rituals to mark the marriages of Ruth and Orpah. Those rituals would have been based on religious, theological and cultural values that shaped the minds and conducts of the people of Moab. Orpah and Ruth would have been formed in the wisdoms and theologies of Moab and, though this does not apply to everyone, they may have remembered something from their wedding rituals. Insights from those events would have shaped their responses to Naomi. Put sharply, Orpah and Ruth were not 'empty women' and their responses to Naomi reflected Moab's religious, theological and cultural teachings.

This observation was important for PBS participants because they see themselves on the side of Moab, a sentiment that goes back to the days when white European Christian missionaries rejected the 'pagan' and 'savage' ways of Pasifika people together with our ancestors. Latter-day native missionaries (whose contributions to the establishment of the Christian movement in Pasifika are largely unacknowledged) also remind us that we are sons and daughters of 'gentiles', the more popular among whom in biblical and traditional theologies are the people of Moab and Canaan. It was therefore *natural* and important for the PBS participants to affirm Ruth as a Moabite, and by extension Ruth became a figure for the natives of Pasifika. In this way, the PBS participants reappropriated the stigma that the narrator gave Ruth: being a Moabite was derogatory in the talanoa (story, telling) of the narrator, but meaningful in the talanoa (retelling, conversation) of the PBS groups.

When Ruth's response uplifts Naomi, putting her high and first, Ruth reflects the values and wisdom of both Moab and Pasifika. With Ruth as 'one of us', the next move was to read her response as if it was by a native woman to one of her white European 'boss women' (as Hagar was to Sarai, and as Naomi is in Figure 4.2). Naturally, the native woman would shower the boss woman with a 'garland of smooching' if she did not want to be kicked out of the job or out of the house. Ruth's response was simply that – a garland of smooching. Ruth strings such a beautiful garland of smooching that it shuts Naomi up – '[When] She saw that she was steadfast to go with her ( ) She eased off from speaking to her' (1.18) – and makes readers forget that Naomi did not want Ruth to come with her to Judah.

Ruth's garland of smooching appears as a sign of loyalty in the eyes of many readers, who are overtaken by her seven-part commitment, but it is also a sign of 'sticking it up to the boss woman' in the eyes of PBS participants. In this case, Ruth also sticks up for herself. She has something to gain by going all the way to Judah, and the metaphorical garland that she presents to Naomi enabled her to step in that direction.

Where you ahh, I will ahh

At the PBS gathering in Munda (Solomon Islands), i learned from the male participants that there is a joke among natives that rewrites Ruth's response to Naomi:

Where you go, I will go
Where you lie, I will lie
Where you die, I will die
Where you are, I will are

Though a joke, this rewrite makes the point that natives are open to playing with and twisting biblical texts. One of the female participants at the same PBS event suggested that the spelling should be changed from 'are' to 'ahh' – *where you ahh, I will ahh*. With a wink she explained that there is more than an 'a ha' moment in the text; there is also room for an 'ahh' moment. Her suggestion sexualizes Ruth's words, and it did not bother the other participants that the suggested ahh moment was between two women. They simply called this in the reading the 'Sol ahh moment' ('Sol' for Solomon Islands).

At PBS events with Pasifika men in prison (Parklea, NSW), the subject of sex frequently comes up. Young men in prison have sex with, or perform sexual favours on, one another, but they do not count themselves as gay. (Homophobia is alive and well in prison as well.) The 'Sol ahh moment' is thus not too radical in the eyes of young men in prison. What is radical for the young men in prison is Ruth's preparedness to go all the way on the journey with Naomi, all the way to Naomi's God and to Naomi's death. What is radical is Ruth's preparedness to die *with* and be buried alongside Naomi. This is similar to a form of courage with which young men in prison are familiar – the willingness to 'take the fall' *for* someone else, for which young Pasifika men are known in the streets of the diaspora. Street gang leaders have several bodyguards for different functions, and the Pasifika member of the team is the one expected to step up and take the fall. That Pasifika bodyguard takes pride in the courage (which actually is stupidity with hormones) of peoples who *once were warriors*. That Pasifika bodyguard is prepared to go all the way into prison and even to death, and this courage – more of an argh moment – is heard in Ruth's response to Naomi.

At the Fōfo'anga PBS (an all-men, mostly Tongan, gathering at Bankstown, New South Wales), there is another controversy in Ruth's response. Whereas couples vow to be for one another *until death do us part*, the Fōfo'anga group reads Ruth as saying that *not even death will part* her from Naomi. Where Naomi dies there also will Ruth die and be buried, and Ruth calls on YHWH to not allow death to part her from Naomi (1.17):

Where you die, there will I die and be buried
Thus may YHWH do to me, and thus add more
For [if] death to separate between me and you

Death will not be able to separate Ruth from Naomi. In Tongan ears, Ruth commits to what we call *fai funga* ('be buried upon', usually on a previously deceased relative or ancestor), according to which Ruth vows to be buried upon Naomi. The real controversy for the Fōfo'anga group is in the word *fai* (to do, to work), which is used as slang for sex. In this crude connection – a mixture of ahh and argh moments – the Fōfo'anga group extends the 'Sol ahh moment' to the grave. Even after death, Ruth will *fai funga* upon Naomi.

In this reading, Ruth's garland of smooching is in preparation for Naomi's death. Lacking from Ruth's response is any indication of time. Will Ruth die at the same time as Naomi, as in the Hindu practice of *sathi* (wives who commit suicide to die alongside their husbands)? If Ruth is to die later, but at the same place, the *fai funga* will take place later.

Onward

Seeing that Ruth's cleaving words are steadfast, Naomi budged. Or did she 'like' Ruth's cleaving? Silently, they walked the rest of the way to Bethlehem (1.18–19a).

Pasifikation

One of the habits shared by Pasifika people is the giving of a *lei* (Hawai'ian for garland) to arriving travellers. The lei (worn around the neck, the waist or as a headband) serves two functions: first, to welcome travellers and, second, to give them permission so that they may participate in whatever event for which they have come. The background for the second function, which tourists do not often sense, is providing protection for outsiders who may not have the appropriate attire for coming on to native land and for participating in ceremonies and protocols. The lei, as a cultural emblem, gives travellers permission and protection, both of which are necessary in (is)lands that are tapu (sacred, taboo). In this regard, the practice of giving guests a lei is testimony to the sacredness of our (is)lands.

I experienced the burden of the second function of the lei when i visited Tuvalu. In all of my visits i received several leis at the airport from my hosts as well as from others who knew my hosts, but they did not come to the airport to receive me. They came with leis for whoever needed to be received into their island. And at every outer island of Tuvalu that i visited, i received more leis as well as clothes, and so did my fellow travellers. And more leis when we departed the outer islands, and when we returned to the capital island of Funāfuti – and, even more, when i departed at the end of my visits. Tuvaluans give leis, which has been commercialized, to both foreigners and locals, travellers and outsiders, giving them welcome and permission to arrive as well as to depart.

In the eyes of locals, the lei also marks the wearer as a guest, someone who will not stay for long. The lei is thus a cultural emblem that welcomes, protects, as well as marks those who are outsiders. It is within this frame that i read Ruth's response to Naomi as a garland (lei) of smooching – it indicates Ruth's acceptance (welcome) of and support (protection) for Naomi, as well as Ruth's push back at Naomi (as a foreigner).

Takeaway

1 How might you draw the scene on the road, when Orpah turned back to Moab?
2 How do you feel when someone that you do not want or like insists on being with you?
3 What do you find irritating in this bible study?

Prompts for further talanoa

1 Amy Laura Hall, 2005, 'Ruth's Resolve: What Jesus' Great-Grandmother May Teach about Bioethics and Care', *Christian Bioethics: Non-Ecumenical Studies in Medical Morality* 11, www.tandfonline.com/doi/full/10.1080/1380 3600590926413, accessed 5.5.21.
2 Jeff Miner and John Tyler Connoley, 2002, 'Ruth loved Naomi as Adam loved Eve', an excerpt from *The Children Are Free: Reexamining the Biblical Evidence on Same-Sex Relationships*, www.wouldjesusdiscriminate.org/biblical_evidence/ruth_naomi.html, accessed 5.5.21.

3 South Pacific Commission, 'Adapting to Climate Change in Tuvalu: The Fresh Water Dimension', www.youtube.com/watch?v=Y1atvZXPUbo, accessed 5.5.21.

Notes

1 Wendt was born in Samoa then migrated with his family to Aotearoa New Zealand. From there, on account of his career, he migrated to Fiji, back to Aotearoa, back to Samoa, and now back in Aotearoa (with short stints in other parts of the world).

2 It may not be an accident that the death of Sarah is reported in the next chapter. Did she die from shock, after learning what Abraham intended to do with their one and only son?

3 In my mind, the 'no hoopla' with their departure says a lot about the narrator's view of the Moabite neighbours. A native storyteller would have put on a feast to farewell the women and shed a few tears (of sadness and/or of joy) as they walked away.

4 Unless she was a Moabite, a possibility noted in Chapter 2.

5 The opportunity for trickery is present in several Pasifika languages. For instance, one of the Tongan words for sex is *fai*, a word that also means 'do' and 'work' (*fai* is used in 1.8 for 'may Yhwh *do* kindness with you as you *did* with the dead, and with me'). In native Tongan ears, when Naomi wishes that they 'find rest' (*m'u ha mālōlō'anga*) in 1.9 they hear the *fai* in 1.8 as both 'work' and 'sex'.

6 There is no kiss in 1.14a, and i assume that Ruth and Orpah were the ones who wept again in 1.14a. There is another kiss in 1.14b, by a different subject, which i will come back to in the next bible study.

7 Acts that violate the *tapu* (taboo, sacredness) of the land may include the shifting of customary boundaries, disturbing of burial grounds, uprooting of sacred plants, compromising rituals, being loud and noisy in the village and ceremonial sites, introducing foreign practices, and so forth. Every Pasifika island has protocols that determine 'the truth' of and for the land, and the land will bite both native and non-native people who violate these protocols.

8 See the image at https://en.wikipedia.org/wiki/Ruth_(biblical_fig ure)#/media/File:1795-William-Blake-Naomi-entreating-Ruth-Orpah. jpg, accessed 5.5.21.

9 See the image at www.swartzentrover.com/cotor/Bible/Dore/doreOT/DoreOTo8.htm, accessed 5.5.21.

10 See the image at www.heqiart.com/store/p120/17_Ruth-&-Naomi_Artist_Proof_.html, accessed 5.5.21.

5

Ruth 1.19b–2.7
Resettlement and (re)connecting

Because (re)migration involves uprooting and moving, (re)settlement involves (re)rooting. Migrants and remigrants face many joys and challenges while they are on the move, on the road, and upon arrival they face the demands of (re)settling into a new and different place, or into an old place that has changed since the last time they were there (so it is an old but different place). They need to set up a shelter with devices and supplies to meet the basic needs of daily living – to eat and drink, to clean up, and to safely rest and sleep. To meet these demands, it helps when (re)migrants get some assistance from friends, neighbours and relatives, if there are any. And they need to draw on resources that they brought with them, and some local resources to which they may have access. They need to be smart and efficient with their relations and resources, and they might have to pull off a few tricks as well in order to get by.

In theory, (re)settlement should be easy for people who are strong because, to borrow a biblical way of thinking, they are like plants by streams of water (cf. Ps. 1.3) – they would easily take root in new grounds (or new pots). But there are drawbacks to being strong. The stronger the (re)migrants are, the deeper they are *set in their old ways*, and thus the different setting (in their next destination) could make them fragile. Those who were strong and established before they (re)migrate experience homesickness more severely, compared to (re)migrants who can cope with less and who can easily adapt. Put another way, as reflected in a native Pasifika way of thinking, the rich have means to facilitate their (re)migration but the poor survive better in (old and new) desperate situations; (re)migrants adapt differently, and it helps if they can 'surf' the demands of (re)settlement.

In the case of Naomi, over ten years have passed since she departed with her family. They departed as a group of (at least) four, and she returns with (at least) one other woman.[1] Ten years is brief enough that the local people would still remember Naomi, but it is also long enough for new things to rise up in the old settlement of Ephrathah of Bethlehem. Since Naomi's departure, there would have been new arrivals. New shelters. New questions. New relations, and other new things. Bethlehem has changed. Naomi returned to an old settlement (Ephrathah of Bethlehem; Ruth 1.1–2) that has become a city (עִיר; 1.19b).

In the case of Ruth, she was coming to Bethlehem for the first time. She was a foreigner, and the narrator is persistent in labelling her according to her ethnic background (a Moabite) as well as according to her family status but in relation to Naomi (a daughter-in-law). Her marital status (a widow), which makes her a responsibility and beneficiary of the clan of her late husband, is not volunteered in the narrative.

Into Bethlehem, Ruth entered along with Naomi. She entered not as a figure of the imagination, or as a shadow of Naomi, but as a full narrative character. With Ruth on her side, Naomi did not return on her own. Alone. Empty. Ruth joined Naomi's *return* on the road, and she entered Bethlehem as a steadfast companion for Naomi. In coming with Naomi, Ruth ensured that Naomi did not arrive empty-handed to her people, and to her land.

(6) Ruth 1.19b–22: City buzzes over marred Naomi

^{19b} { } As they entered Bethlehem
( ) all the city stirred upon them
( ) they said, 'Is this Naomi?'
²⁰ ( ) She said to them, 'Do not call me Naomi
Call me Marah [bitterness], for Shadday has marred
me muchly
²¹ I went full, and YHWH brought me back empty
Why call me Naomi [sweetness]?
– ( ) YHWH has rallied in me
( ) Shadday has dealt evil for me'
²² (Thus) Naomi returned
( ) Ruth the Moabite, her daughter-in-law, with her
Who returned from the field of Moab
– ( ) they entered Bethlehem in the beginning of the barley
harvest

That Naomi and Ruth arrived together seems important to the
narrator for he references it twice in 1.19b and 1.22. Naomi
and Ruth arrived as a pair, along with the range of emotions
and tempers that travellers experience after a long journey.
Together they departed Moab, plus Orpah, and together they
entered Bethlehem, minus Orpah.

The city *stirred over them*, and the women of the city (the
subject that asks the question in 1.19b is the third person feminine plural) came out to welcome them. There was no farewell
at Moab, but the women received them into Bethlehem. For
the PBS participants, the narrator is obviously biased towards
the women of Bethlehem, who carried out what Pasifika
women expected – they welcomed travellers (see Chapter 3).
Compared to the women of Moab, the women of Bethlehem
stir in the narrator's favour. Their welcome, however, was
short-lived because Naomi 'blew up' in their faces.

City women

It is taken to be a custom in Judah that women come out to celebrate victories, as Miriam and other women of the exodus generation did in the wilderness (see Exod. 15.19–21), and to receive victors upon their return home. But the customary celebration by women was not always appreciated, as in the story of Jephthah's daughter. Jephthah had been away from home for some time with his fellow 'empty men' (Judges 11.3), to wage a battle on behalf of his people and land (11.4–33). When Jephthah returned home, victorious from the battle, his unnamed daughter came with joy to receive him, dancing to the sound of timbrels, only to be scolded: 'Alas, my daughter, you bloody cut me low, and I am devastated because I opened my mouth to YHWH and I cannot take it back' (11.35). Jephthah had made a vow to YHWH, but he did not inform his household, and his words have come back to bite him: he vowed that if YHWH gives him victory then he would sacrifice the first one to come out of his house to meet him on his return (11.30–31). That one turned out to be his 'only child, beside her there was neither son nor daughter' (11.34).

With respect to the narrative, Jephthah's only child was precious, and may even be more precious than Isaac (see the binding of Isaac narrative in Gen. 22.1–19). Without saying that any child is unimportant and expendable, the suggestion in the previous sentence is because Abraham had other children: before Isaac, he had another son – Ishmael (see Gen. 16.1–16 and 21.1–21) – and more sons later (see Gen. 25.1–5). The daughter of Jephthah, on the other hand, was his one and only. Without her, the name of Jephthah will survive in stories and narratives but not *in* the land. Without her, the names and memories of his mother and grandmothers are also erased. Without her, her namelessness is excused.

The women of Bethlehem come out in the shadows of Miriam and the women of the exodus generation, and in the memories of the unnamed granddaughter of a prostitute in Gilead (Judg. 11.1), to receive Naomi and Ruth. That the city stirred *over them* suggests that the women's reception was for both of them, together. Of the two travellers, the women recognized one and hence their question addressed only one subject, 'Is this Naomi?' This is a common question with the first sighting of travellers: the women asked, in order to determine who the new arrivals were. If the women had known Ruth before, i imagine that their question would have been different: 'Are Naomi and Ruth returning to us, their people?'

In Pasifika, in the case of the arrival of beloved members of the community, questions of first sighting would bring joy and excitement. Homes would open up, mats rolled out, and the community would gather for feasting and dancing. A fatted calf would be sacrificed, and neighbours would contribute to and help at the kitchen. The ones who were away, or who may have been lost, have come back safely. Celebration. Homecoming.

For the return of not so beloved members of the community, the questions of first sighting would come with grunts and yikes. Nonetheless, Pasifika natives would be tolerant if the not so beloved returnees were members of the family. These returnees might not be liked, but they are family, blood and they need a place to stay. They might not be liked, but they have a home or two to which they may come. In this regard, the question of first sighting is also about alerting members of the community who need to make room for the returnees, or who have to vacate the properties that belong to the returnees. The women's question, therefore, comes to Naomi as well as to others in the crowd who are expected to provide or vacate space for Naomi.

It is not possible to determine, on the basis of the narrative, the mood of the women's question mainly because Naomi did not show any excitement about seeing them, her people. Naomi did not engage with the women, as one would expect from friends who have not seen one another for over ten years. There is no 'good to see you, thank you for coming to receive us, please meet and be kind to my cleaving daughter-in-law'. Instead, Naomi spit on their welcome. She stirred the women back.[2]

Fiepālangi, fie'eiki

Naomi's response was sharp: 'Do not call me Naomi [sweetness], call me Marah [bitterness]' instead (1.20). Any sweetness Naomi might have had when she left Bethlehem did not come back with her. Just as she was in the telling-off event on the way back, Naomi was still bitter. The women of Bethlehem were not to be blamed for her bitterness (unless they have a history with Naomi that is not shared in the narrative). Naomi laid all of the blame on YHWH / Shadday. She is marred and empty because YHWH has 'rallied' (ענה); answered, testified, oppressed) *in* her and Shadday has 'dealt evil' (רע) *for* her (1.21). Inside (*in*) and outside (*for*), she was a victim of the ruthless schemes of YHWH / Shadday.

Naomi drew the attention to herself and to her sorry condition. She claimed that YHWH returned her empty (1.21). But Ruth was there. Whether Ruth was behind or beside Naomi is not as critical as the narrative fact that she was there also. The narrator and the women saw Ruth, but Naomi's bitterness hid Ruth from the attention of readers. Naomi's bitterness wrote Ruth off from the welcome of the women of Bethlehem.

Naomi comes across as a grumpy old woman who fits the profile of fiepālangi (natives who behave as if they were pālangi, referring to foreigners in general and white Europeans in particular). A long time ago, fiepālangi referred to people who return from overseas with the presumptuousness that they were better than the local people, evident in the way that they speak down to them. Nowadays, fiepālangi also applies to locals who have not travelled overseas but think that they are superior to everybody else. In both regards, the sharpness of Naomi's response to correct the local women put her in the company of fiepālangi. She assumed a position of superiority, and this did not sit well with the PBS participants – one should not just come back and shout at a group of local women, some of whom might have been her aunts and elders.

There is a pālangi (foreigner) in the encounter, Ruth, but her presence is not seen. Participants at the PBS events in Tonga suggest that a more appropriate title for Ruth is *sola*, a Tongan term that refers to someone from outside of the community. This suggestion draws on the popular saying *tauhi e sola ke 'oua 'e tataka hono loto*, which translates as 'care for the outsider so that her or his soul does not want to take flight'. As a *sola*, Ruth would be better cared for in Tongan circles than she was in the shadows of her fiepālangi mother-in-law.

In real life, there are fiepālangi women and men in Pasifika who snap at their elders. Some of them participated in the PBS events! They saw themselves in Naomi's snap, which portrays Naomi as a woman of higher status (due to heritage or reputation) than the normal women who stirred in 1.19b. In Tonga, we have a different term for this attitude – *fie'eiki*, someone who demands respect because she or he is of reputable and noble heritage (*'eiki*). Did Naomi snap at the welcoming party because she was fie'eiki?

Blame

Naomi blamed YHWH for her marred condition (Ruth 1.20), a blame that could easily be affirmed given that YHWH had been credited for the return of bread (read: good fortune) to Bethlehem (in 1.6). YHWH is responsible for the land and for the people of Bethlehem. This affirmation invites reconsidering the politics of blame, and the politics of shifting the blame, both in the narrative as well as in readings of the narrative. Of significant relevance here is the blaming of the judges for the famine in Ruth 1.1a (see Chapter 2), and the unwavering trust of most readers in the narrator and the narrative. As it was written, so must it have been. Case closed.

Naomi's confronting snap at the welcoming women poses a different way of reading the politics of (shifting the) blame: could the shifting of blame be evidence of fie'eiki? Looking back at 1.1a, the narrative opened with Naomi snapping, a telling-off, at the judges. It is easy to see the narrator as one who was fie'eiki against the judges. As positioned in the Christian Bible, the narrator favours a shift to kingship.

But against what or whom are readers fie'eiki when we buy

into the blaming of the judges in the narrative? One answer is obvious to my native mind: in favouring kingship (read: empire), one disfavours or is fieʻeiki against judgeship or chief-tainship (read: the forms of leadership in village settings). Consciously or not, the favouring of kingship goes against the canonical flow of the Hebrew Bible (see Chapter 1). And, in PBS village settings among normal readers, bowing to the politics of blame against the judges suggests the spirit of fieʻeiki among readers. That readers are not innocent is a popular conclusion nowadays. That readers are also fieʻeiki (read: supremacist), consciously or not, is a confession that this bible study invites.

The welcoming women did not respond to Naomi's fieʻeiki. Whether their silence was a result of them bowing out to Naomi, or caused by something else, is a theme that will return in later bible studies (see especially Chapter 8).

Harvest

This pericope closes with a detail that situates Naomi's and Ruth's entry to Bethlehem at the beginning of the barley harvest. Barley is foreign to Pasifika, but harvest is not. For us, as in many other contexts, harvest is an occasion to cele-brate the fruits of the land and of the sea. In this connection, the time of harvest unsettles Naomi's claim to be empty. Was her emptiness a ploy to distract the local women? Did Naomi claim to be empty on arrival in order to discourage the women from expecting something from her?

When natives travel, they take gifts. And when they return from abroad, they bring back pālangi gifts for family and rela-tives who remained at home. Naomi's claim to return empty, thanks to YHWH / Shadday, released her from having to give gifts to her people.

Pasifikation

The popular mantra 'our ancestors were navigators' – that is, our ancestors navigated across the *moana* and resettled into different islands – affirms that resettlement is in the veins of the native people of Pasifika. Resettlement is in fact ongoing in Pasifika. Most island groups have talanoa of resettlement of whole communities, for two main reasons: resettlement because of living conditions, and resettlement because of foreign procedures such as colonization, blackbirding (slave trade)[3] and war. These resettlements take place within island groups, as well as across into other islands.

Resettlement to other islands because of impoverished living conditions included, using World War Two as the timeframe and context, communities from Banaba (Kiribati) to Rabi (Fiji) in 1945–83 and from Vaitupu (Tuvalu) to Kioa (Fiji) in 1947–83. International law does not recognize these resettled communities among its lists of refugees ('climate refugees' is not a legal status), but these people were forced to move because of the ecological condition of their homes. Moreover, the international community does not recognize other factors that contribute to the impoverishment of the ecological state of island homes, such as phosphate mining in Banaba. In the case of Banaba, ecology is tied in with economy, and the resettlement of islanders is the consequence of the enrichment of mining companies (from western nations). The international community also does not recognize the legacy of coloniality behind these resettlements: the British empire, which at that time claimed sovereignty over Kiribati, Tuvalu and Fiji, enforced the resettlements and used island resources to pay for the expenses.

Resettlement because of war included some 1,200 natives from Nauru that the Japanese government moved to Truk in order to make room for its war against the alliance led by the USA (see Packett, 1971; Weeramantry, 1992). Japan built airstrips and several oil tanks at Nauru, as a midway point for its fleet. After the war, a little over 400 Nauruan survivors were returned to an island ravaged by war (e.g. oil leaked into groundwater channels) and it is estimated that 80 per cent of the 20.98 square kilometre island has been made uninhabitable by phosphate mining.

Another consequence of the war was the resettlement by the British government of communities from Phoenix and Kiritimati islands (Kiribati) to the Solomon Islands (with the majority to Gizo) between 1954 and 1964 in order to make room for its cold war programme of testing atomic weapons. After this British resettlement, the USA then arrived to test its weapons at Kiritimati as well as at other islands in the Micronesian groups, while France conducted its tests at Ma'ohi Nui. There are more talanoa on the ongoing devastation to the lands and waters of Pasifika because of war and the legacies of militarization, but the lesser known talanoa of Nauru and Kiribati suffice to make the point that resettlement has to do with ecology, economy and the legacies of war.

One of the upshots of resettlement across national borders is that refugees become bi-nationals. The resettled people of Kioa are both Tuvaluan and Fijian, the resettled people of Rabi are both iKiribati as well as Fijian, and the Kiritimati and Phoenix islanders are Solomon Islanders who have not given up being iKiribati as well. Forced migration makes them bi-national and bi-cultural, but this reality has its consequences. For example, the second and third generations do not always feel that they belong back on their parents' or grandparents' home islands. Their parents and grandparents did not return home, like the Nauruans, and they had to raise their families on islands where they were out of place (by appearance, language, practice, culture and custom).

Even when resettlement takes place within the same island group, there are challenges for the refugees as well as for the hosting communities. In Tonga, the resettlement of people from Niua Fo'ou to Tongatapu first, and then to 'Eua (starting in 1949) because of the volcanic eruptions at Angahā that started on 9 September 1946 (with earlier eruptions recorded back to 1929), went on until 1951 (see Rogers, 1986, pp. 11–19). At the beginning, part of the difficulty for the refugees had to do with the ancestors: 'A great wailing arose from every graveyard on the island that night as many people prepared to leave their loved ones for the first time in their lives' (Rogers, 1986, p. 67). Leaving home is not easy, and new homes have difficulties: Niua Fo'ou people spoke different dialects, and the refugees complained that Tongatapu was too cold for them. As a consequence, several went back (against the government's advice) even before the final group of refugees were brought from Niua Fo'ou in 1951.

More recent climate refugees have joined the procession across national borders as well as internally, including the 2005 resettlement of Carteret islanders (Papua New Guinea), the resettlement of Solomon Island communities (at Gizo) after the 2 April 2007 tsunami, the resettlement of communities in Samoa and Tonga after the 29 September 2009 tsunami, and the 2014 resettlement of the climate-affected Vunidogoloa village in Fiji. Given the acceleration of global warming, some environmental scientists project that more communities from Tuvalu and Kiribati (if not both nation groups as a whole) will be forced to resettle by 2050. Many homes in those communities are already flooded by the rising sea level, made worse once a month by the king tide that raises the sea level for four days or more at a time.

From Pasifika contexts that have been shaped by resettlement, the bible study presented above asked several questions of the text that were not of concern to the biblical narrator. The views of PBS participants suggest that the biblical narrator may not have been aware of the challenges of (re)migration and resettlement.

Takeaway

1 How do you feel when you see someone whom you have not seen for a very long time?
2 How did your experience with migration/migrants shape your reading of this passage?
3 Where might Naomi and Ruth have stayed upon entering Bethlehem?

(7) Ruth 2.1–3: Ruth discovers Boaz's plot

¹ ( ) For Naomi was a kinsman of her husband
  ( ) a warrior-like man of strength, of the family of Elimelek
  ( ) his name was Boaz
² ( ) Ruth the Moabite said to Naomi
  'Let me go to the field and glean among the ears of corn
  behind whomever I find favour in his eyes'
  ( ) She said to her, 'Go, my daughter'
³ ( ) She went ( ) she entered
  ( ) she gleaned in the field, after the reapers
  ( ) her luck came to light –
  that part of the field was for Boaz
  who was of the family of Elimelek

Multiple set ups are in play. From the locals' side, Boaz stands above the rest. The passage opens and closes with Boaz. He is introduced as a strong character, and the narrative sets readers up to expect Boaz as *the man* (of strength) who will come to the aid of the two women who, like refugees, have recently arrived. Boaz (riding a white horse) to the rescue. Boaz too was being set up, even before he enters the narrative. The narrator allocated or devoted him 'for Naomi', because he was a kinsman of Elimelek (2.1, 2.3).

From the (re)settlers' side, on the other hand, Ruth the foreign woman sets things up. She takes the initiative to find food for herself and her mother-in-law. Things fall into her favour. She finds a harvest, enters the field, she gleans, and it comes to light that the plot where she gleans belongs to Boaz. In other words, Ruth finds herself in Boaz's plot (pun intended).

Kinsman

The opening of the pericope is quite telling: '*For Naomi*, was a kinsman (מודע) of her husband.' Boaz fits the bill. Because the root of the participle translated as kinsman is ידע ('to know'), an alternative translation for 2.1 reads:

( ) for Naomi, was someone known to her husband
a man of valiant strength, from the family of Elimelek
his name was Boaz

In this alternative rendering, Boaz is set up for Naomi. Boaz is appropriate 'for Naomi' because *he was known* by Elimelek. There might be other kinsmen, but the narrative gives the impression that Boaz would have gained the tick of approval from Elimelek. Boaz was not a stranger to the family (see 2.3). He is the narrator's choice for Naomi.

The text is tricky (in a 'set up' kind of way) because the root word ידע carries sexual nuances as well (cf. Gen. 4.1a, 'The man *knew* Eve his wife and she conceived and bore Cain'). The text is thus open to the possibility of understanding 'a man of valiant strength' (or 'warrior-like man of strength' / גבור חיל איש) with sexual nuances. The 'warrior' (on גבור / warrior, see Gen. 6.4) was valiant and aggressive in the battlefields as well as in the fields of sexual activity. In the past, such 'warrior-like men of strength' were known in Pasifika as 'headhunters' – they went out to raid neighbouring islands and communities, and their raids involved the rape and abduction of women (which also happen in biblical narratives, see 1 Sam. 27.8–11 and Judges 21). As described to me in the Solomon Islands, the headhunters were warriors in the open (read: the fields of battle) as well as in the caves (where they perform rituals of war such as raping enemy women and men, 'skull' enemy leaders, and revel in cannibalistic activities).[4]

On the road, Naomi was open to the possibility of having a husband and bearing more sons. With that possibility in the background, Boaz is introduced as a suitable partner for Naomi. And as the narrative unfolds, the suitability of Boaz is sweetened even more. He has a plot in the field that was being harvested. As a man of strength with a plantation and seeds, Boaz could only be good for Naomi. He has strength, and he has wealth – in many Pasifika bibles, 'man of strength' is rendered as 'man of wealth' and so there is an economic side to the suitability of Boaz.

The reputation of Boaz enters the narrative before his presence does. Naomi is at the foreground of the passage (2.1), and Boaz is introduced as an opportunity for Naomi to be resettled in the land and to be re-rooted in the family of Elimelek. In this regard, Ruth's going out to glean is a side-track from the narrator's pro-Naomi ('for Naomi') agenda.

Toutuʻu

A narrative detail that caught the imagination of the PBS participants is the mention that Ruth came to glean in 'the part of the field [that] was for Boaz' (2.3). This detail suggests that the plantation was a community project, and thus gives the narrative a village feel. To whom the land belonged, whether to a family or to the community, did not matter to the PBS participants. But it made a big difference that the community planted, worked and harvested together. Put another way, ownership is not as critical in Pasifika as evidence of collaboration and communalism, which is at the root of our relational and reciprocal cultures.

In Tonga, community plantations are called *toutuʻu*. Members of a 'block' in the village work together to clear and prepare the ground, then divide (as equally as possible) and allot the plots between the families involved. Each family would plant and keep their own plot, and help out with the others when the need arises. As a community project, one is hardly alone no matter what time one comes to the toutuʻu. And at harvest time (*polopolo*) the community gathers to celebrate but also to compare the fruits of their hands. A crowd is thus expected to be in the field at the time of polopolo (harvest), with prying eyes.[5] Reading from contexts where toutuʻu and polopolo are practised, the PBS participants expected a crowd in the field when Ruth approached.

There would have been other harvesters and gleaners at the same time, in other parts of the field, belonging to other families, and they would have seen Ruth enter the part that belonged to Boaz. For the PBS participants, it would have been interesting to know the proximity of the field to where Ruth and Naomi stayed and how many plots Ruth had to pass to come to Boaz's part of the field. Depending on how early in the day she set out in comparison to the other gleaners, who may have come out earlier and were gleaning at the parts closer to town, Ruth may have come later in the day and only found a place to glean at Boaz's part further down her path. The main issues here for the PBS participants are how many pairs of eyes Ruth passed by to come into Boaz's lot, and how many prying whispers floated on to her path.

Bethlehem may have developed into a city, but the plantation fields would have still been sowing grounds for talanoa and rumours. These were not on the radar of the narrator, who was probably more of a city person than a labourer or gleaner.

Woman of intelligence

Whether Elimelek's family and the Bethlehem community reached out to give Naomi and Ruth food and support upon their arrival, the narrator does not explain. I cannot tell from the narrative if Naomi and Ruth were desperate for food, or if Ruth was bored at home and wanted to explore and meet the people in the field. The text is, however, clear about one matter: it was Ruth's idea that she went to the field to glean. Ruth came from the *field of Moab* and it makes sense that she would be interested in seeing what goes on in the *field of Judah*.

Naomi occupied the focus since their arrival and up to the beginning of this pericope. Then the focus shifts, and the plot belongs to Ruth. The shift began with Ruth making room for Naomi's seal of approval. When Naomi gave her consent – 'Go, my daughter' (2.3) – Ruth set out on a path similar to ones that others have travelled, and on which some (were) abused. Ruth brings to mind the wilderness. In Exodus 16, the people of Israel went out to gather from the daily rain of bread from the sky (16.4). The instruction was clear – gather enough for each day and do not leave any for the next morning (16.19) – but the people nonetheless disobeyed and thus angered Moses (16.20).

Moreover, some of the people went out on the Sabbath and thereby also angered YHWH (16.27–29). Also connected to the wilderness is the teaching in Leviticus 23.22:

> When you reap the harvest of your land, you shall not reap to the very edges of your field, or gather the gleanings of your harvest; you shall leave them for the poor and for the alien: I am the LORD your God. (NRSV)

With the shift of the focus, Ruth opens the narrative towards the wilderness tradition as well as towards Pasifika.

One of the hot topics for PBS participants was where Ruth and Naomi stayed upon entering Bethlehem. The way Naomi was rude to the women in the previous passage suggests that she did not need to stay with any of them. She had her own place, thank you, and she was coming to her own home, to her own family and to Elimelek's family – in whose care she and Elimelek would have left their home and resources when they migrated to Moab. The PBS participants expect that both Naomi's family and Elimelek's family would have provided for Naomi and Ruth, and some members of the family may have continued to live with them. The crucial point here is the strong possibility that Naomi and Ruth came to a space of communal living. They did not have to live alone, and so their movements would have been noticed by their live-in companions. And they did not have to be desperate for food, so Ruth volunteering to go gleaning may be because of curiosity and a desire to build relationships (as Dinah is presented in Gen. 34).

In the PBS scenario, Ruth's going out to glean would have been noticed. She did not (have to) tiptoe out of the home, or sneak into the field. Eyes would have followed her into the fields: eyes of concern, for she was a foreigner and might fall into danger, and eyes of inquisition, because she was a widow (read: available).

The narrator does not give Ruth credit or agency. According to the narrative, it was luck that brought her to Boaz's part of the field. The Tongan rendering of 2.3 suggests otherwise:

pea ʻi heʻene faainoa naʻa ne veʻe tonu
ki he konga vao ʻo Poasi
(in her roaming she falls into step
to the plot-of-bush of Boaz)

The two Tongan words (*veʻe tonu*) that signify luck come from the context of dancing. One who dances well (by moving in tune with the rhythm and the beat) is veʻe tonu. True, veʻe tonu has something to do with luck; but in Tongan ears, veʻe tonu has much more to do with talents and gifts, and stamina (enduring several practice sessions). Veʻe tonu does not come by chance. Rather, it is passed on, practised and perfected. In this regard, Ruth was roaming and, at some point, she 'falls into step' and her skill of adaptability enables her to step into the plot of Boaz. In the Tongan rendering, this was not all nor only luck. It was also because Ruth was gifted, skilful and intelligent.

Ruth went out with intentions – to glean 'behind whomever I find favour in his eyes' (3.2). She was 'roaming' (according to the Tongan rendering) but that does not mean that she was aimless. She roamed with a purpose and, as one might expect, the PBS participants imagine that she was 'going fishing' (not in the sea, but in the bush). Natives fish on land also – in lakes and ponds, and for sea creatures that come on to land (crabs, turtles, birds, eels), some of which even climb up and live permanently on trees (among the favoured in Pasifika are the land-crabs that live on coconut trees). It was therefore not so strange when Solomon Island women suggested that Ruth was going fishing. Against the narrator's presentation of Ruth as coming by chance to Boaz's part of the field, the Solomon Islanders saw Ruth as determined and calculating. She knew what she was doing.

Boaz was not the only person of strength in this passage. Ruth too was warrior-like, a woman of intelligence and purpose, who came into the open space of the plantation-field with the kind of courage that headhunters possess.

Pasifikation

On most islands, burial grounds – which are among Pasifika's sacred grounds – are at or across the path from the beach (see Figure 3.2 on page 69). Those sacred grounds are exposed to the wind and the waves; and the rising sea level energized by climate change is a threat to the comfort of both the dead and their descendants.

Some of the most moving talanoa i heard at PBS events were about islanders going into the sea to collect human bones that have been scattered by the waves after a cyclone or tsunami. The waves had dug up the burial grounds, shattered the skeletons, and carried those sacred relics out to sea. In the case of tsunamis, some of the bones get mangled with other debris and dumped at different places inland. The pains of regathering the bones had to do with not being able to find all the pieces and not being able to identify which bones belong to which loved one. The gathered bones are nameless.

The PBS participants used the metaphors of fishing and gleaning to describe the regathering of bones. What the wind and waves scattered the natives gather, rub clean with coconut oil and tears, then wrap in a warming *tapa* or cloth and rebury in the land, so that they may again rest – but they do not expect that they will find peace. Is peace ever possible for bodies, dead or alive, that have been violated and dismembered? Also irritating for the natives is the possibility that they have wrapped and buried in the same bundle the bones of individuals (e.g. sister and brother) who in life observed tapu (*tabu*, taboo). When they were alive, due to relational protocols, they would not sleep in the same room at the same time. At their first burial, they would 'sleep' in separate graves out of respect for their tapu. But at reburial, they are made to violate one another's sacred space. The metaphors of 'planting the bones' and 'feeding the land' come up in the talanoa of reburial. Those images help islanders deal with the pain, that they were doing something that benefits the land, but they did not expect the bones to grow (unless Ezekiel returns with his magic words, cf. Ezek. 37.1–14).

The talanoa of fishing and gleaning for bones invite expanding the reasons for Ruth's venture. The bible study presented above, and most readings of this passage, assume that Ruth went to gather food – for consumption. The fishing and gleaning of bones suggest another reading: speaking metaphorically, some of the seeds that Ruth gleaned may also be buried so that they grow, and bear fruits and seeds for future generations. For future gleaners. Consumption is not the only reason for gleaning, nor the only concern of islanders. Survival is also important. Did Ruth glean for seeds in order to plant? For her sake, and her survival?

Resettlement is not complete when one arrives. Home, security and daily food are necessary. Looking towards the future, planting and gardening are also important. In this connection, the reburied bones in Pasifika extend Ruth's gleaning venture into the future: some of the seeds may be planted, to provide food for tomorrow (read: survival). Survival makes resettlement meaningful.

These two readings – for consumption, for survival – are not exclusive of each other. Nor are Ruth and Naomi. What is good for one is good for the other; Ruth gleaned for herself and for Naomi. In this connection, Ruth too was 'for Naomi'.

Takeaway

1 Who are the biblical and historical 'warrior-like persons of strength' that you could associate with Boaz?
2 How did your experience of gardening and harvesting (or lack thereof) influence your reading of (or disinterest in) this passage?
3 What difference does it make for your reading of this passage, and of the narrative as a whole, that much of what unfolds happens in public places?

(8) Ruth 2.4–7: Boaz discovers Ruth

⁴ ( ) Behold, Boaz entered from Bethlehem
( ) He said to the reapers
'Yhwh be with you'
( ) They said to him, 'Yhwh bless you'
⁵ ( ) Boaz said to his young man, set over the reapers
'For whom is this young woman?'
⁶ ( ) The young man set over the reapers answered and said
'She is the young Moabite woman
that returned with Naomi from the field of Moab
⁷ ( ) she said, "Let me glean and gather
after the reapers among the sheaves"
( ) she entered [and] have stood
from morning time until this time
she stopped at the house, a little'

Finally, the presence of Boaz enters the story. He returned from Bethlehem, greeted his workers, and discovered a new woman (whom readers already encountered in the previous passage) in his part of the field. Boaz enquired, 'For whom is this young woman?' The young man set above the workers in the plantation did not answer his question, but instead praised her stamina – she was a strong and enduring woman. Boaz did not follow up his question, but he appeared to silently approve of her presence in his plot.

Who knows what and whom are important in the world of talanoa? The storyteller knows more than the characters, and sometimes listeners and storyweavers also know more than the characters. As the talanoa unfolds, some characters grasp the plot and choose to play along. But not all characters do. Some characters opt to disobey (e.g. Jonah headed for Tarshish instead of Nineveh; Jonah 1.3) and some opt to subvert (e.g. the Gibeonites tricked Joshua and the Israelites; Josh. 9) the plot.

With respect to the passage for this bible study, readers know more than Boaz about what happened in his own part of the field. Readers also know that, as suggested in the previous bible study, Boaz was returning to a set-up.

With you

Boaz entered the narrative with the name of the divine, 'YHWH be with you'. His greeting echoes the assertion that Naomi made to Orpah and Ruth while they were still on the road, 'May YHWH do kindness with you' (1.8). Given that he literarily mimicked her, Boaz entered the narrative with a hint that he was 'for Naomi'.

The workers responded in kind, 'YHWH bless you'. This exchange – be with you, bless you – would have been shared on each occasion when they greeted each other, and it clearly favoured Boaz: he wished the presence of YHWH to be *with* his men, and they wished that YHWH *blesses* Boaz. Literarily, Boaz was lined up to receive more from this exchange, and that reflects his status and power in relation to the workers.

The exchange paints Boaz and his men as religious figures, but that does not mean that they were therefore peaceable and just. Even ruthless subjects know, and greet others in, the name of their Gods. Many religious subjects have contributed to the most heinous projects in the history of humanity, including the occupations of Canaan – first by Abram (see Gen. 12.6) and later by the people of Israel under the leadership of Joshua, as well as the Holocaust (concocted at Germany – the homeland of top-end scholarships and high Christian cultures at that time), and the ongoing settlement of Palestine by the modern State of Israel. The pushers of these projects regularly call on the names of their Gods.

The transatlantic slave trade is another example of the ruthless practices of people who function with religious sentiments and rhetoric: the slave traders worship at Christian chapels above the holding cells where hundreds and thousands of black bodies await the arrival of ships and then, as at the fort in Elmina (Ghana), throw water upon African men, women and children to baptize them as they step through the 'door of no return'. Calling on the name of a divine being and/or exhibiting religious characteristics do not make one fair and reasonable.

Boaz may not have been a colonialist or a slave owner,[6] like Abram, but he was clearly a man of strength, wealth and status.

He would have exuded power and drawn respect in return. Entitlement. The narrative links him to a city, Bethlehem, and he could have even been a city dweller who (as a habit) came later in the day to his plantation. He was in no hurry, for he has young men (read: subalterns) who managed his plantation. Or he might be a plantation-dweller (for there is a reference to a house in 2.7) who had business to do early in the day in the city. It is also possible that he had enough wealth to afford him two homes, one in the city and one at the plantation (a country home). These possibilities accentuate his status. Boaz was a significant character, with substance.

For whom

Boaz did not know all that readers know. He did not know the new face in his plantation, so he asked, 'For whom is this young woman?' He assumed that she belonged to or has been reserved for someone, which brings to mind the narrator's earlier assertion that Boaz was 'for Naomi' (2.1; see the previous bible study).

It is rousing that Boaz referred to Ruth as a 'young woman' (נערה). On the one hand, he asked in order to find out who owned this young woman. Being young and a woman, and this reflects the patriarchal culture behind the narrative, she must belong to someone. Boaz was no fool. On the other hand, his question suggests that he might be interested in the young woman, maybe to join the other 'maidservants' (2.13) who worked in his plot. Or maybe for other functions. In this regard, Boaz might step away from the narrator's 'for Naomi' agenda. Whatever the case might have been, Boaz's question did not have to be an innocent one.

The young man (נער) set above the workers sang Ruth's praises. She was the young Moabite woman who returned with Naomi from the field of Moab (2.6b). She was a woman of the field, so she would have known how things work in Boaz's part of the field. She was a hard worker. She has been on her feet since she arrived, working with no break ... except for the time she stopped at the house (2.7). He noticed when she moved, and when she stopped. She must have been irresistible. Ruth had not completed even a whole day in the field, and she already found favour in the eyes of a young man (cf. 2.2). But there were other eyes in the field.

Nameless

The young man did not refer to Ruth by her name, but he has eyed her up since she arrived. He noticed that 'she stopped at the house (בית), a little' (2.7). This detail caught the attention of the PBS participants. What kind of house was it? Did she ask for permission to enter the house, or did she waltz right in as if she belonged? Did other gleaners stop at that house?

Many Pasifika communities distinguish between 'big house' (for community functions) and 'little houses' (for sleeping), and in some cultures 'little house' (*falesiʻi* in Tongan) refers to the toilet (outhouse or house at the back; *faletua* in Samoan). Following the word order in the Hebrew text, the last phrase of 2.7 may be rendered as 'she stopped [at] the little house' and could thus entertain the queering of PBS participants. Whether Ruth stopped at the little house to relieve herself or to rest (nap) is one question; another and more important question is whether she stopped alone or were there others with her? These questions caught the attention of PBS participants because they imagined other gleaners in the field, but they did not catch the attention of the narrator. The other gleaners are faceless as well as nameless, which gives talanoa-folk the impression that the narrator was trying to hide and/or set something up.

Assuming that the house could be for sleeping, does this mean that Boaz was a family man? And how old was Boaz? Or was the house not for his family but for the workers? These questions cannot be answered on the basis of the text, but they raised the suspicions of PBS participants. Looking back over the passage, the house may be read as a Freudian slip that brings to view matters that the narrator preferred to keep hidden (or nameless).

This house would have been a significant and permanent structure for it to be called a בית. It appears in a place where PBS participants did not expect such a structure, and it brings into view a house missing from the narrator's account: the PBS participants expected the narrator to locate the house into which Naomi and Ruth arrived. In walking into the house at the plantation, Ruth brought into view the house that the narrator had hidden.

Pasifikation

So-called seasonal workers have been taken from Pasifika to Australia and Aotearoa New Zealand to provide cheap labour for tasks that local Australians and New Zealanders expect to be paid more for (read: paid appropriately, fairly, or justly). These tasks vary from picking fruits, harvesting vegetables, to slaughtering and butchering livestock.

Seasonal workers are the modern faces of ancient reapers. They get a little, if they are lucky and careful, but the owners of plantations and farms will always take home more. Despite the mechanization of industries, hiring the human touch at times of harvest saves owners a lot of damaged products and money. And hiring cheap labour from Pasifika and Asia, and some backpackers who need extra cash, saves owners more money.

The seasonal workers are given work permits and they are taken across for three to ten months at a time, then they go back to the islands and wait for the next season. They are paid *below* minimum wages for Australians and New Zealanders,[7] out of which they are to pay for their accommodation and upkeep, and they are expected to be grateful to the institutions (governments and cooperatives) that are said to be helping them out financially. In the end, however, these institutions take with one hand what they give with the other hand.

Seasonal workers who work long hours (12 or more hours a day, for six or seven days a week) are able to make some money to send back to their families. But not all are successful. One seasonal worker explained to me that he joined the seasonal workers programme because he had taken out a loan to build his family a house, and after two stints to New Zealand he owed almost twice more than when he started. He had to take new loans to cover his travel expenses, and the cost of living in New Zealand was too much for him to be able to save any money.

Most of the islanders who join the seasonal workers programme have a loan to pay back, mainly for building new houses for their families. They need new houses for several reasons (the old house was falling apart, the family was growing and/or shifting to a different island) but the reason that is not often named is that the family needed to resettle because their old home had been lost to the sea (see Figure 3.2 on page 69).

Losing the family home to the sea, and the wrath of climate change, was brought home to me in my first visit to Kiribati. A retired pastor (Baranite Kirata) invited me to visit him at his home-island of Onotoa, where he remigrated soon after retirement in order to rebuild his family home, so that i could meet his family and see what life was like for his people. When i arrived, he had not started to build his home, but he and his wife were living with his brother and his family. On the second day, he took me to the other end of the island to show me his parents' home. We walked up to the edge of the land, the tide was out at that time, and he pointed to about 35 metres *into the sea* and said, 'That's where my grandmother's house was, the house where I was born'. The sea had taken over 35 metres of land, together with the row of homes that used to be there 70 or more years earlier.

From the struggles of seasonal workers to the displacement of climate-affected islanders, and to the plantation of Boaz, a house, big or little, makes a difference. It is in these kinds of context that the house in Ruth 2.7 was significant for the PBS participants. In other words, the house into which Ruth went brought to light the houses that are 'hidden' from the shores of Pasifika.

Takeaway

1 How are female migrant workers treated in your neighbourhood and society?
2 How has your mind changed or remained the same with
respect to Boaz?
3 How has your mind changed or remained the same with
respect to Ruth?

Prompts for further talanoa

1 Jonathan Magonet, 'Did Jephthah Actually Kill His Daughter?' *The Torah.com*, 2015; www.thetorah.com/article/
did-jephthah-actually-kill-his-daughter, accessed 5.5.21.
2 Tamar Kamionkowski, 'Will the Real Miriam Please Stand
Up?' *The Torah.com*, 2015; www.thetorah.com/article/will-
the-real-miriam-please-stand-up, accessed 5.5.21.

Notes

1 There might have been helpers who went along with the family
and helpers who returned with the two widows, but the narrator does
not divulge this.
2 The majority of participants at all PBS gatherings found Naomi's
response to the women, some of whom might have been older than she,
disrespectful and inappropriate.
3 The Peruvian slave trade reached Tonga around 1862–4 and took
natives from 'Ata (the southernmost island in the Tonga group) and
Niua Fo'ou (at the north end, closer to Samoa than to the capital island
of Tongatapu), but did not succeed at 'Uiha (in the Ha'apai group).
From 'Ata, the Peruvian slave traders (blackbirders) took over 170
islanders; in response, around 200 natives were resettled to Tongatapu
(in Lomaiviti / Matālikufisi) and 'Eua (in Ha'atu'a / Kolomaile). It
was also to the same settlements that refugees from Niua Fo'ou were
resettled after the 1946 volcanic eruptions – this is an example of the
first cause for resettlement.
4 War-situations and violence against women go hand in hand.
Headhunting practices are of course not limited to Pasifika, and definitely not limited to the past. The untold talanoa of the coups and

military regimes in Fiji (since 1987), for instance, is the increase in the number of rapes (by military officers and by civilians). There are similar situations in West Papua, where Indonesian soldiers rape and violate Papuan women (e.g. stick instruments into their genitals). Before i get distracted, the point i am making here is that there are sexual and violent aspects in the characteristics of warriors and men of strength. That Boaz might have been such a 'warrior-like man of strength' is a possibility that the PBS participants could not rule out.

5 The practices of *toutu'u* and the prying eyes at *polopolo* take place (under different names) in all parts of Pasifika. There are different kinds of community projects, on land and in the sea, and they help form and sustain villages and islands. Community projects develop relationships and encourage reciprocity.

6 The young men (נערים; 2.9) that worked for him are usually seen as 'lads' or 'servants' (as in Gen. 22.3) but there is no indication in the narrative that they were day labourers or hired hands. In other words, they could have been Boaz's slaves.

7 If Australians and New Zealanders were paid appropriately (according to local rates) for these menial tasks, i suspect that many of them would join these lines of work and there would be no shortage in the workforce.

6

Ruth 2.8–23
Food and comfort

Food is necessary for peace and comfort. Food, however, is not available for everyone in the same way and ease, or for the same cost. One's wealth affects one's assessment of cost (bear in mind that cost is relative and contextual), and there are cultural elements to the scale of affordability. In Pasifika, for example, an impoverished family would seek ways to secure the expected food items to gift to their pastor or chief (when it is their turn to do so) even if those items are beyond their means (see Pouono, 2021). There is also an expected amount of food items to give (e.g. not three tins of corned beef, but a whole box; not a piece of cake, but a whole cake) because pastors and chiefs are perceived to represent (Christian and traditional) Gods. Cultural and religious expectations make expensive and out-of-reach items affordable only for important people, and as a consequence the poorer families borrow and quickly fall into debt.[1] Pasifika natives are thus trapped by their traditional customs as well as by their religious cultures (see Taule'ale'ausumai, 2021).

Food is a currency in Pasifika. A family might not have any cash, but they could survive if they have access to a piece of land (for planting and hunting) and to the sea (for fishing and foraging). Families usually share what they harvest from the land and the sea with their neighbours and relatives, and they thereby take shelter in the vivaciousness of reciprocity, and they may also choose to sell part of their harvests (whether there is enough food to go around or not). Turning food into cash may be undertaken privately or within corporations, in the shadows of which 'the market' turns food into economic products and converts co-dependent and reciprocating *wantoks* ('one talks')[2] into customers and patrons. In the towers of capitalism, families who own plantations and thus have influence on the production of food, or control over it, do well economically and on the platforms of social power.

In market-driven economies, food is one of the 'goods' (product, value) that testify to the operations of (in)justice. How are food items produced? Are the items priced appropriately? Who takes home the lion's share? In response to such questions, some food products are marked as organic, ecologically friendly, fair trade, farmers' brands, produced locally, among other labels,[3] in order to appeal to conscious and ethical buyers. But for the poorer customers, the bottom line is cost and affordability, which means that the cheaper own-label store brands (called clean- or clear-skins in Aotearoa and Australia) win out most of the time. One of the problems with these brands is that the production and distribution processes are hidden (not even given in the fine print), and therefore customers are blind to the fruits of injustice(s) that they are about to purchase, consume or gift away.

The bible studies offered in this chapter read selected texts at the intersections of food (around matters of production and labour, distribution and currency, profit and (in)justice) with comfort. These bible studies are shaped by the bible studies in the previous chapters on the challenges that situations of remigration and resettlement present. My attention in this chapter is on how food provides and symbolizes comfort for remigrants and foreigners, rather than the comfort of privileged subjects or with so-called 'comfort foods' (which are privileges, because they are in addition to the daily basic foodstuffs that each person requires). Put another way, the following bible studies are more interested in survival than in profit.

(9) Ruth 2.8–13: Boaz comforts Ruth

⁸ ( ) Boaz said to Ruth, 'Have you not heard, my daughter
Do not go to glean in another field
( ) also do not cross over from this one
[but] abide here with my young women
⁹ [keep] your eyes on the field that they reap [then] go
  after them –
Have I not commanded the young men to never touch you?
[When] you are thirsty, ( ) go to the vessels
( ) drink from what the young men have drawn'
¹⁰ ( ) She fell on her face, ( ) bowed to the earth
( ) She said to him, 'Why have I found favour in your eyes
to notice me, for I am a foreigner?'
¹¹ ( ) Boaz answered [and] said to her
'It has fully been told to me
all that you did to your mother-in-law
after the death of your husband
( ) you abandoned your mother ( ) your father ( ) your
  land of birth
( ) you went to a people you did not know up to now
¹² May Yʜᴡʜ fulfil your work
( ) may your reward be fulfilled from Yʜᴡʜ
God of Israel, under whose wings you have entered for
  refuge'
¹³ ( ) She said, 'Let me find favour in your eyes, my lord
( ) for you spoke to the heart of your maidservant
[though] I am not like one of your maidservants'

The exchange between Boaz and Ruth took place out in the open – the plantation belonged to Boaz, but the field was a public place. Seeing that Ruth entered freely and secured permission to glean with no hassles, i imagine that there were other gleaners there who were also within the reach of Boaz's voice. Together with the reapers – young men and young women – as well as the young man in charge of the workers, some of them must have overheard the exchange of words, the expression of care and the extension of attention.

The ears of workers usually tune in to the voice of their master; they would have heard and formed an opinion. Their eyes would have roamed. I imagine that they would have glanced at one another, made facial expressions without needing to state what they were thinking – until they leave the plantation at the end of the day.

Wantoks

The focus of the narrative continues shifting (from Naomi) towards Ruth. The exchange between Boaz and Ruth was not a private matter, discussed in secret. Boaz reached out to Ruth with assurances. He warned her of the dangers in the field and invited her to stay with his young women, in whose company she will be able to glean safely. She may also drink from the water that the young men have drawn. Boaz guaranteed food and water for Ruth if she remained in his plantation and he encouraged her not to be a stranger to the others in there. She would be better off in Boaz's plot.

Boaz was 'pretty smooth', claimed the PBS participants in Aotearoa and Australia. He reached out further 'for Ruth'. She in return was alarmed by his generosity. Why did the owner of the plantation pick (on) her? Her alarm is understandable, for it was her first day in the field of Judah (according to the narrative). They had just met, and they barely know each other.

Sounding like many family elders in Pasifika, Boaz explained that his generosity was reparation for the favour that Ruth had extended for dead members of his family. Ruth accommodated her husband and his family, who were Boaz's *wantoks*, and she has given up almost everything to accompany her mother-in-law back. In doing so, Ruth also became *wantok* with Boaz. Ruth thereby deserved Boaz's favour, and she took him up on his generosity.

Generosity

Boaz's generosity is honourable. He ticked all the right boxes that migrant workers appreciate in an employer. He did not appear sexist or xenophobic, at least not in obvious ways, and was just being kindly towards a (younger?) foreign woman. He took the time to explain her advantages, and her rights, and he did not come across as patronizing the younger Ruth. Boaz spoke to her heart, as a migrant woman, and the narrative even gives the impression that they share the same language or *tok tok* (the root for *wantok*).

In this reading, Boaz stands in the shadows of other caring biblical characters. He shares a welcoming heart with Potiphar, who took the cast-away Joseph (Gen. 37.17b–36) under his wings, and he shares a parental spirit with Mordecai, who became a guardian for his younger cousin or niece (in the Vulgate) Esther after her parents died (Esth. 2.7). Like Potiphar, who trusted Joseph to take charge over his household (Gen. 39.6), Boaz was generous towards a young foreigner. And like Mordecai, who continued to offer advice to Esther even after she had become queen (see Esth. 4.12–14), Boaz advised Ruth on matters pertaining to her welfare.

In the shadows of Potiphar and Mordecai, whose stories unfold around food,[4] Boaz looks out for the welfare of Ruth. Welfare and comfort are linked, and both are presented as common goods for Ruth and Boaz. What is good for Ruth is good for Boaz, and vice versa, even though they do not share 'common wealth(s)'.

Boaz's generosity, however, invites suspicions. Was Boaz selfless, or was he looking to gain something from, through and/or with Ruth? Returning to the shadows of Potiphar, whose unnamed wife (see also Chukka, 2021) had fallen for Joseph (Gen. 39.7), could Boaz have fallen for Ruth and thus used food and water to bait her (with his generosity)? In other words, was Boaz a 'sugar-daddy' or 'blesser' (a term used in contemporary Africa in reference to wealthy older men who give money, expensive gifts and opportunities to young women in exchange for favours)? These questions bring Boaz into the shadows of Mordecai as well who, according to a midrash, may have also been a husband for Esther (see Levy, 2016). Could this possibility have been part of Boaz's motivation?

Boaz was trying to get into Ruth's mind and heart, and the suspicions raised here point to the possibility that Boaz may have been trying to get into *more than her mind* as well as trying to *gain something through her body*. These suspicions were brought home for me by the PBS participants at Nauru (like Banaba in Kiribati, Nauru has been 'raped' by phosphate mining) and Ma'ohi Nui (a group of islands occupied by France): as a plantation owner, Boaz was no fool.[5] Like miners and colonialists, Boaz would have had profit in his mind. He would have had the knowledge of when to plant and when to harvest, and what to do in between to boost his operations. He would have also known how to manage the market, in order to make a profit. For the Nauru and Ma'ohi participants, Boaz's generosity was about building profit. And Ruth was both profit and bonus.

Altruistic or not, Boaz had a chance to profit with and through Ruth. There is no mention of Boaz having any children or spouse(s), and Ruth could help alleviate such lacks (if that were the case) or supplement what Boaz already had. In and with Ruth, Boaz could gain more. Boaz could also redeem Elimelek his kinsman through Ruth, and consequently increase his own wealth. Ruth is thus an opportunity for the expansion of his family and business profiles, and Boaz used food as bait to hook and reel Ruth into his 'plot'.[6]

Boaz manoeuvred in the shadows of Potiphar and Mordecai. Like Potiphar, whom YHWH blessed because of Joseph, Boaz had a chance with and through Ruth to grow 'in the house and in the field' (Gen. 39.5). And like Mordecai, for whose 'plot' Esther risked her life (Esth. 4.4, 4.16), Boaz's move on Ruth put her in a situation with a lot of risks – ranging from sneers and insults from jealous co-gleaners *in the field*, all the way to rejection by Naomi, as number one widow through whom Elimelek may be redeemed, *in the house*. In the shadows of Potiphar and Mordecai, Boaz has something to gain as a consequence of his own generosity.

A Tongan saying appropriately explains the outcome of Boaz's generosity – *piko piko iku mai*, which refers to a path that turns and turns (*piko piko*) and ends where it begins (*iku mai*). Boaz's generosity ends with himself, whereas Ruth, on the other hand, had to face many risks.

Favour

Ruth herself was no fool. In her first response to Boaz's generosity, a hint of suspicion comes through in her question – 'Why have I found favour (חֵן) in your eyes to notice me, for I am a foreigner?' (2.10b). Without giving up the obvious reading, that Ruth was grateful for and humbled by Boaz's generosity, there is room for wonderment and suspicion as well. 'Wow, unbelievable! Why me?' In this twist, Ruth was suspicious of Boaz long before any reader considered questioning his generosity and motivation. By extension, Ruth's wonderment invites readers to be suspicious of Boaz.

The favour (חֵן) that Ruth found in Boaz's eyes matches what she was looking for at the beginning of the day: 'Let me go to the field and glean among the ears of corn behind whomever I find favour (חֵן) in his eyes' (2.2). The young man in charge was favourable to her but, because of the choice of words, the favour (חֵן) that she found in Boaz's eyes was the real deal. In the Hebrew Bible, this special kind of favour (חֵן) is linked with YHWH God, who extends it to key characters like Noah (Gen. 6.8), Abraham (Gen. 18.3), and Moses (Gen. 33.12–13), to name but a few. These characters are the 'more favoured' among the favoured people of YHWH God, thus showing that favour (חֵן) comes in many degrees and shades.

In the Wesleyan heritage to which i belong, the special favour or grace of YHWH God is understood to be free and prevenient. It is a gift. On some occasions, however, YHWH God withholds this special favour and as a result hardship falls upon the people (Isa. 27.11).[7] But with some prompting by the 'more favoured' on behalf of the people (Exod. 32.21, 2 Kings 13.4) the favour of YHWH God may return,[8] which was the setting for what Isaiah announced as the 'year of the Lord's favour' (Isa. 49.8; 61.2). Favour comes and goes, and it may also be (re)distributed and (re)directed. On the other side of the coin, some characters abuse and take advantage of the favour of YHWH God. Among those characters are the special characters named above:

- *Noah*: One of the absurdities in the story of Noah is that very soon after the ark landed and they brought the animals out, he sacrificed some of the clean animals and clean birds that he was commissioned to save (Gen. 8.20). Whether to call that thanksgiving, homage, covenant making, stupidity or something else, one thing is clear – Noah was pushing the limits of YHWH God's favour (but YHWH God did not seem to mind).
- *Abraham*: Instead of waiting for YHWH God to deliver on the promises (Gen. 12.1–4a), this so-called pillar of right-eousness twice passed his wife off (Gen. 12.10–20; Gen. 20.1–17) for his own protection and profit, took another woman as his wife (Gen. 16.3), and he was prepared to cast his first (Gen. 21.8–21) and second sons (Gen. 22.1–19) away. Those acts earned Abraham the title 'father of faith' in my Sunday School days, but they also give evidence of his not taking YHWH God's favour seriously. Put more sharply, in those acts Abraham abused the favour of YHWH God (and here, also, YHWH God did not seem to mind).
- *Moses*: The popular explanation given for why Moses was left to die in the wilderness instead of entering Canaan is that he had fallen out of favour with YHWH God (Num. 20.12). Moses saw the land from a distance, but did not enter it (Deut. 34.4). In the case of Moses, YHWH God did mind.

There are other examples, but the point i highlight here is that favour (חן) is not permanent nor unchanging. Favour is open for negotiation, and this applies to both the favours of YHWH God as well as the favours of humans.

In the Ruth narrative, favour is associated with food. The famine at the beginning of the narrative (1.1) implies loss of favour; the return of food five verses later is described as being a result of the remembrance and visit by YHWH (1.6) – that is, because of the return of YHWH's favour.

In 2.8–13, Ruth went out looking for favour (חן) in the form of food, and found חן in the eyes of Boaz (2.10). But that was not enough for her; some three verses later, Ruth asked for more. Between 2.10 and 2.13, Boaz appealed to YHWH's favour on behalf of Ruth:

'May YHWH fulfil your work
( ) may your reward be fulfilled from YHWH,
God of Israel, under whose wings you have entered for refuge.' (2.12)

Boaz prayed for YHWH's fulfilment (read: favour) upon Ruth. In response to this prayer Ruth asked for more of Boaz's favour: 'Let me find favour (חן) in your eyes, my lord ( ) for you spoke to the heart of your maidservant' (2.13a). With clarity and a comforting tone Ruth sang 'tell me more' into Boaz's ears. She could not have enough of this good thing – favour (חן).

Pasifikation

The honour and shame cultures that shape the minds of Pasifika natives take the subjects, and politics, of generosity and favour seriously. Honour and shame are like the masts to which the sails of relationality (kinship, communalism) are attached, and reciprocity is like the wind that motivates native communities to move (forward, sideways, or round about). At the contact of relationality and reciprocity, generosity and favour are neither free nor detached. There is a cost (read: burden) for generosity and favour, which someone somewhere would have to somehow bear. In this connection, *piko piko iku mai* (see the 'Generosity' section above) comes to mind when generosity and favour are offered or exchanged. What is the cost or the burden? In addition to the appreciation for generosity and favour is a splash of suspicion, all of which are reflected in this bible study.

In the context of climate change in Pasifika, the combination of appreciation of and suspicion for generosity and favour is clearest in relation to foreign donors. Some foreign bodies and foreign nations donate lump sums in the names of 'security' (e.g. to fund the building of seawalls), 'development' (e.g. for desalination projects) and 'sustainability' (e.g. for solar power farms), and expect small island nations not to question their current operations (e.g. seabed mining and the occupation of Pasifika islands), to support them at global forums (e.g. at the United Nations), to purchase accessories from their manufacturers (the equipment is free, but operations, updates and repairs are not), and so forth. Such generosities and favours are reminders of the cost to native lives when colonialists introduced foreign diseases when they 'discovered' our islands, and the cost to native religions when missionaries declared native cultures as forms of paganism that lead to hell (a concept that missionaries brought with them) when they 'converted' our people. All forms of aid therefore invite suspicions in the eyes of natives, and this critical tendency plays out in the above bible study.

Takeaway

1 What are other reasons for Boaz reaching out to Ruth?

2 Who else might have overheard the exchange between Boaz and Ruth, and how might they have interpreted the conversation between the two?

3 In who else's shadows can Boaz be seen in Ruth 2.8–13, and why?

4 Who are other biblical characters who received and/or abused the favours of Gods and humans?

(10) Ruth 2.14–18a: Boaz heaps Ruth

¹⁴ ( ) Boaz said to her at the time of eating
　'Come here [and] eat from the bread
　( ) dip your piece in the vinegar.'
　( ) She sat beside the reapers
　( ) He gave her parched corn
　( ) She ate ( ) she was satisfied ( ) she left over
¹⁵ [When] she rose to glean, Boaz commanded the young
　men saying,
　'Let her glean between the sheaves also ( ) do not shame
　　her
¹⁶ ( ) also, purposely pull out from the bundles for her
　( ) drop them ( ) let her glean
　do not rebuke her'
¹⁷ ( ) She gleaned in the field until evening
　( ) She beat out what she had gleaned
　{ } About an ephah of barley.
^{18a} ( ) She took it up [and] entered the city

Ruth went back to gleaning. Silently. In this passage, she moved, ate, gleaned some more, then returned to the city, without saying a word. What might have silenced her? Did the narrator purposely silence her? These questions arise because she was engaging and talkative in the previous passage, and suddenly she went silent after Boaz's assurance.

Boaz, on the other hand, was not silent. If there are any doubts to his generosity, that is put to rest in this passage. In response to Ruth asking for more favour in the previous passage (2.13), Boaz offered her more (2.14) and more (2.15b–16) food in this passage. He compellingly reached out to Ruth, with words and deeds.

On the other side of the coin, the question of whether Boaz was completely selfless or not returns to the surface. Might he have expected something in return? In other words, what was the cost and burden of his generosity?

Meal

Since the announcement of the famine (1.1) and through the widows' return to and arrival at Judah, it is not until this passage that a meal spreads out in the narrative (2.14). In light of Ruth's firm commitment to Naomi (1.16–17) on the road during their return and given that this narrative was set off by the lack of food, it is curious that Ruth did not also vow 'your meal will be my meal, my food will be your food'. In this regard, Ruth did not go all the way in her commitment to Naomi.[9]

Food returned earlier to Judah (1.6), but it is not harvested, shared and consumed in the narrative world until Ruth came to Boaz's plot. In this reading, two translations of 2.14 are inviting:

> NJPS (my italics): At mealtime, Boaz said to her, 'Come over here and partake *of the meal*, and dip your morsel in the vinegar.'

> NRSV (my italics): At mealtime Boaz said to her, 'Come here, and eat some of *this bread*, and dip your morsel in the sour wine.'

'Come [over] here' implies separation. Boaz invited Ruth to a *meal* (as compared to a *feed* or *kaikai*, to use terms used in Pasifika for a 'snack'), which carries an element of intimacy. The invitation aimed to close the gap. Boaz did not call Ruth to take (as in a pick-up or drive-through window) and go back to her place, but he invited her to come over, sit down and eat the same food – *this bread* – as Boaz. Boaz's 'table' was open to Ruth also, and the meal was an occasion for sharing. And, of course, sharing is caring.

The PBS participants were curious as to whether Boaz sat and shared the same meal together with his workers or, while they shared the same food, he sat at a different place (i.e. at the boss's table). The narrative allows for both possibilities, depending on how one reads 1.14b. Boaz could have sat with the reapers and thus Ruth joined them at the same 'table'; Boaz could have sat away from the reapers, thus with Ruth hanging back from his 'top table' to sit with the reapers. No matter where the reapers sat, the subject of who handed dried/roasted food to Ruth is (in the singular) Boaz. The NRSV accentuates Boaz's generosity: 'So she sat beside the reapers, and *he heaped up for her* some parched grain' (2.14b, my italics). Boaz's heap was so much that Ruth ate to her satisfaction and she left some over; that Ruth left some over appears to have more to do with Boaz's generosity rather than any frugality on her part.

At the meal, Ruth was uplifted. She entered the plantation as a gleaner but at the meal she sat and ate with the reapers, at the boss's invitation. Other gleaners at the plantation did not receive the narrator's notice nor Boaz's invitation. And Ruth did not draw attention to her peers. Ruth silently joined the meal, and silently she ate. When she sat down, did she turn her back on the other gleaners?

The reapers at the meal, on the ground, would have noticed the extra favour that Ruth received. But as far as the narrative is concerned, the reapers too sat and ate in silence. This silence is difficult to grasp in Pasifika because meals among peers are usually noisy with talanoa, jokes and gossip. What might have caused the reapers' silence? Were they too tired to talk, or were they for some reason silenced? At this point, the narrative refuses to *tell me more*.

Silence

After the meal, Ruth got up to glean some more. In silence. For her advantage, Boaz gave clear directions to the reapers: load Ruth up, and do not rebuke nor shame her (1.15b–16). This time also, the reapers were silent (or silenced) and their silence begs the refrain, *tell me more*.

Compared to situations where 'left over' is excess food that the eater missed or cannot eat, Ruth was intentional to 'leave over' (יתר) some of her meal. The same Hebrew verb is used to describe the locusts eating the fruits that the hail 'left over' (Exod. 10.15) and the Passover meal that the Israelites must eat up and *not* 'leave over' anything to the next morning (Exod. 12.10; cf. Exod. 16.19–20); in both instances, יתר refers to food that is purposefully left (compare with Jacob being 'left behind' in Gen. 32.25) rather than excess food that is missed. Ruth left over some food, but in continuing to glean after the meal she appears to want more. She was satisfied with the meal, but not yet satisfied with what to take home. *Give me more, give me more.*

In the field, Ruth continues her ascent. She is not to be treated as a regular gleaner but allowed to glean between the sheaves also. She may step forward, ahead of the other regular gleaners. Better still, the workers are to 'pull' (שלל) from their bundles and drop for her to glean. In this way, Boaz's reapers were to work for her profit. Sweet. Her companions at the mealtime became her helpers when they returned to work. This was nice for her, but potentially upsetting for the reapers.

At the end of the day she beat out what she gleaned, and her profit amounted to one ephah – a biblical measure for dry grain, ten times the amount of an omer (Exod. 16.36). Given that an omer should be enough to sustain one adult per day (Exod. 16.16), Ruth gathered enough for ten people. That amount does not include what she left over at the meal, which the text does not measure. For a day's work, Ruth was well favoured.

The obvious explanation for why Ruth beat (חבט) what she gleaned is so that she did not have to carry the wastage back with her. She would have been tired, and to lighten her burden was to her benefit. The PBS participants add more explanations:

First, she had to beat the bunches because she gleaned so much that she could not carry everything. The emphasis here is on the amount, an ephah of barley would have been beaten out of a big bundle, rather than on getting rid of waste. Since stalks, leaves and sticks are useful for the kitchen fire, she did not have to leave those in the field. The beating is therefore a signal for how much she gleaned (and had to carry), similar to islanders who husk their coconuts in the bush so that they only carry the nuts back to the village.

Second, the beating signals that there was still enough day-light for her to work. She might have stopped gleaning earlier than the other gleaners (who could work longer than the reapers), again signalling her success. She worked until evening (2.17a), but it was still early enough in the evening that darkness was not upon her and home may not have been far away.

Third, she could have been tarrying so that someone would walk her home. She has received so many favours all day long, so why not at the end of the day as well? These *tell me more* ruminations come up because Ruth worked silently in this passage.

Did Boaz's kindness make Ruth silent? Or was she silent because things were working out in her favour? For Ruth, everything was in order so there was no need for her to say anything further.

Pasifikation

Few people have enough time, and fewer people can buy time. For the majority of people who do not even have space for some downtime, time has become one of the, if not *the*, most expensive commodities in life. For that majority, the ancient wisdom teaching that there is a time for everything under the sun (see Eccles. 3. 1–8) is passé. Ancient as. That scripturalized wisdom no longer works. Time is not as expansive for that majority. There is not enough time to go around.

But time ticks to different beats in different settings. Time has a different feel for people who live and work in a city as compared to people who live on a farm, work in a factory, or spend time in a garden or on a beach, and it makes a difference if those lived settings are in a continent or an island. Time moves according to different beats and there are different rhythms for different folks.

While the notion of 'island time' is fluid in Pasifika, the natives are attentive to signs of (day)light and darkness when it comes to talanoa. In this connection the key issue for me in this passage is not what time 'evening' (2.17) begins on the hickorydickory clock – so that i can tell at what hour and minute Ruth stopped gleaning and started beating – but whether she had enough daylight to finish her tasks and return safely home (before it gets too dark). Judging by the tempo of the narrative, seeing that Ruth did not need to rush her beating and to hurry home, it feels as if enough daylight remained. She had worked hard all day long, but she was not rushed at the end of the day. The lack of evidence of rush also suggests that she must have been very tired, too tired to rush.

There also does not appear to be any rush at the beginning of the day (2.1–2). Naomi and Ruth were at their own leisure, and the events of the day unfolded leisurely. No rush, no stress. I thus imagine that the two widows had time to go about their morning business, then at some point towards the middle of the morning (2.7) Ruth proposed to go and look for a set of eyes that will be favourable towards her. This move comes leisurely as an option, rather than because she was desperate.

Because there is no rush in the narrative, and there is no chatter and babble as characters silently move from one event to the next, i am inclined to think that Ruth and Naomi were not desperate for food. Food was a concern, but it was not a struggle to these leisurely ladies. At this stage, Naomi and Ruth give the impression that food may have been a currency for something more – whether for trade and commerce, for something to claim and inherit, or for something else.

Takeaway

1 How do you interpret Ruth's silence in this passage?
2 If you read this passage through the eyes of other gleaners, how would you describe Boaz's words?
3 Could the narrator have silenced Ruth and the reapers in this passage for a particular reason (or reasons), and what might that (those) be?

(11) Ruth 2.18b–23: Ruth feeds Naomi

^{18b} ( ) Her mother-in-law saw what she gleaned
( ) She brought forth [and] she gave to her
what she left over, after she was satisfied
¹⁹ ( ) Her mother-in-law said to her
'Where have you gleaned today ( ) where did you work?
May the one who noticed you be blessed'
( ) She told her mother-in-law with whom she worked
( ) She said, 'The name of the man with whom I worked
today is Boaz'
²⁰ ( ) Naomi said to her daughter-in-law
'Bless him, for YHWH has not betrayed his kindness
to the living and to the dead'
( ) Naomi said to her, 'The man is near to us
he is among our redeemers'
²¹ ( ) Ruth the Moabite said, 'Also, also, he said to me
"With my young men, abide
Until they end all of my harvest"'
²² ( ) Naomi said to Ruth her daughter-in-law
'Better, my daughter, that you go out with his young
women
[so] they do not meet you in another field'
²³ ( ) She abided with the young women of Boaz
to glean until the end of the barley harvest
[and] the wheat harvest
[while] she dwelt with her mother-in-law

An ephah must have given Ruth a sizeable lump or bulge, depending on how she carried her bulk, for it was the first thing Naomi noticed. Naomi saw first that Ruth did not return empty-handed. And when Ruth opened her hands, to give what she had left over, Naomi saw, second, that Ruth had been satisfied. Ruth must have found favour-able eyes and satisfying hands in the field of Judah; her appearance might have reminded Naomi of something back in the field of Moab. Ruth can still deliver, and she can also be satisfied.

Ruth was empty when she went out that morning, but she returned full in the evening. Put this way, Ruth's return invites comparison with Naomi's return some time (and one chapter) earlier. I highlight one difference between the attitudes of these two (re)migrants that will continue to recur, in different ways, in these bible studies: Naomi disregarded Ruth upon their arrival at Bethlehem, whereas Ruth looked out for Naomi on her return from the field. For PBS participants this is evidence of tensions between Naomi and Ruth, which are expected of in-laws from different cultures.

Ruth gave Naomi what she had left over *after she was satisfied*, the narrator reiterates, but the narrative does not refer to Naomi eating anything. Of course, no one feeds on bread alone. In this frame of mind, i have called this bible study 'Ruth feeds Naomi' because Ruth did not have to feed Naomi with food only. She also fed Naomi's hunger for information, for comfort, and for control. Naomi might not have been hungry for food – she might have already been satisfied on her own (see note 9) – or she might have been more interested in Ruth's story and feat than in her feed. In both cases, the function of food in the household of these widows remains ambiguous.

Neighbour

Ruth came out of silence, with a twist. Naomi asked her 'where' and she responded to a 'who' question that was implied – she cut to the chase – Boaz was his name! He is the man that Naomi should bless because he was the one who noticed Ruth (2.19a). And good to her word, Naomi blesses Boaz and then added her own twist – 'for YHWH has not betrayed his kindness (חסד) to the living and to the dead' (2.20a).

In my rendering of 2.20a, Naomi attributed the favour (חן) that Ruth found in the eyes of Boaz to the kindness (חסד) of YHWH. In this twist, Ruth's good fortune is not all about Boaz; it is also about YHWH. While both outlooks – favour (חן) and kindness (חסד) – are valued, biblical interpreters give

more weight to חסד (popularly translated as 'loving kindness')
because that term is used in the context of covenants between
YHWH God and the favoured people (see Bareket, 2017). In
blessing Boaz but giving thanks to YHWH, Naomi brought
Boaz and his favour under the wings of YHWH and into the
frames of covenant relationships. Thanks to the kindness of
YHWH, Boaz was favour-able to Ruth; and, by extension, an
appropriate response to the kindness of YHWH would be for
Ruth to be covenanted to the favour of Boaz. For PBS participants, this is *piko piko iku mai* Naomi-style.

Thanks also to the kindness of YHWH, 'the living' and 'the
dead' connect upon Boaz. It was not all because of the living
(read: Ruth) that Boaz was favourable; it was also because of
the dead (read: Elimelek and his sons) that Boaz was favour-
able towards Ruth. Put crudely: in case Ruth thought that she
caught the eye of Boaz through her own merits, Naomi pointed
out that Boaz was favour-able also because of the dead. In
this reading, Naomi knew something about Boaz and she thus
expected that he would look out for his dead wantoks.

Naomi went on to tell Ruth what the narrator had already
told readers – Boaz was related to them (see 2.1). This time
also, Naomi added a twist: 'The man is near to us' (2.20b).
Whereas the narrator identified Boaz as someone *known to*
and *from the family* of Elimelek (see 'Ruth discovers Boaz's
plot' in Chapter 5), here Naomi described Boaz as someone
'near (קרוב) to us (לנו)'. There are two significant elements to
note in Naomi's explanation: first, Naomi identified Boaz as
one who belonged to them. Elimelek is not in the picture (compare 2.1 with 2.20) so Naomi might as well have said, 'it's now
all about us, Ruth; you and me only'. And second, while קרוב is
usually translated as referring to a relationship (NRSV: 'nearest
kin'; NIV: 'close relative'; cf. Lev. 21.2) the term also carries
the sense of distance ('near' as compared to 'far'). The same
term is used to refer to a town (Gen. 19.20), a settlement (Gen.
45.10) or a neighbour (Exod. 12.4) nearby. The next clause
in Naomi's declaration, 'he is among our redeemers', relates
Boaz to them as kin but that does not rule out the possibility
that קרוב may be understood in terms of physical space and

distance. Naomi thereby declared that Boaz was nearby. He was not far away. Boaz could even be a next-door neighbour. And (to use a Wesleyan motif) the best of all is this: he was also a possible redeemer.

Much has been said about Boaz as a redeemer (גאל) but not enough about the possibility that he may have been a neighbour. This possibility points back to an earlier question about where Naomi and Ruth could have stayed upon their arrival (see 'City buzzes over marred Naomi' in Chapter 5). In my native mind, which flies on the wings of talanoa, Naomi and Ruth had to stay somewhere, maybe with someone else, and they would have had neighbours who helped them out as well as saw and heard what went on around them. As someone 'near' (קרוב) to Naomi and Ruth, Boaz could have been their neighbour. He would have been able to see, hear and know some of the things that happened around Naomi and Ruth.

Earlier that day in the field, Boaz acted as a neighbour to Ruth. And, as stated above, he was no fool.

Also, also

The possibility that Boaz was also a redeemer excited Ruth. She busted out in joy, 'also, also' (גם כי-) and she fed Naomi with details of her feat that day. She told Naomi that Boaz told her to 'abide' (דבק) *with his young men* until they finish his harvest (2.21). Here, Ruth twisted the details. The same form of the same verb (דבק) is used in 2.8 when Boaz instructed Ruth to 'abide' *with his young women*. In switching the subjects Ruth purposely tweaked Boaz's words, and there is room for further tweaking, depending on how one understands the root word דבק (to abide).

There are several options for translating דבק including 'keep or stay close', 'keep or stay fast' and 'keep or stay strong'. Because the Pasifika bibles that i consulted use terms that combine the senses of 'live with' and 'loyal or kindly towards', i opt to use 'abide' (so KJV with 2.8). To PBS participants, this talanoa is not simply about Ruth going back to work with

Boaz's young people, but also about Ruth cooperating with those young people as if they live together and are loyal to one another; this talanoa is about being co-workers who abide in one another. My choice of 'abide' is also in reaction to tensions vexing between Naomi and Ruth which the PBS participants felt, and that i have presented in these bible studies. In using 'abide' i am adding our Pasifika tweaks to this tweaking narrative: abiding plus tensions make for healthier relations.

There is also room for queering Ruth's tweak, on account of Naomi's response (2.22). Boaz instructed Ruth to דבק with the young women (2.8), and Ruth revealed that she prefers to דבק with the young men (2.21); Naomi's response points back to Boaz's young women, but she used a different verb – 'Better, my daughter, that you go out (יצא) with his young women' (2.22). That Naomi uses יצא (go out, go forth) instead of דבק (abide), the verb that Ruth used in the previous verse, suggests that Naomi might have been troubled by the connotations of דבק. Naomi's response put a stop to the דבק business. It is better that there was no דבק (abiding); even better, that there is only יצא (going out or going forth) and only with the young women. Naomi, as said above, was no fool.

Naomi's reasoning – '[so] they do not meet you in another field' – shows her concern for Ruth. This may be read simply as Naomi not wanting people to find Ruth gleaning in another field; better still, that Ruth gleans in the field of their neighbour and redeemer. And at the other extreme, this may be read as Naomi not wanting Ruth to be violated in another field. With the growing number of women being assaulted, violated, raped and murdered in all kinds of fields, Naomi's reasoning should not be taken lightly no matter how one understands דבק and יצא. In this connection, it is safer to be at the field of a neighbour (without denying that some neighbours and family members are also violent towards women and younger people). Not only can neighbours see and hear Naomi and Ruth, but Naomi and Ruth can also see and hear their neighbours.

At the end of the day, Ruth listens to Naomi. She abides with the young women for two harvests, the barley and the wheat harvests, while she dwelled (ישב) with her mother-in-law (2.23). They arrived in Bethlehem at the beginning of the barley harvest (1.22), which was about one month before the wheat harvest (see Exod. 9.31–32) and, if Ruth averaged an ephah every day she went gleaning, she would have built up a decent stockpile by the end of the two harvests. For what other purpose was all that stock?

Widows

Mentions of 'widows' bring to mind images of women who are weak, desperate and vulnerable. These frail images reflect what readers see in human societies and in biblical literature – together with orphans and sojourners, widows are to receive special protection and care (see Exod. 22.21–24; Deut. 27.19).

But not all widows are weak, desperate and vulnerable. There are exceptions, and readers know that there are exceptions, yet most readers still expect widows to be weak, desperate and vulnerable. I do not deny that in life, in general, many widows are weak, desperate and vulnerable. But my question here is why do readers, by default, expect all widows to be that way?

Pasifikation

At most plantations in Pasifika, there would at least be a bush hut (made with branches and leaves) where workers may rest when the sun starts biting during the day and where owners or watchers may keep an eye on the crops at night. Plantation owners who are better off would have something more stable like a tree house, a thatched house or even a *fale pālangi* (European house). So the reference to a house where Ruth stopped while she was at Boaz's plantation (2.7) brought up talanoa among PBS participants of abodes at local plantations, and the various manoeuvres that take place in such places.

Usually by the end of PBS sessions over Ruth 1—2, two questions come up: first, could Ruth have stayed in that house for that night? She worked hard until evening, and it would have been safer for her to stay the night rather than go back on the road in the dark to the city (which no one knows how far away it was). If she had stayed, some of the PBS participants expect that Boaz, a kindly and godly man, would have made sure that she was safe. And, second, could that house be where Naomi and Ruth were staying? They were near to Boaz's plantation. And this means, of course, that Naomi would have watched Ruth that whole day. Ruth did not need to rush home because their house was right there. They were neighbours to Boaz.

As neighbours, they would have been at ease, comfort-able, with one another. But that does not mean that they would see food in the same way. They would have had to hold different views not just because of their different genders and races, but also because they operated different ventures or businesses. Naomi and Ruth had a home to maintain and inheritances to redeem, so food was a currency. Boaz had workers to pay and feed, and a plantation to maintain and develop, so food was currency as well as capital.

This reflection takes me back to the stock that Ruth piled up over two harvests. Even though her storeroom would have been appropriate for a place named Bethlehem (house of bread), the amount of food would be plenty more than needed by two widows. The problem here is with the expectation that their household consisted of only two people. Because families (wantoks) are extended in Pasifika, i expect that there would be several mouths to feed in the household of Naomi and Ruth. One ephah per day might even be less than required, so they would need access to more food, more currency, more capital.

Takeaway

1 Draw an image of what Ruth might have looked like carry-ing her ephah of barley on her return to Naomi.
2 Could there have been others on the road at the time when Ruth returned home, and what might they have thought upon seeing her?

3 Who are strong and courageous widows that you know in biblical literature, in human history, and in your local context?

Prompts for further talanoa

1 Richard Leson, 'Genesis 39: Joseph and Potiphar's Wife', *The Visual Commentary on Scripture*, https://thevcs.org/joseph-and-potiphars-wife, accessed 5.5.21.
2 BibleProject, 'Overview: Esther', www.youtube.com/watch?v=JydNSlufRIs, accessed 5.5.21.
3 Ayla Lepine, 'Esther 8: Esther Pleads for Her People', *The Visual Commentary on Scripture*, https://thevcs.org/esther-pleads-her-people, accessed 5.5.21.

Notes

1 Similarly, a poor mother would fall into economic strain in order to buy the expected amount of jewellery for her daughter's wedding.
2 *Wantoks* are people who share the same language and purpose in the creole tongues of Papua, Solomon and Vanuatu; similar to *whānau* in Māori and *aiga* in Samoan.
3 Halal and kosher are no longer the only specialty food labels in the market.
4 Potiphar's crops and livestock flourished because of Joseph (Gen. 39.5b) and Mordecai's cause led to Esther hosting banquets for the king and Haman (Esth. 5.4, 8).
5 The Nauruan and Mā'ohi participants also stressed that readers too are no fools. Readers can see behind, as well as interrogate, the obvious. As storyweavers (in talanoa), readers may interrogate the motivations for the exchange (of words and actions) between Boaz and Ruth.
6 In this regard, Boaz stands in the shadows of the Gibeonites also (Josh. 9): they were the local people of the land that the Israelites invaded, and they approached the Israelite elders with dried food to trick them into thinking that they had come from a distant land. Falling for the dry bread trick, the invading Israelites made a treaty with the Gibeonites not to expel them from their own land. In the shadows of the Gibeonites, Boaz may be read as trying to trick Ruth into his favour. In this reading, food is currency and Boaz is a shrewd investor.

7 This, however, did not apply to Joseph (Deut. 33.16) and Samuel (1 Sam. 2.26). They did not lose God's favour (even though Samuel was rejected by the people; cf. 1 Sam. 8) nor the favour of the biblical narrator. In the case of Joseph, he received the favour of Potiphar as well as the favour of his wife (Gen. 39.4; 39.21).

8 The exceptions to the rule include Saul and David. Saul lost YHWH's favour and could not get it back (see 1 Sam. 15.22–23). David, on the other hand, did most things wrong, but he just could not shake off YHWH's favour (see 2 Sam. 7.15).

9 On the other hand, in the shadow of Joseph, who was in charge of Potiphar's whole estate except for the food that he ate (Gen. 39.6), this reading finds something behind the narrative: Ruth may not have been responsible for what Naomi ate. She therefore did not go gleaning primarily for Naomi.

7

Ruth 3.1–15
Home and belonging

Home is a place where one belongs. A person might be entitled to a place, but it is necessary that they also feel that they belong in and with that place. Without belonging, an individual's entitlement is agonizing.

A home does not need to be overabundant with milk and honey or lined with endless rows of trees that bear fruits in their season,[1] even though some of those would indeed be appreciated. It does not need to be sparkling with pearls on the gate and pure gold as clear as glass on the path, which would make the place too slick and too cold for most normal people to feel that they belong. Simple food served with the warmth of recognition and welcome suffice to make a place homely, a place where people feel that they belong. For the bible studies in this chapter, belonging is taken as a key requirement for a place to be a home.

For one to belong in and to a place requires that one *is* safe and secure there. In a perfect world, it could be possible for one to both *feel* and *be* safe and secure at a place called 'home'. The real world, however, is not perfect. Global warming gives evidence to the blemishes of the world, and the Covid pandemic proved that the world had become sick and that it seemed to be going mad. Time will tell the full impact of the pandemic (the lockdowns and the effect on world economies) on ecology, but there have been signs that have suggested that Covid will be seen in the long term as a scapegoat for withdrawing environmental care and protection.[2]

I distinguish *being* from *feeling* safe because in Pasifika one could still *be* at home even if the (is)land does not *feel* safe and secure. It is difficult to feel safe and secure when one sees evidence of sea-level rising on the shore, sleeps to the sound of waves bashing the reef, and wakes up to unproductive land and brackish groundwater that one or more cyclones (each time with extra fury) produce each year. Pasifika is not perfect; it may meet the paradisiac ideals in the eyes of tourists, but it is still *home* for natives in our climate-changed world. The government and church leaders of Tuvalu, for instance, have declared that even though their group of islands is in danger of disappearing – so they do not feel safe on the islands any longer – they do not see relocation as an option. They are staying because Tuvalu is their home, the place where they belong – not because it is in the long run a safe and secure place. Tuvalu is a home that is not free of challenges or risks, but for the time being they are staying. This resolution is shared by other communities across Pasifika, and beyond.

In the following bible studies, i draw attention to the intersections of home, belonging and security in the next three stages of this unfolding narrative: in Naomi seeking security for Ruth (3.1–5), in Ruth seeking security under Boaz's wing (3.6–9), and in Boaz choosing to secure Ruth (for himself) from the rightful (nearer) redeemer (3.10–15). These bible studies turn to new stages in the narrative, and at the same time remain within the insights and possibilities presented in previous bible studies.

(12) Ruth 3.1–5: Naomi pimps Ruth

[1] [Then] Naomi her mother-in-law said to her
'My daughter, should I not find for you security
that would do well for you?
[2] ( ) Now, is not Boaz our relative there
with whose young women you were?
Behold, he is winnowing barley at the threshing floor
tonight
[3] [Therefore] wash up, ( ) anoint yourself ( ) put your finest
garment on
put it on yourself ( ) go, go to the threshing floor
do not reveal yourself to the man
until he has finished eating and drinking
[4] { } when he lies down, mark the place
where he lies down, there ( ) go and uncover his feet
( ) lie down, lie down
( ) he will tell you what you will do'
[5] ( ) She said to her
'What you said to me, I will do'

It is expected of mothers to want to see their daughters married, for the sake of their security. This is not because daughters cannot take care of themselves or be secure on their own, but because human communities in general value family life; and, traditionally, family is understood in the heteronormative sense to be made of husband, wife and child(ren). With the child(ren), the family system survived.

I imagine that starting a family was the primary motivation for the first marriage of Naomi, as well as of Ruth and Orpah. Their parents got them married off so that they might find security (cf. 3.1) under the care and protection of a husband. I quickly add here that marriage is for the security of the daughters as well as for the security of the mothers, who would benefit from well-placed and well-endowed sons-in-laws.

Mother-in-law

When the case is that of a mother-in-law seeking to get her widowed daughter-in-law married off, i imagine that there might be additional motivations to finding security. And i imagine that the intention of a mother-in-law would be different from that of a father-in-law. In the case of Judah, for instance, he wanted Tamar his widowed daughter-in-law to bear offspring for his firstborn son through his second son (see Gen. 38.1–11). Judah's concern was for his own legacy and inheritance, which passes on to his sons and their offspring.

Judah's unnamed Canaanite wife – referred to as 'daughter of Shua' in Genesis 38 and remembered as Bathshua in translations of 1 Chronicles 2.3 – was silent throughout the whole narrative. Behind the narrative, Bathshua was seen, married, entered, gave birth three times, and she died in the verse after Tamar returned to her father's house (Gen. 38.11–12). She is silent in the narrative, but she does not have to be silent in the imagination of readers. And since readers come from – and with – different traditions and experiences, she will be made to say different things. How might Bathshua talk back to Naomi is one of the questions that lurk behind this bible study.

I expect the relation between mother-in-law with daughter-in-law to differ between those who come from the same heritage (as in the case of Rebekah and her daughters-in-law, Leah and Rachel) and race (as in the case of Hagar and Ishmael's unnamed Egyptian wife), as compared to those from other classes (like Asenath and Zipporah, who were daughters of priests) or other races (like the mothers-in-law of the foreign wives whom Ezra-Nehemiah ostracize). How might these mothers-in-law talk back to Naomi?

To insert the voices of Bathshua, Hagar and their sisters into the story of Naomi with Ruth requires the working of talanoa imagination, and doing so could serve two functions: to honour the differences between mothers-in-law, and to provide a figure for the silent women who lurk behind the narrative (such as the women who came out to greet Naomi in 1.19, then disappear into silence until they return in 4.14). In line with the previous bible studies, this one also pushes back at the narrator's plot.

Delay

The passage opens with a conjunction – '*Then* Naomi her mother-in-law said to her' – which makes this passage flow from the previous one. Naomi's push for Ruth to go after Boaz (3.2) is thus made to flow from, and in response to, the generosity that Boaz extended in the previous passage; Naomi's plan was to secure Boaz for Ruth's (and by association, Naomi's) security. This view would work well if Naomi's plan was devised soon after Ruth started gleaning in Boaz's plantation. However, there was a long delay before Naomi presented her plan to Ruth.

The night in question (3.2) was not the same night when Ruth came back with food from Boaz's plantation (2.18). It was not even the next night. In the narrative, a second harvest passed (2.23) before Naomi called Ruth to go after Boaz (3.3–4). Naomi did not rush (not soon after Ruth started gleaning at Boaz's plot). What might have caused Naomi to delay making her move?

One possible explanation may be drawn from situations of crisis (e.g. pandemic) when people lose their sources of income, and they seek other ways to earn a living. Harvest times have passed and so have the opportunities for Ruth to glean. From where will future meals come? Naomi's plan was an alternative means of earning a living. Instead of going out to glean during the day, Ruth was set up to go out 'to glean' at night. In this reading, the aim is to gain access to food. This is one way of understanding the 'security' (so NRSV and NKJV) that Naomi was seeking in 3.1.

This explanation echoes in the lives of many people, including black, brown and ethnic minority women and children, who are victims of desperation. They are pushed or sold into prostitution and other forms of slavery in order to survive. They 'earn their living' through insecure and unhomely tasks.

A second explanation may be drawn from the connection between 'security' and 'home' suggested in the translation above (so NIV). Naomi was seeking more than future meals. She was seeking a home for Ruth, in the security of a husband. This raised two points of suspicion among the PBS participants. The first matter of suspicion was Naomi's approach. If Ruth went 'fishing' (a metaphor suggested by the Solomon Islands participants) into Boaz's plantation during the day, Naomi instructed Ruth in this passage to go out at night as a 'ninja' (a metaphor suggested by the Nauru group). Natives fish at night also, but the Nauru group hoisted the conniving feature in Naomi's plan. This is not to say that Boaz was innocent. Rather, the push of both PBS groups was to consider that Naomi and Ruth were not innocent. Moreover, the second matter of suspicion for the PBS participants was Naomi's intention. Could the plan to find security or home for Ruth be an attempt to also push Ruth out of Naomi's household? This suspicion is based on what happened on the road, when Naomi tried to push Ruth away (see Chapter 4, 'Ruth 1.8–14a: 'Naomi pushes her daughters-in-law back'). Was Naomi, again, trying to get rid of Ruth? The harvests were over, and Ruth's chances to glean were no longer. Getting rid of Ruth will save Naomi valuable resources.

Both explanations seek to make sense of Naomi's delay in proposing a move for Ruth to take. On literary and historical bases, the verse that inserts the delay (2.23) is most likely a later addition. But on ideological grounds, the verse gives Naomi a shade of character and attitude that appealed to PBS participants. Naomi had something to gain and, as it were, she waited for the right wave to surf.

Ninja

The target was Boaz, the 'relative' (from the Hebrew ידע / 'to know'; 3.2) with whose young women Naomi instructed Ruth to be (2.22). Boaz was 'near' (2.20), and Ruth had personally come to know him.[3]

Naomi knew that Boaz would winnow barley that night (3.2), and the PBS group in Tonga suggested that this was the opportunity for which Naomi had been 'stalking' (in Tongan, *lama*). That evening, Boaz was expected to spend the night at the threshing floor. That night was at that time of the year when plantation owners spend the night away from home. What usually happens on that kind of night would have been known around town. This leads to a third explanation for Naomi's delay (in addition to the two suggested in the previous section): she was 'waiting' (in Tongan, *lama*) for the opportune time, when Boaz has a sleepover outside of his home, to make her move.

Traces of the story of Potiphar's wife – she is unnamed in Genesis 39, but Hebrew and Islamic scriptural traditions name her Zuleika – ricochet in this story (see Chukka, 2021). While Potiphar was outside of the house, Zuleika acted on her desire for Joseph – who was (playing) hard to get. The biblical narrator's favour was for Joseph, and by privileging YHWH's favour for Joseph (39.21) the narrative discredited Zuleika. While the Qur'an is understanding of her desire, it too snubs Zuleika (see Sura 12.23–32, 50–53). Because of her ethnicity, which is not revealed but most readers assume that she was an Egyptian, readers do not question her portrayal in these two scriptural traditions.

What these scriptural traditions do not consider is where Potiphar might have gone, and in order to do what. Potiphar was a public officer who left everything in Joseph's charge 'except the food he ate' (39.6). He expected Joseph to do everything for him. I expect that whenever he was out of the house, day and night, he would mix business with pleasure. Naomi expected the same in the case of Boaz: that at the threshing floor he would mix business with pleasure. That was the opportunity she had been waiting for.

With a eunuch as her husband, i understand why Zuleika would have wanted Joseph to lie with her – not only because he was well-built and handsome but also because Potiphar could not lie with her in the ways that a heteronormative society expects of a husband. In a different situation yet under the shadow of Zuleika, Ruth was a widow with no access to a functioning husband. Juxtaposing the lack in the sexual experiences of these foreign women makes me expect Ruth to be open, if not eager, to Naomi's plan. Ruth may not have had much action since the death of her husband, but that does not mean she was ready to 'retire'.

Naomi's plan is clear. She instructs Ruth to pimp up then go to the threshing floor and look for Boaz, but not reveal herself 'to the man' until he finishes eating and drinking. Ruth is to mark the place where he lies down to sleep then at some point go over, uncover his feet, lie down, and wait for Boaz to tell her what to do. To the Nauru PBS group, this ploy was a ninja move. Entrapment.

I imagine that Bathshua would have also seen entrapment in Judah's appeal to the levirate marriage practice in order to give Tamar to his second-born Onan (38.8), for the sake of raising an offspring for first-born Er. There is a different form of entrapment when Judah sent Tamar to her father's house until third-born Shelah grows up (38.11). 'Many days' after Tamar returned to her father's home, Bathshua died (38.12). The narrative thereby silenced Bathshua. But she died with the knowledge that Judah wronged her daughter-in-law, who could have been a Canaanite woman like her. Bathshua would have grieved not having her own grandchildren, for which the narrative blamed Tamar. But withholding Tamar from Shelah did not help resolve Bathshua's grief (for not having grandchildren), and the blame for that fell on Judah (see 38.26). Double entrapments thus take place in Judah's move: Judah turned Tamar's father's home into a trap for Tamar, and he also trapped Shelah in Bathshua's home. Would Bathshua have approved of Judah's ninja move?

By extension, would Bathshua have endorsed Naomi's ninja move? The narrator does not entertain this question, but the canon invites reading across the two narratives. No one knows if Bathshua was indeed silent behind the narrative. Who knows, Judah might have only put Bathshua's plot into play. If Bathshua endorsed Judah's move to trap Tamar in her father's home, i imagine that she would have suspected Naomi of trying to get rid of Ruth. In this regard, Bathshua would have seen and endorsed Naomi's ninja move.

Yes boss

Naomi had waited, but Ruth was eager to go. When Naomi presented her plan, Ruth responded with confidence – 'What you said to me, I will do'. Ruth was in, and her response brings Isaiah's response to mind – 'Here am I, send me' (Isa. 6.8). This is not to say that Ruth was selfless. She had something to gain. Security. Home. Rest. The comparison with Isaiah, who did not feel suited to the task (see Isa. 6.5) and was pushed to consent (after the seraphim put a live coal to his mouth; Isa. 6.6–7), highlights Ruth's eagerness regarding Naomi's plan. Unlike Isaiah, Ruth was not coerced to consent.

To her credit, Ruth had a say in the matter. This distinguishes her from Hagar, who was not consulted. Sarai decided for Hagar, and she also decided for Abram. Sarai told Abram to take her Egyptian maidservant (Gen. 16.2), and he did not object. One could almost hear the reverse of Isaiah: 'Here am I, send *to* me.' 'Then Sarai took Hagar, the Egyptian, her handmaid ... and gave her to Abram her husband to be his wife. He entered Hagar, and she conceived' (Gen. 16.3b–4a). Hagar was to Abram as Ruth was to be for Boaz.

Juxtaposing the cases of Hagar and Ruth raises the question of consent. Did Hagar consent? This question draws readers' imagination into the shadows of the Bible where the biblical narrator does not appear too concerned about the will of women, both local and foreign. In the shadows of the Bible also, the 'taking' of a foreign woman – whether Hagar, Tamar daughter-in-law of Bathshua, or Ruth – is not considered as problematic as the 'taking' (read: rape) of other women like Dinah (Gen. 34) and Tamar daughter of Maacah to David (2 Sam. 13). Foreign women carry two crosses – the cross of gender, and the cross of race.

My musings invite another question: how would Hagar react to Ruth's hasty consent? I raise this question in light of Hagar's courage to flee from her abusive mistress (Gen. 16.6), which she openly declared (16.7). Hagar was not shy to admit that she was a runagate slave woman. The angel of YHWH made her go back and submit to Sarai but, to her credit, there was a short while when Hagar decided how to appropriately respond to abuse. In this connection, i imagine Hagar seeing herself in Ruth's consent. Naomi has opened for Ruth a window that was not available for Hagar.

I consequently imagine two possible responses to my earlier query. First, it is reasonable to imagine that Ruth saw Naomi's ploy as an opportunity for her to leave. This is not just the matter of Naomi wanting to get rid of Ruth, but also an opportunity for Ruth to get out. And Ruth took up the opportunity (how quickly she replied), willingly and sounding enthusiastic. Ruth was ready to be out. Second, it is also possible that the narrator has done a 'fake news' number on Ruth. Like other colonial subjects, Ruth is at the mercy of a Judean narrator who stands to gain from her consent to Naomi's plan. Ruth thus stands in the shadows of Zipporah and Rahab, foreign women who are portrayed as willingly serving the interest of the Judean narrator.

These two responses (exhibiting the hermeneutics of suspicion) open a window for airing a tension in the characterizations of Ruth. Earlier on the road (1.7–18), Ruth would not let Naomi have her way; but in this passage, Ruth is willing to do what Naomi concocts. For the Ma'ohi Nui PBS group, this tension is not evidence only of a character with two different emotions. This tension may also be read as evidence of the shifting in the character of Ruth. She was strong and feisty at the beginning; but in this passage she has been worked over and softened down. In the shadow of Hagar under the words (see Gen. 16.9) and eyes (see Gen. 16.13) of YHWH, the narrative submits Ruth to her mother-in-law.

Pasifikation

Pasifika communities have back-up sources of food (in the bush and on the reef) for when they run out of their preferred staples, for when they are in between harvests, or when they face lack due to damages and disruptions by negligence or 'bad weather'.[4] In my home island, for example, breadfruit and bush cassava are seen as food for pigs and the impoverished.

But when there are no taro and yam, Tongan families harvest bush cassavas and pick breadfruits to eat along with bizarre proteins from the lagoon and the reef.

In situations of desperation and crisis, natives find relief in what are otherwise seen as below standard in an everyday perspective. In those situations, the land and the sea come to the rescue of the natives; the land and the sea play active roles in the rescue because those food items were not planted or tended. Those items are the free offerings of the sea and the land. In situations of desperation, therefore, the land and the sea rise up to rescue islanders.

In the native Tongan calendar, the moon cycle before the arrival of the rains is named *'Uluenga* (when the leaves are yellow, between November and December) to signify one of the times when we will need to draw upon our back-up resources, from the land and in the sea. During this time, and several other occasions during the year (e.g. the hurricane season), what are usually seen (during times of plenty) as rubbish and a nuisance become nourishment and means for satisfaction.

Food plays a critical function in Pasifika natives' understanding of home. A place is not a home if food is not available there, and the land and the sea can provide food irrespective and independent of the labour of islanders. There are therefore natural connections between home, food, land and sea. In seeking home, one also expects to find food, land and sea. One cannot seek one without also expecting the other elements.

The foregoing reflection locates the 'security' that Naomi proposes for Ruth at the intersection of food, home and land (the sea was not obvious to the biblical narrator, but it intertwines with the land in the minds of PBS participants). Security is not empty nor does it come by accident. Security comes with home, food and land, and in Ruth 3.1–5 these intersect in the body of Boaz. It is thus natively understandable why Ruth was enthusiastic regarding Naomi's plan.

Takeaway

1 Does Naomi remind you of other literary, movie or biblical characters?
2 Who are other biblical in-laws that this passage brings to mind?
3 How far would you go in order to belong or to be free?

(13) Ruth 3.6–9: Ruth uncovers Boaz

⁶ ( ) She went to the threshing floor
( ) she did as all that her mother-in-law commanded her
⁷ ( ) After Boaz ate ( ) drank ( ) cheered his heart
( ) he went to lie down at the edge of the heap of grain
( ) she came softly ( ) uncovered his feet ( ) laid down
⁸ { } in the middle of the night
( ) the man startled and turned himself
( ) behold, a woman was lying from his feet
⁹ ( ) He said, 'Who are you?'
( ) She answered, 'I am Ruth your maidservant
( ) stretch your wing over your maidservant
for you are a redeemer'

The 'saying(s)' of Naomi in the previous passage (see 3.1 and 3.5) become, following the narrator's interjection, a 'command' (צוה; see 3.6) in this passage. There is a legalistic feel to the Hebrew term צוה (the root for 'commandment', מצוה), suggesting that there is a power difference between the two subjects, between the one who commands (commander) and the one who is commanded.

The narrator's interjection is straightforward: as the mother-in-law has commanded, so is Ruth said to have carried out. But why make this declaration at this point, before reporting what unfolded (in 3.7–10)? It would make better sense if the narrator made his declaration at the end of his report, to sum it up. Both the placement of the declaration and the shift from 'saying' to 'command' thus feels like a double signal, that something has changed. In that light, i offer the following explanations:

First, i read 3.6 as an opportunity to revisit Ruth's quick consent in the previous passage (3.5). In referring to Naomi's plan (proposal) as a 'command' the narrative invites readers to consider the possibility that Ruth's response was out of respect and/or fear for her mother-in-law. Ruth was the subaltern who has been commanded to lay her body on the line for her commander.

Second, i read 3.6 also as a flag for the report that follows (3.7–15). It invites readers to take note of the extent to which Ruth fulfilled and/or diverted from Naomi's command (3.1–5). Ruth could have interpreted Naomi's command differently. It is one thing (for Naomi) to give a command (rather than stay at home) and another (for Ruth) to carry out the command (on the threshing floor) and to adapt as the evening unfolds. In the case of the latter, diverting from the command is required by the situation and Ruth reacted as she saw appropriate. To use a Pasifika image: Ruth was dunked into the water, and she had to swim or drown.

The shift to 'command' places Naomi on top, and also flags Ruth's manoeuvre. This one narrative interjection thus produces two effects. For the PBS participants, these two effects raise suspicions towards Naomi as well as praise for Ruth who had to swim beyond the eyes (but she still had to carry the weight) of her commander. This narrative thereby highlights the various ways in which Ruth negotiated some of the differences between her and Naomi.

Softly

Time still does not factor in the narrator's account, but silence does. No one speaks in 3.6–8 except the narrator, whose report swiftly moves Ruth from the face of Naomi to the feet of Boaz. When silence is filled with swiftness (passage of time), readers may slow the flow of the narrative down and fill in the gaps or hurry the flow along and ignore the gaps. In my case, i do not expect the narrator to provide all the details but i take the gaps in the narrative as opportunities for talanoa (conversation, storyweaving).

Ruth went to the threshing floor in silence, and the narrative presents Boaz to also, in silence, have eaten, drunk and be cheered up. The narrator then swiftly moved Boaz from where he was (among his fellows) and laid him down at the edge of the heap of grain (3.7a). Herein is another silence in the narrative: the narrator does not report if Boaz had fallen asleep before Ruth came (3.7b). This silence lets Boaz be awake still, and this was also anticipated by Naomi's instruction (3.4):

> when he lies down, mark the place
>> where he lies down, there ( ) go and uncover his feet
>> ( ) lie down, lie down
>> ( ) he will tell you what you will do.

Go there, lie down; lie down, and he will guide you. According to the flow of the commands, Naomi did not expect Boaz to have fallen asleep yet. In this regard, the 'stir' in the narrator's account is how 'softly' Ruth was in her approach. Boaz was still awake (and may have been too drunk), but he did not notice when Ruth 'came softly, uncovered his feet, laid down' (3.7b).

Ruth's approach could also be characterized as 'stealth' – she was sneaky and calculating, intentional about taking advantage of Boaz.[5] While stealth is also part of it, i opt to use 'softly' because of the kind of condition that i expect of the threshing floor. The narrator does not state if the threshing floor was outdoors (most likely) or indoors, but i expect that it would have been littered with husks, branches and twigs that would crack and make a noise when someone stepped on them. In the dark Ruth could step on such kindling materials and break the silence of the night, but she approached so softly that she muted her movement and Boaz (and others at the threshing floor?) did not notice. She moved so quietly that he did not feel her presence or her uncovering his feet, nor her lying down – Ruth was that soft(ly). This reading affirms the ninja image proposed above because ninjas are known to be soft in their *approach*, but vigorous in their assault.[6] The Tongan PBS group at Gisborne imagined Ruth's approach to have been 'more gentle' (*moulu ange*) than the approach of 'a thief in the night'. They associated a popular Sunday School rhyme with the silence of the narrative:

Sētane ena tolotolo mai (Satan is there creeping in)
tāpuni ho loto ki ai (close your *loto* to it)

The controversy in this group's extra-biblical turn is that the word *loto* refers to 'heart' (in a metaphorical sense) as well as to 'inside' (in a physical sense). The rhyme is thus about guarding the soul or will as well as guarding the body. As children guard their *loto* from Satan, this PBS group of migrants imagines that Boaz too should guard his *loto* from Ruth. It was not critical for this group whether Boaz was awake, or that Ruth should not have taken advantage of him. Rather, their emphasis was on how gentle Ruth was in her approach. She was as gentle as Satan.

Space also does not factor in the narrator's account. That Boaz laid down at the edge of the pile (3.7) suggests that Ruth may have simply walked around (in the dark) on the outside of the threshing floor, to get to the edge where Boaz was. It would not have been much of a challenge to creep up to where Boaz laid, uncover his feet and lie down. The issue here is not Ruth's approach, but Boaz's failure to feel her presence and what she did.

There is a temporal gap, marked with '{וַיְהִי} and it came to pass, in the middle of the night' (3.8a), between when Ruth laid down and when Boaz realized that she was there. Was Boaz too drunk to notice (compare with Noah in Gen. 9.20-21 and Lot in Gen. 19.33-35), or too cheery to ask (as Israel was in Exod. 32.6)? On the other hand, what might Ruth have done for Boaz to drop his guard?

Woke

Something startled Boaz in the middle of the night. He turned
and discovered a woman lying near his feet. She was the same
woman who was at his plantation. She identified herself with
conviction: 'I am Ruth your maidservant ( ) stretch your wing
over your maidservant for you are a redeemer' (3.9). Ruth
went further than Naomi had instructed. She did not wait for
Boaz to guide her but she gave it to him straight: she told him
what he needed to do – he has a responsibility to fulfil, for he
was a redeemer (גאל).

Boaz's response comes in the next bible study, but i pause at
this point to highlight Ruth's *loto* (heart, inside) which turned
the narrative. Naomi targeted Boaz because he was a 'relative'
(3.2) in whom Ruth could find security; Ruth went further, and
she obliged Boaz because he was a 'redeemer'. This was more
than a personal matter of seeking home and security; this was
a matter of redeeming family heritage and inheritance. This
was not just about Ruth alone; this was also about Elimelek
and Naomi.

It is not how Boaz was 'woke' that matters in this reading,
but how Ruth startled many of the PBS participants. For the
Māori PBS group at Gisborne, for example, there was nothing
riveting about the possibility that Ruth may have jumped
on Boaz. Such manoeuvres happen in camps and even at the
wharenui (the communal house usually at the centre of a Māori
marae). So what if they had sex? It does not help to debate or
loathe the possibility that they did. What woke (in an energiz-
ing way) the Māori PBS group was the simple fact that Ruth
went straight in, to the *loto* of the matter – redemption, which
had to do with inheritance. This woke the Māori group in part
because Ruth as a Moabite was *manuhiri* (guest, foreigner),
and because the group associated inheritance and heritage with
ancestors. In the history of the Māori people, their inheritance,
heritage and ancestors have not been redeemed. The Māori
PBS group therefore appreciated that Ruth did not beat around
the bush, but they also lamented that this opportunity has not
been available for their people.

The other PBS group at Gisborne was also startled, but the weight of their 'woke' had to do with their status as migrants. They reflected back to their homes in Tonga: they did not leave any wealth behind, but their (is)land is precious and they panic because of the threat that global warming poses for their Tongan heritage. Fifty years from now, from where will redemption come?

Pasifikation

In Pasifika, a home is a gathering place for a family. To this, i must add a qualification – in Pasifika, a family (in the sense of *whanau* and *aiga*) is always extended, with many branches. A home is thus like a crossroad where generations meet (intersect). The current generation births the next generation as well as cares for the previous generations and, at some point, farewells them. It falls on the current generation to prepare the next generation (or tomorrow people) to 'carry the line', and to keep the home as a site of meeting and transitioning.

The current generation passes the home on, and what it represents, to the next generation. If there is no next generation, the line ends. Dead-end. When there is no next generation, the home is not secure(d) for its traditional holders. In this regard, and in addition to the readings suggested above, one may see Ruth also seeking security for the line and for the home of her late husband (hence, of Elimelek and Naomi as well). At this juncture, the line could end or it could continue with Ruth. When Ruth worked her way into and under Boaz's wing, she made a move that could secure the line and home of her late husband.

The foregoing musing suggests another reading of Ruth's unrelenting (stubborn) response in 1.16–17. In insisting on going back with Naomi, Ruth took on the responsibility of keeping the line going. Ruth was therefore not as self-centred as suggested above (see Chapter 4). She was not all for herself only. Rather, she played a role in the redemption of the household of her late husband and father-in-law. She did for the household of Elimelek as Tamar did for the household of Judah. Both of these foreign women contributed to securing lines and homes in and of Judah.

Takeaway

1 How might you (in your bible study group) enact this passage, especially the mention that 'she came softly' and laid down from Boaz's feet?
2 Does it matter if Boaz and Ruth had sex (or not) that night?
3 What other words (in other languages) can substitute for 'redemption' and how do those words add meaning(s) to or subtract from your interpretation of this passage?

(14) Ruth 3.10–15: Boaz (re)covers Ruth

¹⁰ ( ) He said, 'Bless you of YHWH, my daughter
your kindness was better at the end than at the beginning
that you did not go for young men, poor or rich
¹¹ ( ) Now, my daughter, do not fear
all that you ask, I shall do for you
for the whole town of my people know
for you are a strong woman
¹² ( ) Now, it is true I am a redeemer
( ) however, there is a redeemer nearer than I
¹³ Stay tonight { } in the morning, if he will redeem –
good, let him redeem –
( ) if he does not want to redeem you
( ) I will redeem you'
¹⁴ ( ) She laid from his feet until morning
( ) she arose before anyone could recognize anyone
( ) He said, 'Let it not be known
for the woman came to the threshing floor'
¹⁵ ( ) He said, 'bring the shawl that is on you ( ) hold it'
( ) She held it ( ) he measured six barleys ( ) put on her
( ) He went into the city

It is easy to imagine this story as a seedy one-night stand. Ruth spent the night at Boaz's feet, and both suspicious and patronizing minds can go wild with the silences of the text. For this bible study, i focus on textual details related to home and security. The passage opens with Boaz blessing Ruth with assuring words (3.10–13) and it closes with Boaz blessing Ruth with six measures of barley (3.15). Boaz spread more than his words over Ruth; he also poured 'the wing' of his harvest into Ruth's shawl (on 'wing' as 'edge', see Num. 15.38). The old man was generous. One may accordingly argue that Boaz showed more kindness to Ruth at the end of the night than he did in the middle of it.

Strong woman

Boaz blessed Ruth for coming after him. She already knew that he was a man of substance and, that night at the threshing floor, she did not count his age against him. There were other men on site, but she went for him only. In coming after him, Boaz testified that her kindness (חסד) 'was better at the end than at the beginning' (3.10). The text, however, is ambiguous regarding to what 'the end' and 'the beginning' refer. At the end and at the beginning of what? There are several possible responses, but i here reflect on two options that caught the energy of the PBS groups:

First, Boaz could be referring to the beginning of Ruth's association with Naomi and her family. At the beginning of their association, Ruth was 'lifted' (1.4) to be a wife for Mahlon. This time, at (the beginning of) 'the end', Ruth is the one who has done the lifting. She lifted the cover from upon Boaz's feet, and for that Boaz blessed Ruth.

Both Naomi (3.4) and the narrator (3.7) expected that there would be a cover over Boaz's feet, but the text does not specify what that cover was. This missing detail enticed the musings of several PBS participants, and they tossed between reading the story literally or metaphorically. Ruth referred to Boaz's 'wing' in 3.9, and the same word could be translated as 'covering' (NASB), 'garment' (NIV), 'cloak' (NRSV), 'robe' (NJPS) or 'skirt' (KJV). Any of these options could be taken as the unspecified cover over his feet, and the text leaves to the imagination of readers how or whether to decide; the text also leaves to the imagination of readers the possibility of reading it metaphorically. Does it matter what the cover was? Does the cover have to be material only, and not figurative also?

The majority of PBS participants prefer 'wing' because it was different from how their vernacular bibles rendered it and also because it amplifies Boaz's character.[7] As a metaphor, 'wing' turns Boaz into a 'big man'. It presents him as someone with the capacity to soar above others, and to shield and transport those who, like refugees, come under his care. The wing metaphor also brings Boaz under the wingspan of the seraphim in Isaiah's vision, each with six wings – two for covering their faces, two for covering their feet, and the two with which they were flying (Isa. 6.2). The six wings suggest that the seraphim had triple the expected dominion of other flyers.

The PBS participants did not expect Boaz to have the equivalent of six wings but, chasing after the metaphor, they had an alluring question: to what was *lifting his wing* (in order to 'uncover his feet') a metaphor? That night, at 'the end', Ruth did something that made Boaz soar. It is in the spirit of metaphors to invite yet be open-ended, and the drive of the question from the PBS groups is to suggest that whatever Ruth did to Boaz 'at the end' was better than what she was lifted for 'at the beginning'.

Second, the other event to which Boaz could be referring was the beginning/end of the season of harvest. Ruth's kindness was better at the threshing floor (the end) than at the plantation (at the beginning, when she was gleaning). This does not deny that she extended kindness at the beginning of the harvest. The point here is that her kindness at the end of the process was better and, for Boaz, that she did not go after younger men was evidence of her kindness. Ruth was kind, and it was critical for the PBS groups to highlight her kindness. She was not an empty woman, and Boaz affirmed her character: 'the whole town of my people know ... you are a strong woman (אשת חיל)' (3.11b).

Thus far in the course of the narrative, Ruth proved her stamina, courage and endurance. And on that special night at the threshing floor, Boaz's description of her strength (אשת חיל) matches the narrator's description of Boaz as 'a warrior-like man of strength' (איש גבור חיל) in 2.1. Ruth and Boaz could thus be a narrative match. They would make a strong (חיל) couple. Her description also echoes the sages' dream wife, a 'woman of valour' (אשת חיל, Prov. 31.10). Boaz responded to the strengths of Ruth – she was kind and strong – and the proverbial link suggests that whatever lifting she did that night made her a perfect wife. 'At the end' she did better than 'at the beginning'.

Nearer redeemer

Ruth called Boaz out, and he fessed up. He was a redeemer, but another man was first in line ('nearer' than he; 3.12). Judging by Boaz's confession, the nearer redeemer was a barrier to Ruth's plan (compared to the nearer redeemer being in Boaz's way). She already has a redeemer, didn't she know? Similar to the unspecified cover over his feet, Boaz does not name who the nearer redeemer was. The other man is 'true', but he is not named.

Being unnamed in a biblical narrative may be read in two ways. First, it demeans and shows disrespect for the character in question. He or she is not worthy of being named, and this is implied in the way Boaz refers to his rival. Boaz did not name him in 3.12 and called him 'Mr So-and-so' in 4.1. In not naming the nearer redeemer, Boaz both hides him from the eyes of readers as well as discredits him in the eyes of Ruth. Being unnamed means that, later on (in the narrative world and in the afterlife of the text), the character could not be found to verify what was said about him.[8]

Second, and this is the explanation that the PBS groups favoured, this suggests that those who are involved know who the character is and so do not need to name her or him. This is a common experience in village and small-town settings. The whole town would know who the nearer redeemer was, so it was not necessary to name him. He is the one who does not need to be named. Ruth too would have known who he was and, as suggested in previous bible studies (see Chapter 5), she and Naomi may have been staying with him.

One of the implications of the second explanation is that Ruth and Naomi were working against the system (or protocols). They knew who the near redeemer was but they preferred Boaz, and thus made a move on him (making both of them ninjas in the PBS sense). This brings to mind Laban's cheating on Jacob, who had offered to work seven years for Rachel's hand in marriage (Gen. 29.15–30). On the evening when Jacob expected to receive Rachel as his wife, after he had feasted with 'all the people of the place' (Gen. 29.22) and felt as merry as Boaz was on the threshing floor, Laban brought Leah instead. Leah and Rachel, as far as the narrative is concerned, did not object. It was only in the morning that Jacob realized that Leah was the one 'he went in to' that night (Gen. 29.23).

Ruth, on the other hand, revealed herself to Boaz in the night. Boaz knew who laid near his feet, and he did not object. It is thus understandable why Boaz was prepared to bat for Ruth:

> Stay tonight – in the morning, if he will redeem – good, let
> him redeem –
> if he does not want to redeem you – I will redeem you
> (3.13)

Measures for the return

Ruth got up early – 'before anyone could recognize anyone' – but the text does not rule out the chance that others may have already woken up before her. They may not be able to recognize who is who, but they would have been able to see figures moving in the dark (outdoors, under the open sky, one can see figures even in thick darkness). I expect that they would have known who usually slept in which part of the threshing floor, and with whom. So if someone got up early, they would have imagined possible explanations. Call of nature? Call of duty? In Ruth's case, she arose early because Boaz did not want anyone to know that she spent the night there.

However, Ruth did not hurry in leaving. She took her time, because Boaz did not want her to go back empty-handed:

He said, 'bring the shawl that is on you – hold it [out]'
She held it – he measured six barleys, put [it] on her
she went into the city (3.15)

Boaz did not have to sit or stand up to do his part. All he had to do was to turn or roll across to the pile of wheat, and scoop some up with his hands. But Ruth would have had to kneel or bend down for Boaz to pour six measures of barley into her shawl. Outdoors, under the open sky, others who were already awake would have seen the movements at Boaz's edge of the threshing floor. Those closer by would have heard Boaz's voice – 'bring the shawl that is on you – hold it' – and may have looked over to see who he was speaking to.[9] Since the main reason why they spent the night at the threshing floor was to guard their harvest, i imagine some of the people who were still asleep would stir at the sound and whiff of Boaz scooping up and pouring out seeds (sound and smell travel in the quiet of the early morning).

Ruth was stealthy in the middle of the night, but she hassled at the end of the night. She did as she was told. She knelt or bent down to receive scoop after scoop, measure after measure, to a total of six measures of barley. She did not say 'enough, stop'. She was prepared to take home everything that Boaz would pour into her shawl.

Boaz's generosity testifies to the abundance of his harvest. This aspect reminded PBS participants of stories from previous generations, when some islanders planted and harvested enough for their family's needs and had spare to feed the rest of the village. Back then, the land was so fertile that crops yielded plenty. The generation of our forebearers were generous because the land was generous to them, and this is one way of reading Boaz's generosity.

Boaz's generosity also reflects a shared custom in Pasifika – one receives and sends guests away with gifts. The gifts say something about the host as well as about the guest. Boaz gave six measures out of his abundance; for her merits, Ruth went home with a generous gift. She deserved the six measures of barley, and this is another way to read Boaz's generosity – he paid due respect for Ruth's merits.

With the confirmation of Boaz's generosity, the narrative comes full circle. Boaz is the 'relative' (3.2) with whom Naomi proposed to find 'security' (3.1) for Ruth. And Boaz provided security with his words (3.13), and with his harvest (3.15). When Ruth returned home that morning, she was a secured woman.

Hurry

Boaz loaded Ruth up, then he went to the city (3.15). The text gives the impression that he left before her. He did not want anyone to know she was there (3.14), and his early departure was a chance for him to slip away undetected. If at daylight his fellows found his edge of the floor empty, they could assume that he did not spend the night there. Maybe he left straight after the evening meal? Maybe he wanted to return to his family?

For what reason was Boaz in a hurry? The narrator inserts the reference to his early departure, then the focus of the narrative goes back to Ruth's return to Naomi. The reason for Boaz's hurry is uncovered later, in Ruth 4.

Pasifikation

The (is)lands and seas of Pasifika are not as generous to my generation as they were to the generation of our grandparents. If our grandparents were to return and see how things are today, i suspect that they would snigger at our disconnection from (read: failure to collaborate with) the land and the sea. They would also lament the way that some of us have spoiled our island homes and security or miscarried the tasks of securing the generational line. I anticipate their lament here not in order to lay the blame on the (is)lands and seas, nor upon the islanders, but to acknowledge that the situation has changed and that there are many contributing factors.

Urbanization and migration have taken many of today's natives away from the land and the sea. The pride of being able to *live off the land and the sea* is the stuff of legends for many in my generation. Western education and professional lifestyles do not leave much space for native fingers to get dirty on the land or shrivel in the sea. The economic demands of survival and the routines of daily living make us lose touch with, and become out of step with, the land and the sea. Our grandparents, if they were to return, would see the changes and some might even wonder what make us natives stay. Time and ways have changed, also in Pasifika.

Technology and development have provided easier ways to prepare the land for cultivation (agriculture) and to increase harvest (agronomy), and these have contributed to the deprivation of the land and the acceleration of climate change. Climate change has made it more difficult for the land and sea to be generous to current and future generations, and we in Pasifika have contributed to the impoverishment of the (is)lands where we live. Moreover, we have also contributed to the impoverishment of lands where others live, in our region and across the seas.

Boaz's harvest may be read as an opportunity to critique our disconnection from the land and the sea. I saw evidence of this disconnection in 2020 when modern communities and borders locked down to prevent the spread of the Covid-19 virus. People rushed to supermarkets to stock up on their 'essentials', and one of the 'hot items' was toilet paper. This essential item is a far cry in comparison to the home and security that were essential to Naomi, Ruth and Boaz.

Takeaway

1 How do you imagine Boaz 'stretch(ed) his wing' over Ruth (as she asked in 3.9)?
2 Whose security and honour did Boaz secure when he asked Ruth to stay the night?
3 Who are biblical or local figures that Boaz's generosity brings to mind?

Prompts for further talanoa

1 Rebbetzin Leah Kohn, 2017, 'The Matriarchs Rachel and Leah: Tears of the Jewish Mothers, Part I', *torah.org*, https://torah.org/learning/women-class48/, accessed 5.5.21.
2 Rebbetzin Leah Kohn, 2017, 'The Matriarchs Rachel and Leah: Tears of the Jewish Mothers, Part II', *torah.org* (https://torah.org/learning/women-class47/, accessed 5.5.21.
3 Susanna Snyder, 'Ruth 3—4: New Life from Outside', *The Visual Commentary on Scripture*, https://thevcs.org/outsider-source-new-life, accessed 5.5.21.

Notes

1 In Pasifika, trees that bear fruits out of season are also appreciated. They raise the expectation for the seasons that are coming and testify that there are alternatives to the so-called normal (in season).

2 See, for example, Brooke Fryer, 'As protests raged across the US, Donald Trump quietly wound back environmental protections', *SBS News* (10 June 2020; www.sbs.com.au/news/as-protests-raged-across-the-us-donald-trump-quietly-wound-back-environmental-protections, accessed 5.5.21).

3 The rare form of the verb ידע used in 3.2 conveys Naomi's affirmation that Boaz 'is known to us' in the discerning sense of the term, but the sexual connotation of the term (as discussed in Chapter 5) nonetheless hovers in the context of the narrative.

4 What is considered bad weather depends on context, and the perspective taken. Bad weather from a human perspective – for example, rain – can be good weather for plants and pigs.

5 'Stealth' would be appropriate for the story of Leah, whom Laban gave as part of his deception of Jacob (Gen. 29.14–30). Jacob was awake and knew what he was doing, and only in the morning did he realize that he had been doing it with a different woman. He had been tricked by Laban.

6 The ninja image fits Potiphar's wife in a different way, for she was aggressive in her approach (upon Joseph) and fallacious in her assault (against her husband).

7 This is another example of normal people being open to alternative renderings to their authorized bibles. It is a mistake when scholars assume that normal people do not have the faculty or courage to think outside of the traditional lines.

8 Along this line of thinking one may understand the reason why, for example, the guards at the tomb of Jesus were not named in the biblical account (Matt. 27.62–65) as compared to the Gospel of Peter (31) and Book of the Bee (44).

9 They did not have to expect a woman because, as in Asia and Pasifika, 'shawl' was for both men and women.

8

Ruth 3.16−4.11a
Resolutions and inheritance

Boaz loaded Ruth up then hurried off to the city (3.15). The narrator, on the other hand, did not hurry after Boaz. Instead, the narrator turned to Ruth's return home. In so doing the narrator takes the attention away from Boaz's rush. In a way, the narrator paused Boaz's rush. Rush. Pause. Delay. In other words, stay tuned!

The following bible studies give attention to the resolutions of some of the observations raised and/or problematized in previous bible studies. In the worlds of talanoa and biblical narrative, resolutions arise in response to unsettlements (problems, tensions) and some resolutions invite and bring more unsettlements; unsettlements and resolutions interweave, back and forth, as well as spiral, roundabout and onwards. Moreover, resolutions sought by some people (e.g. mainline and traditional interpreters) may be experienced as unsettlement by other people (e.g. PBS groups). In the first bible study in this chapter, 'Ruth 3.16–18: Naomi and Ruth unsettle Boaz', the resolution for Naomi was unsettling the hurrying Boaz. And in the second and third bible studies, 'Ruth 4.1–6: Boaz unsettles the redeemer' and 'Ruth 4.7–11a: Boaz un-sandals the redeemer', the resolution that Boaz sought resulted in the unsettling of the nearer redeemer.

At the intersection of resolutions and unsettlements in the following bible studies is the matter of inheritance and the problematics of redemption. What does redemption mean in these texts? What does redemption affect? No matter who performs the act or duty of redemption, an act or duty that could be handed over in/like a transaction, the inheritance is still treated as property (which is sold, bought and owned) and the proprietors (landowners or property owners) are still dead. The act/duty of redemption does not benefit the proprietors. Rather, the benefits of the process of redemption fall on the redeemer, who steps up because there is no heir to inherit.[1]

Many readers, however, shy away from calling out the egotism of biblical redeemers. The religious settings in which biblical narratives of redemption are read make readers expect that redeemers will be gracious and selfless. Interest in opportunities or profits is seen to demean or de-grace the practice of redemption (גאל). The upshot is that any interest in profit on the part of the redeemer goes unnoticed and unquestioned.

The following bible studies turn to three passages in which resolution and unsettlement intersect, with close attention to the problematics of redemption on the landscape of inheritance. Across these three passages, Naomi and Ruth (are) moved from being active and determined subjects to becoming parts of the booty in the inheritance of their late husbands. As they lose their voices and agency, Boaz becomes more assertive. The transformation of these characters evokes the questions: What does redemption mean? For whom?

(15) Ruth 3.16–18: Naomi and Ruth unsettle Boaz

¹⁶ [When] She came to her mother-in-law
( ) She said, 'Who are you, my daughter?'
( ) She told her all that the man did for her
¹⁷ ( ) She said, 'these six barleys, he gave to me
for he said to me,
"Do not go empty-handed to your mother-in-law"'
¹⁸ ( ) She said, 'Stay my daughter
until you know how the matter turn out
for the man will not rest
for until he resolves the matter today'

Naomi greeted Ruth with a question: 'Who are you, my daughter?' This question, compared to the question with which she greeted Ruth when she returned from gleaning (see 2.19), has troubled interpreters. The easiest way to make sense of Naomi's greeting is to divide it into two parts of question and answer – Naomi asked and then she answered her own question: 'Who are you ... my daughter?' A more complex connotation of her greeting is also possible, and more challenging, in which Naomi has a dig at other subjects and other concerns (see below).

Ruth responded with a talanoa. She told Naomi what Boaz did for her, and that he wanted her to bring something back – for Naomi. Ruth did not return empty-handed the first time (2.18), and this time she stressed that it was Boaz's initiative. He sent her back with more than the first time, for Naomi. Naomi sent Ruth to Boaz the previous evening so that she might find rest (3.1), and Ruth returned that morning with evidence that rest was available in Boaz's domain.

Ironically, at this point in the narrative, rest was not an option for Boaz. Something in Ruth's talanoa gave Naomi the impression that Boaz has become restless. She sensed something serious, and she expected that he would seek to resolve it that very day. Naomi's assessment helps put the pieces together: the urgent matter at hand must be the reason for Boaz rushing off to the city.

The narrative presumes some kind of 'click' between Naomi and Boaz. They have not met physically in the narrative since Naomi returned from Moab, but they have heard of each other (and not only through Ruth) in the narrative world. Behind the narrative, they could get into each other's mind and under each other's skin. Through Ruth, they communicated with and understood each other as if they were old friends. Nothing in the narrative prevents them from being of the same generation, or from having a history.

Who are you?

Naomi's question was not so strange for the PBS group in Tonga. It echoes one of the greetings that friends use as a jocular exchange when they meet up again after not seeing each other for some time:

Question: *Ko hai koe?* (Who are you?)
Response: *'Oku 'ikai te u 'ilo 'e au au!* (I myself don't know me!)

This exchange is one of the Tongan versions of 'Long time no see', and it sparked talanoa in the PBS group that raised different options for understanding Naomi's question. I share three alternative readings here:

First, Naomi's question could have been because Ruth looked different when she returned that morning. Something must have happened, and Naomi wanted to know what had changed her appearance. Naomi was fishing – 'Tell me more ... what happened?' Her question was an invitation for Ruth to 'spill the grains' (appealing to the six measures of grains that she brought back).

The narrator did not explain if Ruth looked happier or sadder, better or worse, than she did when she left the night before. Since she looked and smelled pretty decent when she left, i expect her to look less neat when she returned. At one extreme, she may have appeared troubled and 'roughed up'. This was a painful reading for one of the PBS participants who had been raped, and she recalled similar questioning the morning after. Her mother and sister saw that she was upset and disturbed, and they wanted to know what had happened. Having a disturbed look would have been enough to trigger Naomi's query. At the other extreme, Ruth could have arrived with a big smile on her face and i imagine that Naomi would have asked the same question. In this way, Naomi's question was a way of saying – '*Look at you*, Ruth. So, what's behind the big smile?' In both options, Naomi's question was in response to a change in Ruth's physical appearance.

Second, Naomi could have interpreted Ruth's early return as a sign that she had failed to entrap Boaz. She expected Ruth to reach the point of no return. Along this line of thinking, Naomi's question expresses disappointment. Not only did Ruth return, but she returned with a heavy load. The six measures of barley would have affected her posture and appearance. She would have appeared like someone going out for a sacrifice or across borders away from desperation.

Did Ruth return alone? The Ma'ohi PBS group imagined that Boaz, if he was a real gentleman, would have sent one of his lads to carry her load. This is a Pasifika custom (more so in the past) – one shows respect by taking the load or burden from a person that one favours. Such a gesture was not because Ruth could not carry the load but sending a helper would have shown what kind of gentleman Boaz was. From a distance, that would have indicated that Ruth did not fail. I imagine that it would have moved Naomi if she saw someone escorting Ruth back, and that is a reasonable context for her question.

Third, Naomi's question marks the point when she came to terms with who Ruth has become (for her). The stress of this reading, shared across all PBS groups, falls on Ruth being a daughter. Whereas the narrator presented Naomi as mother-in-law (3.1 and 3.16), and hence Ruth is a daughter-in-law (see also 1.6, 7, 8), Naomi on the other hand referred to Ruth as 'my daughter' (1.11, 13; 2.2, 22).[2] At the beginning of the previous evening (3.1), Naomi also referred to Ruth as 'my daughter'. These references reflect cultural courtesies, that an older person refers and relates to a younger person as son or daughter (so was Boaz's reference to Ruth as his daughter in 2.8 and 3.10).

The morning in question was different. Naomi's question – 'Who are you, my daughter?' – marks the point when it dawned on Naomi (read: when Naomi 'woke' to the fact) that Ruth has acted as her daughter (more so than as her daughter-in-law). The penny dropped. Naomi realized that Ruth returned as the one who holds the generational line (see '(14) Ruth 3.10–15: Boaz (re)covers Ruth', in Chapter 7). Before that morning, Ruth was Naomi's daughter by virtue of her age; that morning (and from then on), Ruth was her daughter by virtue of her being prepared to secure the inheritance of Elimelek and/in Naomi's household. Ka-ching! For the Solomon Islands PBS group, the majority of whom were subsistence farmers, the six measures of barley signified the inheritance that Ruth *brought back* into Naomi's house.

Naomi's question may also be rendered (taking the אֶת-particle as a preposition rather than as an object marker) as 'Who are *with* you, my daughter?' This rendering (compare with the NJPS: 'How is it with you, daughter?') may be read as a solution to the Ma'ohi group's wish for someone to escort Ruth back (see above), as well as a symptom for the reading by the Solomon Islands group. Ruth did not return alone. She was accompanied, but by whom? The Ma'ohi group wanted a living person to accompany Ruth; the Solomon Islanders have space for Ruth to bring back the ancestors (read: the ancestral line to the inheritance that she and Naomi were seeking to secure). In the end, there is room for both options. Along these lines, Naomi's question was not because she did not recognize Ruth or because she wanted to push Ruth away, but a sign of her awareness, and willingness to (finally) receive Ruth as her daughter. Ruth went to glean in the field as a responsible daughter-in-law, and similarly the previous evening; but that morning, she returned as a (fitting) daughter.

Hands filled

Ruth's response to Naomi was not about herself or who might have returned with her (or not), but about what Boaz had done. Boaz is the 'who' that mattered, and he has been 'rushed'. The six measures of barley are Ruth's proof, but there are other ways of reading Boaz's gift.

First, if Ruth's report was factual, Boaz was a wise operator. He would have known that Naomi was the first in line to the redemption that Ruth requested; Naomi was old/older, but she was the one that he needed to ingrain (impress, sweeten) hence the six measures of grain. Ruth held Elimelek's ancestral line, but the line goes through Naomi. To use a threshold metaphor: Ruth was the door to Elimelek's household, but Naomi was the key that Boaz needed to turn. Hence the elaborate gift. Boaz knew what he was doing. He made Ruth stay the night. Rest. Tick. Then he sent her back with grains for the future. Food. In his world, food was currency. Food buys comfort. Tick.

Gift-giving is common practice in Pasifika, as in other parts of the world, where gifts are given and received in the context of relationships. A gift is given in the matrix of reciprocity, so gift-giving also has something to do with exchange (on top of expressing generosity). A gift obliges, and it can be a burden upon the ones who do not have much to give back in return. A gift of one fish or one mat may easily be reciprocated; on the other hand, a gift of six fish or six mats would burden (read: enslave) a less endowed recipient. In response to elaborate gifts, Pasifika natives will of course admire and covet but they will also feel the burden of reciprocity.

Boaz's gift may thus be read as an ambush. Six measures of barley would buy the heart of many widows. While Boaz's gift showed off his generosity, it would have also put Naomi in debt to Boaz. Entrapment. This is a shared reality among many impoverished families in Pasifika, like other parts of the world, who get into debt in order to give gifts (including to churches) and reciprocate (for instance, in marriages and funerals). In some cases, the debt rolls through several generations. And in many of those cases, the later generations are not able to pay these family debts. Enslavement. In the context of poverty, therefore, any attention to inheritance needs to take into account the reality of indebtedness.

Second, the Fiji PBS group asked whether Boaz may have been trying to buy the silence of the widows. Buttering up was one thing; being silenced was the upshot. Pasifika natives are familiar with both effects in the 'aids' that foreign governments and mission bodies 'donate'. In the name of development, for instance, 'noble' foreign governments provide assistance and expect local Pasifika governments to not question their policies (e.g. on climate change) and practices (e.g. ongoing occupation of Pasifika islands). This 'silent money' approach is different from the 'buy up' approach when votes are taken at global forums like the United Nations and the World Council of Churches, but both approaches are under the shadows of 'noble donorship'. The donor is seen as noble, and the natives are expected to be humble (if not humble, we are seen as savages). In the case of Boaz, were his gift and concern for Naomi evidence of his being a noble donor?

Third, what if Ruth made up all that Boaz is alleged to have said about Ruth not going back empty-handed in order to butter up and/or silence Naomi? Ruth crossed the spaces between Naomi and Boaz, and she knew what made both of them tick. She made Boaz 'tick' the previous night, and that morning she made Naomi 'tick' as well. In both places and occasions, Ruth was a smooth operator. This alternative reading was affirmed by the PBS groups, who were more interested in seeing Ruth as a wise and intentional migrant than in being seen as readers who exercise some form of hermeneutics of suspicion.

What appealed to the PBS groups in this reading is the possibility that Ruth *tricked* her elders. This possibility was seen in the 'fishing' and 'ninja' readings in previous bible studies, and it is appealing here because the story has to do with inheritance. Food is the merchandise in question, but food is the bait for something larger. In Pasifika, also, the stomach is a point of vulnerability.

Restless

Mission accomplished, as far as Naomi was concerned. Naomi told Ruth to stay (ישב), settle down or be still (Ruth must have been excited), and wait to see how things turn out. Then she added, 'the man will not rest (שקט) ... until he resolves (כלה) the matter today' (3.18). Naomi expected Boaz to complete (כלה) the matter on the same day. Naomi's assessment is believable, for Boaz was in a rush to leave that morning.

The (safety) pin dropped. Naomi was calm and calming, suggesting a shift in her character. Her plan was falling into place, and she became more accepting of Ruth and of their situation. That morning marked the point of her beginning to calm and settle down.

Ruth did not fail. But Naomi did not give Ruth any credit. For Naomi, Boaz was who mattered. He will complete and resolve the matter.

Pasifikation

In diaspora, migrant Pasifika communities go through a long period of settling down. Their lingering state of unsettlement plays out on two fronts: first, they struggle to fit in with their diaspora homes and, second, they seek to keep their ties with their old island homes (the second contributes to delaying the first). Pasifika people are deeply relational, and they cannot move and switch off (cut) their ties with relatives and home island communities.

Pasifika migrants are expected (and many feel obliged) to support their parents and families back on the home island, and so their struggle to belong in the diaspora is aggravated by heavy financial burdens. The cost for belonging in two homes, in two worlds, is a major struggle for the first generation of Pasifika migrants. Home and belonging intertwine with finance and capital, which require sweat and labour.

In the case of the diaspora-born generation(s), their struggle is largely about identity. They do not speak the native language as well as their grandparents (back on the island) do, and they do not understand the island ways nor like the island food. They try to fit in and keep ties to the island home of their grandparents on the basis of their talents (compare this with the migrant generation upholding kin-relations with financial gifts), and this has lately been evident in athletics and sports (e.g. Rugby Union and Rugby League). Diaspora-born islanders, many of whom are top athletes in their countries of birth, go back to play for the island home of their grandparents. At some point, the devotion and loyalty of Pasifika people in diaspora to the native home islands will change and stop. Until then, settling down into new homes takes a long time and several generations to materialize. Neither the penny nor the pin has dropped.

In the case of Ruth and Naomi, Ruth 3.16–18 marks the point at which the long process of settling down began. Their arrival took place in 1.19, but it was only at 3.16–18 that they began to settle.

Takeaway

1 What does gift-giving convey in your community and culture?
2 How long would it take you to settle down when you move to a new place or move back to an old place that you left over ten years ago?
3 What needs and concerns would delay your settling down in such places?

(16) Ruth 4.1–6: Boaz unsettles the redeemer

4.1 ( ) Boaz went up to the gate [and] sat down there
{ } the redeemer, of whom Boaz had spoken, came by
( ) Boaz said, 'turn here, sit down here, "so and so"'
( ) He came [and] sat down
2 ( ) He took ten men, from the elders of the city
[and] said, 'Sit down here', so they sat down
3 ( ) He said to the redeemer
'The piece of land that was to our brother Elimelek –
Naomi has sold, she who returned from the field of Moab
4 ( ) I thought to say to your ears, saying
"Buy it back before the inhabitants
and before the elders of my people
If you will redeem it, redeem it
[but] if you will not redeem it, tell me
[so] I may know for there is none beside you to redeem
( ) I am after you"'
And he said, 'I will redeem it'

⁵ ( ) Boaz said, 'On the day you buy the field from the hand
   of Naomi
   ( ) from Ruth the Moabite, wife of the dead
   ( ) you must buy to perpetuate the name of the dead
   through his inheritance'
⁶ ( ) The redeemer said, 'I am not able to redeem for myself
   lest I ruin my own inheritance
   redeem for yourself my redeeming rights
   for I am not able to redeem'

Boaz got straight down to business. He sat down. He called
the redeemer over and told him to sit down. He gathered ten
elders and told them also to sit down. He pressurized the
redeemer to make a decision on the spot. Then he added more
information, which made the redeemer change his mind. Boaz
was in a hurry, eager to resolve the inheritance matter. Naomi
was correct. Boaz was restless. But was his restlessness out of
loyalty for Elimelek? The question cannot be answered with
any confidence, but it suggests that other matters may have
been nagging Boaz that morning.

Much has been made of the gate as a significant public place
in biblical literature. Various activities take place at the gate –
from resting (cf. 2 Sam. 11.9) and begging to selling products
and merchandise, to gossiping and receiving reports (2 Sam.
18.24, 19.8), to rebelling (cf. Esth. 4.2) and discerning on social
and political matters, to gathering labourers and celebrants.
The gate is a crossing. As a space, the gate is both inside and
outside, and it is not always safe for people from outside the
town or city (as implied in Gen. 19.1–3 and Judg. 19.20). The
gate is the combination of a transit terminal, a market, a town
hall and a registry. The gate was a business place. It was also
a place where deeds over land were exchanged and witnessed
(see Gen. 23.17–20), and such transactions are the background
of Ruth 4.1–6.

Not enough attention, however, has been given to the postures
and positionings (physical and ideological) of the male bodies
that gather at the gate in Ruth 4.1–6. These positionalities
ignite the imagination of the PBS groups mainly because they

listen to the words and 'see the flow' of the narrative. Pasifika natives, too, read with our bodies and senses.

Sit down

Boaz operated with authority at the gate. The atmosphere feels like a court setting. Boaz was the presider. He said 'sit down', and people sat down. And they sat in silence until he called upon, or made space for, anyone to speak or make a gesture. The posture of Boaz and the other men fired up the imaginations of the PBS participants. The people all sat down (4.1–2), but how they were positioned makes a difference in how the story unfolds. In Pasifika, to sit down signifies respect and humility (even when it is requested) but it makes a difference if the other men sat in a row (or rows) facing Boaz (as in a classroom), or to the side of him (like a jury in a court room) or if they sat in a (semi-)circle as friends do in a story-circle. When Boaz said 'sit down', the PBS groups imagined that he also motioned to them with his hands, face and eyebrows – indicating to them where to sit and how to position themselves. Where and how was the redeemer seated in relation to Boaz? Where and how were the other elders seated in relation to the redeemer? And where did the crowd sit? Or did they stand? The indeterminacy of the narrative gives room for the PBS groups to imagine the men playing multiple roles in the narrative.

When members of a community sit down, recline or lie back, their postures signify that they are comfortable with one another. The opposite of this lowering posture is when people 'stand up' (as in the title of one of the reggae signature songs) to resist or rebel. At the gate to the city that morning, according to the flow of the narrative, there was no passing 'traffic'. There was no buzzing and no hustling about. Boaz made the men sit. In silence.

Pasifika people who sit down together signify that they are prepared to talanoa or to eat together. It could simply be an occasion to tell and weave stories, to shoot the breeze and to share a few laughs. And it could also be an occasion to discern and make critical decisions. Sitting down does not signify that they are in agreement but, rather, that they are open to discerning together.

When 'elders' sit down together, something important must be taking place (or about to take place). Such a gathering would draw listeners and observers, to stop and sit down. On the morning in Ruth 4.1–6, at least 12 elders sat down at the gate. Such a scene would draw a crowd of both men and women, and they would have quickly figured out who was directing the gathering. Boaz. They did not have superfast communication technologies back then, but words of the event would have gathered people from the edges of the ancient grapevines.

Up for grabs

The narrative is not clear as to what Boaz was after or where his emphasis fell. When he gave his opening remarks, the crux of his case was that the land that belonged to Elimelek needed to be redeemed. But Boaz did not explain whether he brought the case up because of his respect and loyalty to Elimelek (man, ancestor), or because he did not want a piece of customary land (inheritance) to be lost. The land was up for grabs. Did Boaz simply want to make sure that the inheritance was redeemed, or did he want to redeem it for himself? The answers to these matters are not obvious.

Elimelek had been dead for several years, which would not have been a secret to the gathering. As far as the narrative is concerned, Elimelek's inheritance is wherever it was, and with whomever he left in care of it when he moved to Moab. No one has claimed or confiscated his inheritance, and his widow was still alive. Because Elimelek's inheritance has not been claimed, there is no need to redeem it. What, then, was Boaz up to? And why at this point in the narrative? The urgency of Boaz's opening statement suggests that he was on to something.

The importance of keeping the inheritance within the tribe is emphasized in the two-part story of Zelophehad's daughters.

They appealed to Moses and the elders to allow them to inherit the property of their father, who did not have any sons and he was not a rebel (Num. 27.1–11). Moses presented the daughters' appeal to YHWH, who judged that they were right and so they could inherit their father's inheritance. This introduced a law for the Israelites: daughters have the right to inherit if their father did not have any sons.

Later on, the heads of their clan appealed this decree, because they were afraid that the daughters might marry outside of their tribe and hence their ancestral inheritance will be lost to a different tribe (Num. 36.1–12). The emphasis of those elders fell on the land (inheritance) over against their dead kinsman. YHWH approved the elders' appeal and so the law was supplemented: the daughters of Zelophehad were to marry within their clans. This condition applied to all daughters who inherit their father's inheritance, in order to keep the ancestral inheritance within the tribe of their father. The motivations for the daughters and for the tribal elders do not come across as Boaz's motivation as well.

The text does not explain the relationship between Boaz and 'so and so' (the redeemer), the one expected to be responsible for Elimelek's inheritance. In bringing the case into the open (gate), Boaz took upon himself a task expected of the redeemer. Boaz thus fits the profile of someone that Tongans call *kāimumu'a* – one who speaks out of turn on something that she or he did not have the right or knowledge to do so. And Boaz sounds pushy: 'If you will redeem it, redeem it.' Like, right away! The redeemer simply needed to speak up – if he will not redeem it, Boaz was next in line and he will step up (4.4).

Boaz slipped in a piece of fake news. He alleged that the proposition was about the land that had already been sold by Naomi (4.3). This allegation was not substantiated in (nor by) the narrative, and no one at the gate calls Boaz out. The immediate response by the redeemer portrays him as a responsible family elder: 'I will redeem it' (4.4). If Naomi had sold the land, then he will get it back. That was his responsibility.

Did the redeemer not know his responsibility? For the Nauru PBS participants, the answer was simple: Naomi was back and, up to that point, the text had not said that Naomi sold the inheritance. Both of the Gisborne (Aotearoa) PBS groups assumed that Naomi as a widow had customary right over Elimelek's inheritance. The redeemer was therefore not ignorant nor irresponsible. He knew his place, and he was respectful of Naomi. It was only at the gate that morning that he learned the fake news, alleging that Naomi had sold (מכר, Qal perfect tense) the land. So the redeemer put his hand up to carry out his responsibility – he will redeem the land. Simple. Case closed.

Fishy

The PBS groups found Boaz's opening statement very fishy. They were troubled that Boaz projected Naomi in a bad light: he alleged that she sold the land without consulting Elimelek's family. She should have consulted, at the very least, the redeemer. Boaz also put the redeemer in a difficult spot, addressing him as one who did not know what had been transacted in his domain. Boaz's opening statement condemned the redeemer – something is alleged to have happened under his nose, and he did not know about it. The redeemer's quick response may thus be read as an attempt to save face.

Boaz added another spin to his fake news. On top of the land and inheritance, the redeemer must also 'buy' Ruth in order to 'perpetuate the name of the dead through his inheritance' (4.5). Ruth was part of the package, for the sake of the dead. Immediately, the redeemer withdraws: 'I am not able to redeem for myself lest I ruin my own inheritance; redeem for yourself my redeeming rights for I am not able to redeem' (4.6). Why the quick change of mind? How was Ruth going to ruin his own inheritance?

It is no secret that Ruth is a Moabite, and her cultural background has not been an issue in the narrative. No one questioned or condemned Naomi for taking Moabite women as wives for her sons, or for bringing Ruth to Judah. In fact, the narrative has welcomed Ruth since she was 'lifted' to be a part of the family. Nothing in the narrative suggests that Moabites were seen as god-forsaken people. The redeemer's change of mind seemed to be something other than a symptom of racism. He too seemed to have caught a whiff of Boaz's fishiness. The redeemer was concerned for his own inheritance, and that is easy to understand if he had learned that Ruth spent the previous night with Boaz. That morning, Boaz rushed to get the process going but the ancient grapevine would have beaten him. What if they had sex and, that morning, Ruth was carrying Boaz's seeds? How could the redeemer 'perpetuate the name of the dead' if Ruth was on the way to becoming pregnant to Boaz? In that case, Boaz is the one to 'perpetuate the name of the dead through his inheritance' (4.5). It thus makes sense that the redeemer told Boaz to keep what he has already grabbed: 'redeem for yourself my redeeming rights' (4.6). Boaz grabbed the functions of a redeemer in two instances: by letting Ruth stay the previous night with him (read: by lying with Ruth the previous night), and by officiating the hearing at the gate that morning.

In this reading of the text, the redeemer acted wisely on behalf of his own inheritance (which would be damaged if Ruth becomes pregnant by Boaz) and on behalf of Elimelek. If the redeemer cannot establish that Ruth's next child is his (and the town knew what happened the night before), he will not perpetuate the inheritance of Elimelek (which required the fathering of Ruth's child). The redeemer thus plays into Naomi's plan (as suggested in the previous bible study) – that Boaz be the one to redeem Ruth.[3]

Pasifikation

The key irritation of climate trauma for Pasifika natives is that the inheritances of our ancestors are claimed (read: bought) by the so-called forces of nature, which we strive to understand and with which we seek to be in partnership. How could anyone redeem land that has been impoverished as the consequence of someone (or more than one person) producing something (or the plural) to be sold and bought somewhere else? How could we pray the Lord's Prayer on islands that the sea eats as daily food? How could we sing our songs from the drifting edges of the world?

One of the irritations of this bible study is the ease with which the redeemer passed on his responsibility to redeem. The shifting of responsibility – in the context of climate trauma – is painful. What good are interesting readings of ancient stories to climate-affected (is)lands and waters? This is one of the haunting questions that remained with the PBS groups.

Takeaway

1 Has your home country (been) claimed or redeemed by another state?
2 If 'redemption' refers to taking back something that has been taken (possibly wrongly) or bought, what does it mean to take something that has *not* been sold or bought?
3 What parallels and differences do you find between this story of redemption and the story of Jacob grabbing Esau's birthright and blessing in Genesis 25.19–34?

(17) Ruth 4.7–11a: Boaz un-sandals the redeemer

⁷ ( ) This – in the past, in Israel, concerning redeeming and exchanging –
to establish all matters a man took off his sandal ( ) gave it to his fellow
( ) this was a binding testimony in Israel
⁸ ( ) The redeemer said to Boaz, 'Buy it for yourself'
( ) He took off his sandal
⁹ ( ) Boaz said to the elders and to all the people
'Witnesses you are today – that I have bought
all that were of Elimelek ( ) all that were of Chilion and Mahlon
from the hand of Naomi

[10] ( ) also, Ruth the Moabite – wife of Mahlon – I have
bought for me as wife
to raise up the name of the dead upon his inheritance
[that] the name of the dead may not be cut off from his
brothers
[nor] his place from the gate – witnesses, you are today'
[11a] ( ) All the people who were at the gate ( ) all the elders
said, 'Witnesses ...

Boaz incriminated Naomi in 4.3, but she is left out of the picture as the case of inheritance is resolved. This was most likely because of gender biases on the parts of Boaz and the narrator, but the PBS participants were not satisfied with that explanation. Boaz's character became fishier as the proceedings continued. He took over the functions of the redeemer in the previous passage and he left Naomi out in the cold in this passage – no doubt, he was up to something.

Matching Boaz's haste to resolve the matter was the redeemer's swiftness to hand over his right and privilege to redeem. The PBS participants were suspicious with both characters because the case was about land, which is associated with women in Pasifika. The disregard for Naomi raises questions about the value of Elimelek's land for Boaz. Boaz himself was a plantation owner, and his own inheritance was secured. Boaz was set, even if there was no additional land to add to his inheritance. The narrative witnesses to his productiveness with the land, and he was not afraid of whatever it was that caused the redeemer to change his mind.

Sandal

The association of women with land is problematized in this narrative. Two women are involved. Their characterization shifts in the course of the exchange at the gate. Naomi is first introduced as having sold the land (4.3). It was presented as a done deal, and the land thus needed to be redeemed. Two verses later, Boaz's story shifted: Naomi was selling the land that morning (4.5). Naomi was the landlord and Boaz acted as her real estate agent. She did not need to be present, because Boaz was there to speak and decide on her behalf. Naomi was not named as part of the package, but she held the title over the inheritance and land. She was the key. Naomi too comes along with, and above, Elimelek's inheritance.

Ruth will come with the land in question (4.5), but not for her own sake. The land was to be sold in honour of the deceased and Ruth was to be bought for the same cause, for the sake of the dead (4.5). The redeemer's change of mind (from consent in 4.4 to dissent in 4.6) gives the impression that the addition of Ruth devalued the land. Ruth was the extra baggage that made the redeemer withdraw, as was suggested in the previous bible study. What was not addressed in the previous bible study is that Ruth was to be sold like a slave.

Both Naomi and Ruth were named at the gate, but they were also silenced. They were suspended between being agents and being pawns in men's business. The suspension of the two women reflects the suspension of the land, which was neither sold nor redeemed. Rather, the land was handed over as if it was used footwear.

The scandal at the gate is in the way that the land and the women are presented as if they were the main concern of the event. But their worth, rather, is equated to a sandal. The text explains that this was a tradition in Israel, in the past, 'concerning redeeming and exchanging – to establish all matters a man took off his sandal and gave it to his fellow; this was a binding testimony in Israel' (4.7). That was the tradition, and it served the agendas of the men. The land and women, on the other hand, were scandalized in the name of the tradition of Israel.

Scandal

The scandal of the transaction is that Boaz received the women and the land, as well as the redeemer's sandal, but he did not pay anything to anyone. The narrative speaks of buying, selling and exchanging, but Boaz did not give anything. He had given a fair amount previously, but all that he gave at the gate were his words and his directions.

Once Boaz received the redeemer's sandal, he turned to the elders: 'Witnesses you are today – that I have bought *all* that were of Elimelek, *all* that were of Chilion and Mahlon, from the hand of Naomi' (4.9, emphasis added). The 'all' in Boaz's charge is telling. Boaz started with Elimelek but made no mention of Chilion and Mahlon in his opening remarks. Whatever wealth the sons gained on their own, after the death of their father, Boaz added to their father's inheritance with his 'all'. The most significant addition is Ruth, whom Boaz also 'bought … as wife' (4.10), and he needed the confirmation of 'the elders and all the people' (4.9a). The narrator adds his 'all' to confirm Boaz's case: '*All* the people who were at the gate and *all* the elders said, "Witnesses"' (4.11a).

The PBS groups sniffed two scandals in this narrative. The first scandal is the seizing of Ruth (reflected in the rhetoric of redemption and purchase) and as a consequence the trapping of Mahlon. Ruth became a daughter for Naomi in the previous passage (as suggested in the previous bible study), but in this passage she is bought and made Boaz's wife (4.10). There is no letting up in her favour, and the PBS groups were sympathetic to her because she continues to be passed around as *the* outsider. In the context of the Covid-19 pandemic, Ruth is like the frontline worker who is disposable. In seizing Ruth, Boaz also trapped Mahlon.

While native Pasifika worldviews orient towards the extended family and foster deep relationships, 'on the ground' and 'in life' we give space for latter generations to do their own thing. Children are expected to care for their parents, to continue the family trades, but also to divert as the context conditions them and as their spirits lean. For the PBS groups, Boaz could have redeemed the land of Elimelek *from Naomi* but that should not have included the inheritance of Mahlon. To redeem the land of Mahlon, Boaz needed to negotiate with Ruth. Hence the first scandal, seizing Ruth trapped Mahlon in the shadows of his parents.

The second scandal is the abandonment of Chilion. He is named (4.9) and his inheritance is seized along with Mahlon's, but there is no concern 'to raise up' his name 'upon his inheritance' so that he 'may not be cut off from his brothers [nor] his place from the gate' (cf. 4.10). Put directly: all the elders and all the people gathered at the gate abandoned Chilion. Orpah his widow is not named and as a consequence she too is abandoned. To be forgotten. Independent of the #SayHerName movement, but driven by the same spirit, the PBS groups wanted to be the witnesses to the abandonment of Orpah and Chilion. Alongside the witnesses to the seizure of Ruth and Mahlon, the PBS groups wanted to create a scandal of their own: to raise up the names of Orpah and Chilion – lest we forget.

Names are important in Pasifika, and many families give the names of biblical characters to their children. Each family has talanoa and rituals for adopting biblical names, and Ruth is among the popular ones. All the PBS participants knew at least one Ruth, and at least one participant from each group knew someone on their island with the name of Mahlon. Across the region we identified four persons whose names sounded similar to the vernacular translation of Chilion, but no one could come up with someone named after Orpah (nor Oprah). It thus became an element of the PBS participants' scandal, to consider the names of Orpah and Chilion the next time they have the opportunity to name a newborn. (This will be among the first queries to raise when i go back to the same communities in the future.) The PBS narrative is straightforward: the names of Orpah and Chilion should not be cut off from their brothers and sisters – Ruth and Mahlon.

Witnesses

The surrender of the sandal symbolically served two functions – to establish or to make stand (קום in 4.7) as well as to bind (עוד in 4.7) the agreement between the parties. The sandal ritual thus represented two seals being placed upon the agreement.

On top of those, *all* the elders added their weight, in their witness, to make the agreement all the more binding (also עוד in 4.11a). In other words, the witnessing elders were more than observers. They added a third seal upon the agreement. They were called upon to cement the agreement, and they concurred through their unanimous response – 'Witnesses [we are]' (4.11a).

Witnesses are necessary when a case contests a custom or position,[4] and accordingly Boaz's case was read in the previous bible study as contesting the redeemer's customary privilege. In the end, however, the effortless reaching of agreement and resolution in 4.7–11a favoured both Boaz and the redeemer. Boaz acquired Ruth as his wife, which helped to calm his restlessness, and the redeemer dodged a bullet. But what might the witnesses have gained from the resolution at the gate? What difference did the resolution make for the community? The PBS participants imagined three ways in which the community benefited:

First, the resolution confirmed that someone was endorsed to be responsible for Elimelek and this, for the PBS participants, was necessary in order for Elimelek to 'rest in peace'. The resolution enabled one of the dead relatives to be represented in the realm of the living (cf. 4.10), which was the primary concern of the gathering at the gate. The resolution calmed any restlessness in the realm of the dead, and calmness in the realm of the dead benefited the realm of the witnesses.

Second, the resolution meant that someone was endorsed to be responsible for Naomi as well. Boaz will give Naomi security and rest. And with one word and in one voice, the witnesses bound Boaz to that responsibility. His name was respected at the gate, among his brothers. In this regard, she was not to be the burden of the community at large. They do not have to provide and look out for her. The resolution consequently allowed the community to dodge a bullet. In this reading, what goes around comes around. Boaz gathered the elders to establish and to bind his case, and this PBS reading imagines the witnesses using Boaz to get them off the hook with regard to Naomi.

Third, drawing upon the second reading above, the resolution marked Naomi's arrival. She is no longer the returnee or remigrant who needed someone to glean for her upkeeping. With the resolution, Naomi's position was set.

Boaz was concerned that the name of the dead was remembered and respected among his brothers, whereas the PBS participants imagined Naomi coming back into the narrative and into the men's business. The PBS readings imagined Naomi in a profitable situation, and they interweave her profits with the profits for the community. The benefits of the community are bound with the benefits of Naomi, and vice versa.

Pasifikation

There is a village feel to Ruth 4.7–11a. It would not be difficult to gather and seat ten elders, even in smaller villages. A villager with Boaz's status could easily send a message around (through word of mouth or drumming), and 'ten' (actual or symbolic) elders would gather at the village green. In village minds, the storyline is possible. But it raises suspicions. Why did Boaz need witnesses, and why did he seat them before he addressed the redeemer? Why didn't he invite the redeemer first, and then together agree on the witnesses?

In talanoa settings, we are suspicious of people who call witnesses to verify or certify their claims. Effective orators provide details that situate (in terms of location, time and condition) their assertions, and this works in villages where people know one another as well as know something about what happened near their village (and near the next villages). At the village green, there are no fools. But many could be fooled by wise orators. And elders could smell rats from afar.

What if, on the other hand, the redeemer was the one who called the elders to sit and witness? The narrator does not name who the active subject in 4.2 was, and many translations (including the NIV and the NRSV) and readers assume that he was Boaz. However, the redeemer could also have called the ten elders to join him in seeing what Boaz was up to – Boaz called the redeemer, and the redeemer then called the ten elders. Boaz was not the only subject in this narrative who understood the protocols. The redeemer, on his own, was on top of the sandal tradition, and the narrator presented his move with favour (4.7–8).

The proposed alternative invites seeing the redeemer in a different light and i raise it here in order to call attention to another scandal in this narrative: the redeemer does not redeem, and readers do not feel the need to redeem him. He is not named, so he literarily represents many Judean men who withdrew from redeeming Elimelek and his family.

In closing, i put forward the unnamed redeemer as a figure for subjects who are not redeemed in scripture nor in reading communities. In biblical literature, they make up a long list – from Eve and Cain to the children of Ishmael and the children of Leah, to the Canaanites and the Gentiles, to the sons and daughters of darkness, and to the serpent and other creatures in life deemed expendable in the story of the kingdom of God. When the redeemer in Ruth 4.7–11a gets the chance to be redeemed, these other deemed unredeemable subjects can help reading communities understand the thrills of redemption more fully.

Takeaway

1 What might the reasons be for not involving Naomi in the rituals in Ruth 4.7–11a?

2 What function(s) do witnesses play in your context, and how is that similar to or different from the function of witnesses in this passage?

3 In your context, what rituals are performed for deemed unredeemable subjects?

Prompts for further talanoa

1 Kimberly D. Russaw, 'Zelophehad's Daughters', Bible Odyssey, www.bibleodyssey.org/en/people/related-articles/zelophehads-daughters, accessed 5.5.21.
2 Samuel Tongue, 'Sibling Rivalries and Younger Sons', *Bible Odyssey*, www.bibleodyssey.org/people/related-articles/sibling-rivalries-and-younger-sons, accessed 5.5.21.

Notes

1 Notwithstanding, even when there are heirs, inheritance is contested in biblical literature – as in the cases of Ishmael (Gen. 21.9–10), Esau (Gen. 25.29–34) and Zelophehad's daughters (Num. 36.5–9). The right to inheritance is a matter of concern even with Jesus' parabolic 'kingdom of God' (Luke 18.18–23), and those who benefit from the takeover of inheritance – Isaac, Jacob, descendants of Joseph, children of God – are seen as models of righteousness.

2 In 1.15, Naomi told Ruth to go and follow her sister-in-law Orpah, but Naomi did not stop referring to Ruth as her daughter.

3 Unless the redeemer collaborated with Naomi, and thus there is still something fishy in this narrative. Naomi was not at the gate, but things played into her hands.

4 Witnesses will be helpful later on if the agreement is contested.

9

Ruth 4.11b–22
Roots and lineage

Boaz secured the land and inheritance of Elimelek for himself, but the narrative did not end there. This story is not only about Boaz, nor is it a story only about land and inheritance – subjects that are very important to Pasifika natives. At the end (Ruth 4.11–22), this story returns to the subjects of women and sex[1] – two subjects that are arguably more interesting than land and inheritance. At the end, the story draws (ancestral) lines that circle back (*pikopiko iku mai*) to lines that were suspended (when Elimelek and his two sons died) at the beginning. From the end, the story invites readers to read back to the beginning and, in talanoa fashion, to draw more lines.

In the hearts of Pasifika natives, one of the subjects that makes a talanoa meaningful and deep is lineage (*whakapapa*). In the context of climate change, the concerns for lineage are traumatic because the potential loss of native (is)lands could erase whakapapa. When climate change runs its course, and some island nations are washed away or drowned, what will it mean to belong to a whakapapa from native (is)lands that are no more? These concerns interweave in the final three pericopes of this narrative.

From the gate, the story goes into the town. The hub and temperament shift. At the gate, men were in charge and 'all the people' affirmed. In the town, the elderly women of the neighbourhood took over. These women returned (from behind) to the story (after they came out to receive Naomi and Ruth) because a son, an heir, has been born in accordance with the patriarchal agenda. But in their return, the women subverted the patriarchal agenda as well as encouraged reading against the patriarchal project.

Ruth bore a son in order to keep the name and memory of the dead alive (Ruth 4.11–13), but the women of the neighbourhood took that child and gave him to Naomi (Ruth 4.14–17). This son was for the living rather than for the dead. Naomi took that child and nursed him as her own son, until the narrator (or his genealogist) took the child to become the catalyst for the male-only whakapapa for David (Ruth 4.18–22). In the taking and repurposing of this son, the memory that he was born to keep alive – the patriarchal agenda – dies.

Lurking behind the male-only whakapapa are women – Rachel, Leah and Tamar (Ruth 4.11–12) – who built the house of Israel by bearing and begetting (ילד) sons. The female-only function of bearing and begetting is the spur that transitions one generation to the next in the male-only whakapapa (Ruth 4.18–22). The narrative closes with a double move to feminize the fathers of David: the fathers, as the ones who begat, are literarily introduced as mothers and this (presenting fathers as if they are mothers) problematizes the masculinity of the patriarchal project. The narrator, reflecting Davidic tradition(ing)s, took Ruth's son from Naomi, but the *accounting* of the whakapapa would not let this story end as a male-only affair. The story ends with reminders of begetting (ילד), thus taking readers into the domains of women and sex. This is not to say that women are only appreciated because of their role in the begetting (ילד) cycle, but to propose that the male-only whakapapa fulfils the patriarchal agenda by at once feminizing it.

The following bible studies explore and play with the implications of the son being taken away (abducted, hijacked) in the three closing pericopes of this narrative. Taken by the women first (Ruth 4.14–17), the child helped feminize the story; taken by men second (Ruth 4.18–22), the same child helped feminize patriarchy. The whakapapa is the third and final take on this son, whose repurposing effectively wiped out the memory of the dead who were meant to be remembered through him. In the whakapapa, among the fathers of David, Obed and Boaz are given the place of Mahlon and Elimelek. The lineage that the whakapapa draws also erases. The whakapapa links and remembers, and it also overlooks and forgets.

(18) Ruth 4.11b–13: Yʜwʜ gives Ruth a son

¹¹ [All the people who were at the gate ( ) all the elders said, 'Witnesses!']
May Yʜwʜ give the woman who is coming to your house like Rachel and Leah, the two who built the house of Israel
( ) may you do strongly in Ephrathah and
( ) may your name be called in Bethlehem
¹² ( ) may your house be like the house of Perez whom Tamar bore to Judah
– from the offspring that Yʜwʜ will give to you from this young woman'
¹³ ( ) Boaz took Ruth [and] she became his wife
He entered her ( ) Yʜwʜ gave her conception
( ) She bore a son

On top of being witnesses, *all* the people with the elders at the gate prayed for outcomes similar to those brought by three women in the history of Israel. Upon Ruth, they prayed that she would become like Leah and Rachel; upon Boaz, they prayed that he would become strong and memorable (Ruth 4.11); and upon the expected son (read: Boaz's house), they prayed that he would be like the house of Perez whom Tamar begot (4.12). These three women built the houses of Israel and Judah, but their stories were not straightforward.

Thanks to all the people at the gate, the names and influences of women returned into the story-world. The witnesses and the gathered crowd together called upon women to 'witness to' (make stand, establish) the house of Boaz. In the next verse Boaz took and entered Ruth (4.13), and then he disappeared from the story. One Rabbinic tradition suggested that Boaz died that night (*Ruth Rabbah* 3.5). He was vigorous for one evening, unlike Jacob (in Gen. 29–31) and Judah (in Gen. 38); the prayer of the people (that he 'do strongly') did not work.

Ruth lived on until her son was born, and then she too disappeared from the story-world.

Tricksters

As a woman shepherd who had to wait until the other flocks come before she could water the sheep (Gen. 29.8), when she followed the expected practice, Rachel would have developed her threshold of patience. She could wait. But as a woman who 'had a lovely figure and was beautiful' (Gen. 29.27), she would have been a man-magnet who, in my heterosexual head, occasionally delayed reaching the watering hole so that she strolled into the admiring eyes of the other shepherds. Oh yeah.

I imagine Rachel as a complex character, the kind of woman who would look out for her sister. She could calmly hold back and let her older sister go first, and i imagine that their relationship would have been mutual and reciprocal (including the willingness to share a man, see Gen. 30.14–15). At the same time, Rachel could also be playful if not cheeky. She could hold back by nature and, also, because she had the struts. She knew that Jacob was already a bird in her hands. He would again break the routines in order to please her (Gen. 29.10), as he did at his first sighting of her. She indeed captured Jacob's engrossment and the narrator gave evidence of his testosterone: 'Give me my wife … I want to make love to her' (Gen. 29.21, NIV). He was whipped.

Leah and Rachel must have known of the gentlemen's agreement between Laban and Jacob (Gen. 29.15–19), and they could have collaborated with their father to trick Jacob (Gen. 29.22–24). The sisters knew what they were getting out of and into, and they may have even suspected that their father was looking for a chance to ditch Leah (as excess baggage, cf. Gen. 31.14–16).

Rachel was complex, but Leah was the trickster that night. Laban brought Leah to Jacob, and she did the rest. Leah had weak eyes (Gen. 29.17), but weak eyes are irrelevant in the dark; what mattered was that Leah had the stamina to stay the whole night (and for many nights afterwards) with Jacob. Jacob complained the next morning about not getting Rachel (Gen. 29.25), but he did not complain about getting Leah first. He did not send Leah back to her father's house. A second, unmarked, female is not a problem for Jacob. Leah was secured even before YHWH helped her to conceive (Gen. 29.31).

Two generations later, Tamar entered the story as the wife for a grandson of Leah (Gen. 38). Tamar was taken to marry Er, first-born of Judah (fourth son of Leah). But because Er was wicked in the eyes of YHWH, who swiftly put him to death (Gen. 38.7), Judah told his second son Onan to go into Tamar in order to fulfil the duty of a brother-in-law (that is, to father a son for his dead brother). However, Onan spilled his seed on the ground and thus displeased YHWH, who put him to death as well (Gen. 38.10). Because Shelah, the third son, was still young then, Judah sent Tamar back to her father's house to wait until the lad grew up. But it was obvious that Judah did not intend for Tamar to marry Shelah.

After some time, Tamar heard that Judah, after mourning the death of his wife (Bathshua), was coming her way. Tamar took off her widow's outfit, put on a veil, and came to sit on the side of the road at the entrance to Enaim ('opening of the eyes'). Judah mistook Tamar as a prostitute, turned to her, and asked to let him enter her (Gen. 38.16). They agreed to a price and a pledge, and Judah went into her and she conceived by him (Gen. 38.18). From behind her veil, Tamar did not reveal her identity (compared to Judah, who surrendered three significant markers of his identity – his signet, cord and staff). Tamar was resolved, similar to how i imagine Leah to have been that first night. Tamar pulled a trick on Judah, as Leah did on his father Jacob.

The primary interest of all the people at the gate who recalled the names of Leah, Rachel and Tamar (Ruth 4.11–12) was with these female characters being the builders of the houses of Israel and Judah. That honour and privilege cannot be taken from them. In this reading, i revisited their stories as female characters with the guile to trick the men in their story-worlds. I highlighted how Leah was a trickster mainly because she does not receive a lot of credit, owing in part to her weak eyes. But Leah had the courage to negotiate with Rachel (in Gen. 30.14–15) and to trap Jacob (to sleep with her in Gen. 30.16). Leah had weak eyes, but her will was strong.

Eclipsed by her sister Rachel, the enthralment of Jacob, Leah in this reading is a figure for marginalized and overlooked female characters. In her own story-world, Leah is a reminder for her very own daughter Dinah who is named (Gen. 30.21), raped (Gen. 34.1–2) and then abandoned. In the story-world of Tamar, Leah is a replacement for her mother-in-law Bathshua (see also Chapter 7).[2] And in the story-world of Ruth, Leah is a figure for Orpah, the 'older sister' of Ruth (see Chapter 3), whom the narrator and many people at the gate would have preferred to forget (together with the redeemer, see Chapter 8). In this reading, Leah is a builder of the house for marginalized, overlooked, unredeemed and forgotten female characters. In this connection, Leah may be redeemed, and her story may be read for opportunities to redeem (as the dead who were to be redeemed through Ruth). Leah did not have Rachel's struts or eyes, but she was complex in her own way.

Breachers

After Tamar cleared herself from Judah's accusation that she was pregnant because of whoredom (Gen. 38.24–26), and in the process exposed Judah as the one who treated her as a whore and also made her pregnant, she completed her pregnancy and gave birth to twins (Gen. 38.28–30). The boys did not struggle in her womb like Esau and Jacob (Gen. 25.22–23), but they jostled upon their exit. During labour, a hand popped out and the midwife tied a scarlet thread to it in order to mark it as the first to come out. This hand, however, (was) pulled back and out came his brother to whom the midwife said, 'What a breach (פרץ) you are against yourself!' That is why he was named Perez (פרץ, to breach). His brother came out afterwards with the scarlet thread upon his hand, and he was named Zerah (זרח, to rise or shine).

All the people at the gate wished that the house of Boaz would become like the house of Perez, but they did not mention Tamar's other son. The naming of Perez in Ruth 4.12 adds to the breaching of Zerah. Zerah is among the male characters who are overlooked in the story-worlds of the Bible and forgotten down the line, unredeemed by readers. Zerah is an older sibling whose very own brother breached.

As far as breachers in the Bible go, Perez comes into the shadows of Jacob. Jacob fought against Esau in the womb (Gen. 25.22–23) and breached him in their youth, buying Esau's birthright (Gen. 29.29–34) and their father's blessing (Gen. 27.1–36) with food. And in his latter days Jacob deceived Esau again, telling him to go back to Seir and wait for him there (Gen. 33.12–16) but he instead went on to Succoth and Shechem (Gen. 33.17–18). Jacob breached his brother on several occasions, and their story ended without reconciliation.

Jacob breached his father-in-law also (Gen. 30.25–43). Laban agreed that the speckled and spotted flock will be for Jacob his payment, but Laban did not expect Jacob to be able to manipulate the eating, drinking and mating practices of the flock so that the lambs come out speckled and spotted. Moreover, Jacob put the stronger of the flock into his scheme so that his dividend was assured, and his stock quickly multiplied: 'Thus the man grew exceedingly rich, and had large flocks, and male and female slaves, and camels and donkeys' (Gen. 30.43, NRSV). Jacob breached beasts and humans both.

The people at the gate wished for Boaz's forthcoming son to become like Perez and, because Tamar is named together with Leah and Rachel in the same pericope, i hear their wish in relation to Jacob's ingenuity. I hear the people wishing that Boaz's son would make a profit, and they would not be bothered if he also made a breach by, for instance, manipulating genetic compositions and/or amassing slaves. The people at the gate had just witnessed Boaz making a profit, and i imagine them wishing the same success for his son.

There is another way to read the people's reference to Perez. At the gate, the people looked forward to the son to come but Boaz was in their presence and so their words may be read as a reaction to Boaz. In the previous bible study ('Ruth 4.7–11a: Boaz un-sandals the redeemer'), Boaz passed as a breacher. He pushed the redeemer to give up his responsibility to the dead, and he used Ruth as an opportunity to add Elimelek's inheritance to his own. In another way, one may also say that Boaz used the dead as an opportunity to secure Ruth under his wing. Whether to take this reading as judgement and/or praise is up to readers, but there is no denying that Boaz too was a breacher. To echo the wonderment of the midwife at the birth of Perez – what a breach Boaz was to himself.

The foregoing readings are not innocent, nor pretentious. Breaching others is common in the Bible and in daily life, and the ones who struggle are more open to breaching other people and their ways in order to get up and to stay up. Even the loyal Rachel (by staying back to let Leah be married first) breached her father at the end, by stealing and then sitting on the household gods so that Laban would not find them (Gen. 30.32b–35). Breaching is also done by people with power, to build their estates and control. Owning slaves and taking advantage of others is part of Perez's heritage; even Abram was a slave owner (Gen. 12.5) and settler among the people of the land (Gen. 12.6). This is the heritage that the people wished upon the house of Boaz, a wish that could be a blessing and/or a curse on the future son of Ruth.

Conceivers

Time passes quickly in this narrative. Conception is followed by birth in the same narrative breath (Ruth 4.13b), a hastening that gives evidence to the maleness of the narrator. He writes quickly to get the product out – a son. I, on the other hand, propose to dilly-dally in order to see and name some of the shades of conception.

All the people at the gate were confident that Ruth would deliver a baby. They trusted the couple, and they ended their good wishes by declaring that the 'seed' (זרע) would come from YHWH and Ruth 'the young woman' (הנערה) would do the rest

(Ruth 4.12b). Boaz might have been as old as Judah, but Ruth was still young. Boaz did his part by taking Ruth to be his wife and entering her, but according to the narrator the conception had nothing to do with Boaz. Rather, the show belonged to YHWH and Ruth: 'YHWH gave her conception (הֵרָיוֹן), she bore (ילד) a son' (4.13b). YHWH gave the conception to her, and Ruth delivered. Given the reflection above on breachers, YHWH looks like a breacher (by taking the fathering credit from Boaz).

The word translated as 'conception' (הֵרָיוֹן) appears in only two other places in the Bible. In Genesis 3.16, YHWH Elohim cursed the woman: 'I will greatly increase your pain and your conception (הֵרָיוֹן); in pain you will bear children (ילד) and your desire will be for your husband, but he will have dominion over you.' YHWH Elohim will increase her conceptions – that is, YHWH will make her have a lot of sex – but the pain is linked to bearing and giving birth to children (ילד). Hosea 9.11 goes further and distinguishes between bearing children (ילד), becoming pregnant (or 'wombing', בטן) and conceiving (הֵרָיוֹן). In the context of Genesis 3.16 and Hosea 9.11, one may read Ruth 4.13b in three ways: first, that YHWH *allowed* Ruth to conceive; second, that YHWH *helped* Ruth to conceive; third, that YHWH *made* Ruth conceive. With all three options, the narrator attributes Ruth's conception to YHWH. Was the narrator, at the end, another breacher (if not the real one)? For at the end, the narrator is the one who took the credit for the conception away from Boaz.

There is a phonetic connection between the offspring (זרע, seed) that the people expected YHWH to give and the name of Zerah (זרח) the brother of Perez. Whether this connection was intentional on the part of the narrator or a result of the accident of language, i cannot determine, but the breached brother is echoed in this conception narrative. This conception narrative, in this reading, would not let Zerah be forgotten. This reading conceives Zerah upon the words of the people at the gate, encouraged by the concern that the dead are remembered. In this turn, Zerah serves the same function as Leah in the previous section: they are figures for characters who are forgotten and breached.

Pasifikation

One of the explanations that natives give for the land or sea being cursed is that the ancestors may have been wronged. Wronging the ancestors results in the cursing of our island world. In the context of climate change, even in today's world, this explanation applies. There is a delicate link between the ancestors with the land and the sea, that wronging one also wrongs the others. Similarly, on the other hand, fostering and flourishing one sphere benefits the others. In this native way of thinking, the ancestors are strong and key characters in the systems of retribution and justice. Following that line of thinking, this bible study gave special attention to Leah and Zerah as ancestors who were wronged (breached) in different ways, the consequence of which is that the land and inheritance redeemed through Ruth and Boaz were also wronged. In other words, the 'redemption' that was conducted will not last because 'breaches' were involved.

To correct the wrongs done to the ancestors, the living perform rituals, the easiest but most delicate of which is to revisit and retell their stories. We do so with the energies of talanoa, and i have presented examples of talanoa at work in this bible study (which is also inspired by the talanoa with PBS groups). My aim is not to fix (determine, heal) the text, but to provide readings that invite further engagement with breached characters in (Leah) and around (Zerah) – Ruth 4.11b–13.

Takeaway

1 If Leah and Rachel masterminded the scam (to give Leah to Jacob first instead of Rachel as agreed in Gen. 29.14b–28), could you consider them 'righteous' like Tamar (Gen. 38.26)?
2 Who are other tricksters and breachers in the Bible that this passage brings to mind?
3 In what ways is reading an act of tricking and breaching the text, or isn't it?

(19) Ruth 4.14–17: The women give Naomi a son

¹⁴ ( ) The women said to Naomi
'Bless YHWH, who did not withhold from you a redeemer
   today
( ) may his name be called in Israel
¹⁵ ( ) may he be a restorer of life for you
( ) a nourisher of your old age
for your daughter-in-law, who loved you, has borne him
for she was better to you than seven sons'
¹⁶ ( ) Naomi took the child
( ) laid him on her bosom
( ) to him she nursed
¹⁷ ( ) The women-oldies called him a name saying
( ) 'a son is born to Naomi'
( ) they called his name Obed
he is the father of Jesse, father of David

After giving birth, Ruth disappeared from the narrative. The women of the neighbourhood took over the story. They made reference to Ruth, but did not name her. They approached Naomi and gave her the child; Naomi received the child as a newborn (ילד, Ruth 4.16), and she nursed him. The women made Naomi his mother when they said that 'a son is born to Naomi', and they gave him a name – Obed, meaning 'one who serves'. In this context, and in his condition, Naomi is expected to 'serve' the newborn.

Boaz too disappears from the narrative. As Naomi replaced Ruth, so did Obed – who is also presented as a father-to-be – replace Boaz. The disappearance of Ruth and Boaz from the story-world released the dead – Mahlon, Chilion, Elimelek – into non-remembrance. The names of those whom Ruth brought into Boaz's house are officially buried in the past, for Obed is named into the service of somebody else.

Redeemer

The women came to Naomi and celebrated the arrival of her redeemer (גאל). This redeemer was unlike the two older, endowed and (self-)interested redeemers at the gate; this redeemer was a male child who did not yet know what he was being put into. This redeemer was bicultural and he began his storied life without his mother and father; the women of the town, whom we in Asia and Pasifika would call 'aunties', put him into the care of his grandmother.

In Pasifika, many children grow up under the care of their grandparents. In the past, it was expected of grandparents that they foster their grandchildren. That was one of the ways through which the wisdoms of the grandparents are passed on to future generations. The grandparents are mentors, and some even claim special privilege over their grandchildren. They tell them their stories and show them their ways, and the grandchildren learn the secret recipes, trades and protocols. Later in life, the adult grandchildren are expected to care for their grannies. In more recent times, the fostering of grandchildren is out of necessity – to free parents up so that they may work and earn a living. This form of assistance is especially helpful for single mothers, who may be unmarried, divorced or widowed.

The house of Perez has stories of children being claimed by their grandparents. Laban claimed to own his grandchildren and he established a covenant with Jacob for their sake (Gen. 31.43–54), before he kissed and blessed them (Gen. 31.55). When it was his turn, later in Egypt, Jacob took the two sons of Joseph as his own (Gen. 48.5) and promised them the double portion that he allotted for Joseph. In blessing (read: taking) the grandchildren as his own, Jacob switched them – he put his right hand upon Ephraim even though he knew that Manasseh was Joseph's first-born (Gen. 48.8–22). Against Joseph's protest, Jacob decided who was to be(come) first. He decided, simply, because they had become his children – his household, his children, his blessing, his decision. Despite the difference of gender, i imagine a similar understanding in the narrative of Obed: the women gave him to his grandmother, to become her son. For Naomi, as for Laban and Jacob, this grandson would have been 'the crown of the aged' (Prov. 17.6a).

There are also cases of parents having died and the care for the surviving children fall upon other relatives, as Mordecai was for Esther (Esth. 2.7; compare with the Pharaoh's daughter for Moses, Exod. 2.10). Orphans, together with Levites, widows and sojourners, receive special attention in the Bible (see Deut. 14.29). This raises the possibility that Ruth and Boaz had died and left Obed as an orphan, which makes sense of why it was the women who brought the child to Naomi rather than Naomi who brought the child, and announced to her neighbours that he was her son. Echoing the earlier story of the unnamed sister bringing the mother of a child to nurse him (Exod. 2.7–8), the unnamed women of the neighbourhood brought the child to his grandmother so that she would nurse him. In doing this, the women signalled that Ruth was no longer around. She might have died.

All of these explanations could apply to Obed. He was given into the care of Naomi with the expectation that Naomi would care and 'serve' him. Naomi will serve (deliver) the boy first. And down the line, he would nourish Naomi in her old age. At which point, the lad would be a redeemer (גאל) for Naomi.

Shifts

The women echoed the confidence that the people at the gate expressed in a previous bible study ('Ruth 4.7–11a: Boaz un-sandals the redeemer', Chapter 8). They paid tribute to YHWH first, for having delivered a redeemer for Naomi. And in their tribute, the women changed the subject of concern – this redeemer was *for Naomi*, and not for Mahlon or Elimelek (the main agenda at the gate). Naomi is the genuine subject, and her redeemer is from the generation that reggae artists call the 'tomorrow people'. Whereas the event at the gate reflected patriarchal concerns, the gathering of women some nine months later shifted the focus to a woman and to a child – neither of whom was at the gate.

There are other stories where women upturn the patriarchal agenda, the closest one in terms of subject matter is the birth narrative of Moses (Exod. 1.15—2.10). The Pharaoh was on a campaign to control the Hebrew population so he ordered the midwives Shiphrah and Puah to kill the male Hebrew babies, but let the daughters live. The midwives did not do as the Pharaoh commanded. They let the boys live, and Pharaoh upped the ante: he ordered that Hebrew boys be thrown into the Nile, but let the girls live. A Levite woman did not follow this order; instead, she hid her son for three months. When she could not hide him any longer, she put him into a papyrus basket plastered with bitumen and pitch, then put the basket among the reeds on the bank of the river. The Pharaoh's own daughter found the basket, determined that the boy was a Hebrew,[3] hired his own mother to nurse him, then took him as her son when he had grown up. She named him Moses because she 'drew him out of the water' (Exod. 2.10b). There might have been other mothers who hid their sons, and other sons adopted by other daughters of Egypt, but the story of Moses's deliverance tells of women collaborating to overturn a patriarchal agenda. The women turned a story in which death was expected to become a story of deliverance of a male child by daughters. The narrative does not provide any detail about the daughter of Pharaoh: Was she married? Did she have other children? Was she old? But one thing is clear: like Naomi, she received a son that she had to serve.

The female neighbours of Naomi also paid tribute to Ruth. They reminded Naomi that Ruth was 'your daughter-in-law, who loved you ... she was better to you than seven sons' (Ruth 4.15b). If Ruth had already died as suggested above, this tribute amounts to the allegation of openness, if not consent, on the part of Ruth. To the women, Ruth loved Naomi so much that she would not mind Naomi taking her son. Adding that Ruth was 'better than seven sons' was the icing on the cake (or the knockout punch). How could Naomi refuse to take the son of a daughter-in-law who meant so much to her?

Juxtaposed with the story of the Egyptian women, the manoeuvre by the neighbourhood women allowed Naomi to take the boy – he became Naomi's son. This manoeuvre was necessary given the openness of the previous passages concerning whose son he would be. The elders at the gate witnessed to a transaction according to which the expected son would be the son of Mahlon (Ruth 4.10); when they made their witness, all the people at the gate expected him to be the son of Boaz (Ruth 4.12) and so did the narrator (Ruth 4.13). At the gate, the son was not expected to come into Naomi's domain. With the possibility that both Ruth and Boaz had already died, the female neighbours cleared the way for the boy to be 'lifted', and for Naomi to consent: she took the child, laid him on her bosom, and she nursed him (Ruth 4.16).

The women resolved one issue but ignored another one. Was Naomi the grandmother or the mother of the boy? The women decided on the latter when they declared that 'a son is born to Naomi' (Ruth 4.17) but they did not rule out her merit as a grandmother. In theory, she was both. This paradox reflects a similar situation in the story of Perez, for whom Judah was both father and grandfather. Whereas the people at the gate wished for the son to be like Perez, the women in the neighbourhood put Naomi in a position comparable to Judah.

In this reading, the women put several shifts into effect. Their manoeuvres are reminders that shifts do take place in the unfolding of a whakapapa. Shifts are expected, even though the dominant drive of a whakapapa is to establish and to root.

Server

With Naomi's silent sanction, the women named the boy Obed (one who serves). Juxtaposed with the story of Perez, it is possible that Ruth's son was named at birth (by his mother or a midwife) and so what the women did was to rename him to reflect a purpose they had in mind. For Ruth's son to become Naomi's son, he had to be renamed. The name Obed marks him as the one who, first, Naomi will serve and, later, he will serve Naomi. His renaming is a repurposing.[4]

Renaming is a practice in biblical narratives, the better-known ones are the renaming of Abram as Abraham, Sarai as Sarah, and Jacob as Israel. Renaming is presumed in the case of Moses as well. His mother would have given him a name, and the Pharaoh's daughter called him Moses after he had grown up for several months, if not years. The women named Naomi's son with the expectation that he would be 'a restorer of life (נפש)' for Naomi and 'a nourisher of her old age' (Ruth 4.15a). In modern terms, the women expected Obed to make Naomi feel young again.

Against the women's agenda, the narrator shifts the focus away from Naomi and made the boy serve David – 'they called his name Obed – he is the father of Jesse, father of David' (Ruth 4.17b). The narrator puts forth the patriarchal agenda at the close of this passage, but that does not erase the shifts that the women initiated.[5]

Pasifikation

The overturning of the patriarchal agenda by the women is similar to the subverting of conventional thinking about the parts of trees as metaphors for generations in the 'roots and leaves' body of works by the late Donatus S. Moulo Moiwend (aka Donet), a West Papuan artist, educator and activist. In conventional thinking: the roots represent the ancestors, the trunk represents the parents, the branches represent the current generation, and the fruits and leaves represent the children.

Giving expression to traditional Papuan wisdom, Donet overturned this conventional way of thinking. For Donet, the leaves represent the ancestors because leaves give air for breathing and sap for healing. The leaves (ancestors) sustain and heal the current generation. The ancestors have died but they continue to be present in the healing powers of (green) leaves, in the whispering and singing of leaves in the wind, and in the rattling of dry (brown) leaves under the feet of living creatures. The world of the ancestors is not separate from 'this world' of the current generation. Rather, the current generation lives in the world of the ancestors.

Figure 9.1: Donatus S. Moulo Moiwend, Tree of Life (oil on bark).
Used with permission of the Moiwend family.

The trunk (body) and branches represent the current generation. They provide the base and veins for and from the leaves (ancestors), while the roots represent the children (future generation) because it is out of the roots that shoots (new life) spring. In Donet's *Tree of Life* (Figure 9.1), the roots are also green to indicate that new life starts from the roots. Roots represent new beginnings and the life that waits in the future (read: tomorrow people, future generations). Life comes out and up from the roots. Even when a new plant springs from dried seeds, the roots unfold before the shoot rises.

Following Donet's way of thinking, Obed (as redeemer, nourisher, server) is the roots for Naomi. But also, in the conventional sense (read: patriarchal agenda), Obed is the roots for David.

Takeaway

1 What are possible explanations for Ruth's disappearance from the narrative?
2 What does the mention that the women gave the child his new, different name mean for you?
3 What else does the act of renaming convey?

(20) Ruth 4.18–22: Tradition gives David a heritage

¹⁸ ( ) These are the generations of Perez; Perez begat Hezron
¹⁹ ( ) Hezron begat Ram ( ) Ram begat Amminadab
²⁰ ( ) Amminadab begat Nahshon ( ) Nahshon begat Salmon
²¹ ( ) Salmon begat Boaz ( ) Boaz begat Obed
²² ( ) Obed begat Jesse ( ) Jesse begat David

A whakapapa (lineage) is drawn up in order to remember but also in order to forget, in order to relate but also in order to unrelate. For instance, as explained above, the remembering of Perez is accompanied with the forgetting of Zerah. Likewise, as far as the whole narrative is concerned, the affirming of Ruth contributes to the forgetting of Orpah.

A listing of names is not free of ideologies and politics. Nor is it innocent. The saying that 'winners write history' applies to whakapapa as well, and the gender of the winners (writers, genealogists) makes a difference in who is included and who is not. The fathers are named in Ruth 4.18–22, going back to Perez and forward to David, but the mothers are not named. Gender privileging in this final pericope is apparent, given that in the previous pericope the women named the mothers but not the fathers.

Map

A whakapapa takes readers on a journey. With the image of journey, i draw attention to the storied roads that come to mind with the naming of the fathers in Ruth 4.18–22. The journey starts with Perez, who was conceived on the side of the road. His son Hezron was among the 70 Israelites who moved, taken on a journey, to Egypt with Jacob (Exod. 46.12). That journey was meant to be temporary,[6] until the famine passed, but Joseph restrained the family in Egypt for longer ... long enough for Joseph to be forgotten by a later Pharaoh (Exod. 1.8).

The next two generations, represented by Ram (Aram) and Amminadab, were born away from home (in exile), in Egypt. Amminadab's son Nahshon is remembered in the wilderness during the return journey, on the road back, as the first one to bring his offering at the dedication of the Tabernacle (Num. 7.12–17). Nahshon's son Salmon (who married Rahab, according to the Matthean whakapapa) was most likely born during the crossing of the wilderness, on the road.

Boaz entered the narrative at the end of a journey, arriving back from town (Ruth 2.4), and then made his exit from the narrative after the event at the gate. Not much is known about Obed, except that he was born at the crossroads of two wealthy families (he inherited the family wealth of Elimelek and Boaz), and the name of his son testifies to his wealth – the name Jesse (ישׁי) means 'substance'. David comes at the end of this whakapapa, and biblical traditions favour him as an innocent shepherd boy who was chosen to be king over God's people.

Ruth 4.18–22 maps a journey, from Perez to David; from the side of the road to a throne expected at the end of the road. The whakapapa maps a journey but cannot determine if and how readers may (or may not) take it. In my case, descendants and history do not appeal to me as much as talanoa and ideologies do. The following reflections are thus driven by the politics of whakapapa and masculinity. Who are hidden from this map? What impacts do the hiding strategies have on the patriarchal agenda?

Hidden mothers

'Public transcripts' and 'hidden transcripts' are conceptions that James C. Scott (1990) introduced into the discussion of power relations. Public transcripts (that uphold hegemony and orthopraxy) are the official records, favoured and enforced by the people in power (who are few in number, but they are the rulers, mostly white Europeans). The public transcripts do not include dissentions and anti-hegemonic positions (by the ruled, who are many more in numbers). Hidden transcripts, on the other hand, are dissenting and resisting murmurs by the ruled (such as labourers, subalterns and natives), kept at whispering levels to avoid being picked up and picked on by the rulers and their cronies. The dissenters perform the roles prescribed for them by the rulers, for the sake of their survival, but they do not endorse the ideologies that inform or result from those practices.

In Pasifika, hidden transcripts are homed in the circles of talanoa among normal people. Hidden transcripts are remembered and passed on, and over time they creep into public forums (e.g. through orators and preachers). When hidden transcripts break through hegemonic lines, natives are encouraged to go back over the public transcripts looking for gaps and fractures that give evidence to, or provide opportunities for, dissension and resistance.

The whakapapa in Ruth 4.18–22 is an example of a public transcript, with two significant tweaks. First of all, Ruth 4.18–22 is a selective recalling of the whakapapa in 1 Chronicles 2 (which itself is a selective remembering). The Ruth 4.18–22 whakapapa trims the archived transcript of the chronicler; this public transcript is therefore fractured and fracturing. And, second, the act that links the list of fathers in this shortened whakapapa – יֹלִד (to bear, bring forth, beget; compare with γεννάω in Matt. 1.2–6a) – can only be achieved by women.[7] I read this discord as a symptom for hidden transcripts and thus ask of the whakapapa, who and where are the mothers? This question arises also in response to the chronicler's archived whakapapa (1 Chron. 2) which lists several women: a daughter (unnamed daughter of Sheshan), sisters (Zeruiah and Abigail, sisters of David), mothers (wives of Caleb: Azubah, Ephrath and Jerioth; Atarah, mother of Onam; Abihail, mother of Ahban and Molid; unnamed second wife of Hezron) and a concubine (Maacah, concubine of Caleb). Even as it serves the patriarchal agenda, including presenting Caleb as a biblical playboy, the chronicler's whakapapa nonetheless names some of the women. My gendered question – who and where are the mothers? – therefore comes with an invitation to engage with the politics of whakapapa.

Except for Perez, whose mother Tamar was discussed in previous bible studies, the mothers for the other fathers in Ruth 4.18–22 are not named in other parts of the Hebrew Bible. There is only one instance in which a woman was related to two of these fathers – Aminadab had a daughter named Elisheba, the sister of Nahson. Elisheba was the wife of Aaron, and she bore him four sons (Exod. 6.23). There is no further reference to her in the biblical narrative, and it is obvious that she was named because of her famous husband – Aaron was the older brother of, and the one whom the angry YHWH appointed to speak for, Moses (Exod. 5.14–16) – and sons.[8]

Elisheba was named because she had a place in the patriarchal agenda, but there are mixed vibes concerning her husband and sons. Aaron was Israel's first high priest, but he was also involved in two major rebellions – he cooperated with the people in the golden calf event (Exod. 32), and he collaborated with his sister Miriam to question the authority of Moses (Num. 12). Elisheba's first and second sons, Nadab and Abihu, offered 'foreign fire' and as a consequence YHWH burned them (Lev. 10.1–3). Her third son Eleazar eventually found favour, and he succeeded Aaron to become Israel's second high priest, but he and his brother Ithamar were in trouble with their uncle, Moses (cf. Lev. 10.16–18). The men in Elisheba's life were shady, and there are two ways to read their shadiness: first, subjects who find approval in the patriarchal agenda are not exempt from trouble; second, shady subjects are appropriate for pulling the patriarchal agenda through. Both readings apply to the men in the lives of both Elisheba and Tamar.

Ruth 4.18–22 provides the generational lines that the whaka-papa in Matthew 1.2–6a follows, but the latter stretches back to Abraham and adds some of the mothers. The Matthean whakapapa names Tamar and Ruth, and claims that Rahab (presumably of Jericho, in Josh. 2.1–21) was the mother of Boaz. Juxtaposing the Matthean whakapapa with Ruth 4.18–22 raises a question concerning the witness of the people in Ruth 4.11–13. Why did the people name Tamar but 'hide' the mother of Boaz? This is a critical question given that Boaz was the person of interest at the gate. My question could easily be thrown out, by showing that the Matthean whakapapa made things up. However, *making things up* is precisely what a whakapapa does, both by naming and by hiding names. In this regard, one may rightly argue that the Matthean whakapapa made things up as did the whakapapa in Ruth 4.18–22.

Did the people at the gate have a problem with Boaz's mother? Were they ashamed of Rahab being a Canaanite woman? Rahab was a 'real' prostitute but that did not seem to be an issue in so far as Tamar, who was 'seen' as a prosti-tute, was concerned. Rahab assisted Israel, by deceiving her own people, and Israel fulfilled (Josh. 6.17, 23–25) the pact that their two spies made with her (Josh. 2.8–14). She was then hidden from biblical literature until she reappeared in the Matthean whakapapa, and then recognized as righteous (James 2.25) and a woman of faith (Heb. 11.3). The only thing that counts against Rahab was her ethnicity, and i suspect that her ethnicity had something to do with the people at the gate not naming her as the mother of Boaz. It was not a problem that she, as a Canaanite, delivered Israel. Biblical memory accepts her among Israel's redeemers. The problem, rather, is when she, as a Canaanite, became a mother for a father in Israel. Put directly, the problem with Rahab was ideological: she could redeem, but she was not appropriate to be mother for a father of Israel.

Might ethnicity be the reason also for why the people did not name Ruth in their witness? Ruth is identified as a Moabite woman up to Ruth 4.10, then the narrator did not mention her ethnicity the last time she is named (Ruth 4.13). This suggests that she stopped being a Moabite woman when she became a mother to a son of, and an heir in, Judah. After she became a mother, the people at the gate (Ruth 4.11–12) and the women in the neighbourhood (Ruth 4.14–17) stopped calling her by name. At the end, her Moabite heritage was a problem when she became a mother in Judah. It was at that point that she was hidden from the story-world. Like Rahab, Ruth was another hidden mother.

Hiding masculinity

What kind of man begat only a man?

In terms of the patriarchal agenda (which i have labelled without specifying or limiting it), such a man would be ideal. That man has won against his siblings to represent his generation. His shadiness defines the marks of right(eous)ness, and his sins are quickly hidden. He is presented as the winner, for whom a part of history is written, and at the sound of his name readers are expected to say 'amen and amen'.

Owing to the politics of whakapapa, the mention of that ideal man's name seems to be all that is needed. If he had a shady story, his inclusion in the whakapapa makes him and his story acceptable. As a matter of fact, he does not even need a story. The patriarchal agenda needs him to provide the link from one father to the next, and somewhere along the line one man trumps him and all the other men. In Ruth 4.18–22, David is the 'trump'. All the other fathers are links that legitimize and trump up David. David is made to be the winner before his story is told, even before his history arrives; put another way, in so far as the whakapapa in Ruth 4.18–22 is concerned, history is written before history is.

Each father named in Ruth 4.18–22 is an ideal man because each one is a trump, lined up to be trumped. In this reading, the whakapapa in Ruth 4.18–22 is 'hiding masculinity' in the sense that it conceals how each of these ideal men are both top and bottom, in the service of the big man. In another sense, this reading is 'hiding masculinity' in the way that it also *has a go at* (or gives a hiding to) masculinity. In association, this reading also has a go at hiding the patriarchal agenda.

Unhiding mothers

Thanks to the neighbouring women, Obed had two mothers – Ruth and Naomi. I suggested above (following a Rabbinical tradition) that this might have been out of necessity, because Ruth had died. But Ruth did not have to die yet, and so Obed ended up with two living mothers. In this reading, the neighbours saw what many queer readers suspect: that Ruth and Naomi may have been a couple.

Thanks to the politics of levirate marriage, Obed had two fathers: Boaz and Mahlon (by being the son of Ruth). The women gave him a third father, Elimelek (by being the son of Naomi). Boaz had not been pronounced dead yet, but Mahlon and Elimelek were dead and gone. In giving Obed a third father, the neighbours assured that he inherits the whole house of Elimelek. In this reading, the women of the neighbourhood left Orpah out in the cold.

Pasifikation

The taking(s) of a son at the end of the narrative 'returns' the attention to the taking of daughters (Ruth and Orpah to be wives for the sons of Naomi) at the beginning. In the mindsets of Pasifika natives, reflected in Donet's artwork above (Figure 9.1), taking sons and daughters amounts to the taking of 'roots' (which has to do with land and inheritance). In the current context of Pasifika, this is what climate change is doing. Climate change is taking over, and taking away, the roots of Pasifika.

Climate change is not just taking our land and inheritance, waters and resources, but it is taking our sons and daughters as well. One of the challenges for us, with respect to the tasks of bible study, is to read biblical texts in ways that help us keep our sons and daughters, hear the hidden transcripts, and unhide subjects that sacred traditions ignore and forget. In that spirit, i close with a cluster of questions that were critical for the PBS groups: To where else might Ruth have disappeared? Did she die? Did she quietly disappear behind the narrative, to be co-parent to Obed? Did she return to Moab?

Takeaway

1 What function does a whakapapa (family tree, lineage) serve in your community?
2 What does a list of names from a whakapapa to which you do not belong do to you?
3 How has your mind changed or remained the same about this narrative?

Prompts for further talanoa

1 Joanne Palmer, 2014, 'The three faces of Ruth', *Jewish Standard*, https://jewishstandard.timesofisrael.com/the-three-faces-of-ruth/, accessed 5.5.21.
2 John E. Anderson, 2010, 'Jacob and the Divine Trickster: A Theology of Deception and YHWH's Fidelity to the Ancestral Promise', Dissertation, Baylor University, Waco, https://baylor-ir.tdl.org/bitstream/handle/2104/8017/John_Anderson_PhD.pdf?sequence=1&isAllowed=y, accessed 5.5.21.

Notes

1 In biblical literature, women and sex are presented as a means for fulfilling the patriarchal agenda of reproducing and multiplying sons to carry the family and tribal lineages. This agenda is shared by other patriarchal cultures.
2 As far as character replacements go, Tamar gave birth to two sons, Zerah and Perez, in the place of Er and Onan (sons of Bathshua).
3 It is not clear how she made this decision, because circumcision was an Egyptian ritual as well.

4 This brings to mind one of the practices that mark independence. Following independence, many nations, towns and streets were renamed. However, the legacies of coloniality continue.

5 In the next and final bible study, i will argue that the male narrator could not erase the impact of feminization upon this narrative.

6 That journey is echoed in the journey of Elimelek and Naomi, with their two sons, to Moab. They too were seeking refuge because of a famine in the land.

7 The NRSV avoids this discord by rendering γεννάω (to beget, to bring forth) with 'father of'.

8 Compare with Nitzevet Bat Adael, mother of David, who is only named in the Talmud.

PART 3

Interpretation Prolongs

10

Reading humilities

> I have argued that the biblical story is an unfinished story: it invites its own continuation in history, it resists the covers of our Bibles and writes itself on the pages of the earth. On these grounds, it is legitimate to hold that various biblical reader-actors from different moments in history should illumine the meaning and implications of the text for us. (Dube, 2014, p. 142)

The book of Ruth ends with a list of names intended to close the narrative down. The roll call ushers the future in. The end.[1]

However, as shown in the bible study on Ruth 4.18–22 (see Chapter 9), the names function as prompts that hold the narrative open for more talanoa (see also Chapter 2). The narrator's name dropping did not shut the narrative up. On the other hand, the 'big talanoa' berthed by the Ruth narrative breaks free from the name calling of the narrator to find 'its own continuation in history' (Dube, 2014). In other words, the big talanoa does not end at the end of the narrative.

In a sublime way, the Ruth narrative does not let itself end. There is something cleaving and 'returning' in the narrative, which even death cannot part nor end. For example, death ended the life of Mahlon (Ruth 1.5) but death did not (de)part his presence from the narrative. Actually, one of the drives of the narrative was to keep Mahlon – through his name, rights, inheritance and widow – alive (4.10). Mahlon survived his death. He lived on, despite the onset of death, thanks to the tradition and process of kinship redemption. Death does not have the final say in this narrative. Put in terms of the parameters of this work, *losing ground* is not the final word nor the final world.

In a humbling way, the Ruth narrative unfolds on a path that was taken by other biblical narratives that do not end where they are supposed to end or are expected to end. The garden story, for instance, does not end at Genesis 3 but extends into Genesis 4 (see Chapter 3). YHWH's words and curses did not bring the end to, or close down, that formative narrative. On a broader biblical scale, the narratives of the judges extend into the books of Samuel (see Chapter 1 of this work, and Jobling, 1998) and the Bible's first story extends from Genesis to Kings (see Fewell and Gunn, 1992). Ruth is therefore in good company, among biblical narratives in which the final word does not come at the end.[2] These narratives live on, and they 'return' at other narratives and in other events.

The Ruth narrative has the capacity to prolong itself and problematize its closure, to free and release itself from the end that the narrator has written. I appreciate this capacity as one of the impacts of scripturalization.[3] Here, scripturalization is about prolonging and recovering rather than about authorizing and shutting things up at 'the end'.

End

In a haunting way, talanoa (as interpretation event, in the bible studies above) helped carry the die-hard Ruth narrative further and further, on and on, thereby upending what the narrator wrote and stepping through 'the covers of our Bibles' (Dube, 2014). To be clear, our Bibles have many covers – historical, literary, narrative, theological, ideological, and many hidden covers. In the PBS events, the big talanoa birthed by the Ruth narrative broke through the many covers, physical and metaphorical, of our Bibles. In this regard, talanoa is a form of scripturalization.

Readers, too, operate under many covers. In my case, they include my commitments – to talanoa, to the marginalized, to queer, to dirt, to tomorrow, to climate, to Pasifika, to natives, and to more. At this juncture, i metaphorically string my covers together into a lei (garland) and symbolically put the lei around the character of Orpah. This symbolic lei is given in due respect to a foreign woman character who departed the narrative with no farewell. This symbolic lei is a gesture of recognition that her presence in the narrative was unjustly ended – she was lifted to be a wife, widowed by death, and dumped on the road to go back to uncertainty – but she did not have to consequently lose her ground in the eyes of readers nor in the circles of talanoa.

PBS participants did not let Orpah lose her ground. Orpah stayed with the above bible studies in obvious and sometimes not so obvious ways, and other characters were made to meet her as the ones who departed from the narrative. The last of the characters (made) to depart or disappear was Ruth, whose departure from the story-world in Bethlehem was read as possibility that she may have returned to Moab – where she could meet up with Orpah. If Ruth were to carry back the symbolic lei metaphorically strung (above) and place it on Orpah, Ruth could embrace and recognize Orpah in Pasifika-style. On the wings of talanoa, possibilities are many.

Interruption: my symbolic lei is obviously a figment of my imagination, which i strung up with the help of a native muse who was high on talanoa. To suggest that the Ruth narrative did not end that way in the biblical world, which *must* have been historical, would be a fair response to – and rejection of – my musings.

My imagination is nothing close to the biblical narrative, which must have been strung up with the help of an ancient muse. That the figment of my imagination is nothing close to the narrative world created with the help of a muse (puns intended) is a fair assessment.

What a text makes to disappear, readers can bring forth; in the same way, in the reverse, readers can ignore or hide what texts proclaim and stress. These readerly conducts are practised in all the harvesting fields and threshing floors of biblical studies, but my motivation in this work is talanoa as a reading event. The PBS bible studies presented interpretations that talanoa with and around, and as a consequence *Pasifikate*, the Ruth narrative. Each bible study invited further talanoa, and each bible study furthered, extended and prolonged the big narrative. In talanoa, there is no hard and fast line between text (story) and interpretation (telling, conversation). They interweave. Upend. And extend.

The linear frame of mind according to which a story or event starts at one place and ends at another does not collaborate well in the world of talanoa. Talanoa entangles (knots) and unfolds, and then comes around; talanoa encourages pikopiko iku mai. It may break and rest, until it catches another draft upon which it furthers the narrative. The emphasis here is with taking the narrative further, compared to injecting meanings into the text (or eisegesis). In this regard, the text is talanoa rather than a container of meanings to be unpacked or extracted (as imagined by traditional biblical scholarship).

Invitation

The PBS insights in the previous chapters come with an invitation to reconsider the 'ends' of biblical studies (to mimic Avalos, 2007). The privileging of the written text, of the author's meanings or of the narrator's agenda, do not allow normal readers (like the PBS participants) to 'go native' (see Chapter 2). However, the PBS bible studies show that there is much to gain by engaging normal and native knowledges (roots) and ways (routes). Natives of Pasifika and natives of other (is)lands can further the ends of biblical texts and consequently enrich the practices and the ends of biblical studies.

In a sublime way, the PBS bible studies did not let those who depart from the narrative (e.g. Orpah) disappear. Nor let the ignored (e.g. Zerah) and minoritized (e.g. the redeemer) disappear in the erasures attempted in the interests of the patriarchal agenda. On the one hand, the PBS bible studies mimic the narrative's spirit and drive for redemption, for extending and for keeping alive (some of the forgotten characters). On the other hand, the PBS bible studies resist the other agenda of the narrative – to forget and write off some characters. Both the mimicking and the resisting, which together expose double standards in the narrative, collaborate to upend the narrative. Who knows, if upending the narrative is not what the narrator wants in the end.

Humility

With what attitudes or moods does one read biblical texts? I raise this question because it is one thing to *out* one's perspectives and own one's contexts and something different to catch one's moods (attitudes, personalities) shaping one's interpretation. The invitation to reconsider the ends of biblical texts and of biblical studies is an opportunity to check the moods with which one interprets biblical texts, including the Ruth narrative, and to consequently read humbly.

The drive to determine and fix (rigidify, heal) the limits and meanings of biblical texts does not respect the capacity of texts to end *and then* reach beyond itself. A healthier drive is to be humble and let the texts escape their own limits, and thus lose their own grounds, as well as the limits that one's reading places upon the text. This drive can serve readers in the halls of biblical criticism as well as readers in the circles of bible studies, among both experts and normal people.

Obligation

Confession time: when i began publishing through English mediums and platforms, i could not resist the missionary temptation to offer reflections and readings *from and for* Pasifika (contexts, peoples, cultures). I knew then, and admitted early, that Pasifika is more than my home(is)land of Tonga, and that Tonga is more than the views that i prefer. In those regards, this work is partial remittance for my missionary and colonialist indulgences.

This work privileges the insights and wisdoms of Pasifika natives rather than (re)presents those insights as illustrations for foreign and western ideas and concepts, and the overall work affirms that Pasifika is a collective. We are altogether small, but we are many. This is to say that, in my humble opinion, readings and theologies that claim to be of or from Pasifika need to be in collaboration and to embody communitarianism (see also Havea, 2021c). This work performed both – collaboration and communitarianism – without falling into the trap of the politics of identity, to individualize (e.g. by naming who said what). The wisdom of one person is the wisdom of the collective, and in our case the collective includes the departed ancestors, the tomorrow people, together with fanua (land), moana (sea), lagi (sky) and lolofonua (underworld). This collective and communitarian approach was urged by, and agreed with, the PBS participants. In a Pasifika way, i serve as their orator.

Reminder: the obvious – no orator is isolated nor innocent. This assessment applies to me as well as to each of the PBS participants who participated and contributed *also* on behalf of someone else or for some other cause or subject. We are few altogether, but we are connected. And we all are orators.

This is not to say that we do not understand or exercise ownership – for example, ownership over land, resources, properties, ideas, and other island matters – which has been used to justify our dispossession.[4] The issue here is not ownership but privatization, whereby an individual lays claim to what belongs to, and is owned by, the collective (e.g. nuu, whānau, hapu).

In the realms of biblical studies, my confession is a way of saying that interpretation is served well with a dish of obligations. This assertion flies in the face of objectivism and the presumption of innocence. In the courts of law, these positions – objectivism and innocence – privilege the culprit(s) to the aggravation of the victim(s); in the halls of interpretation, these positions are protective shields for privileged readers; and in the circles of talanoa, these positions are out of touch (see Chapter 11).

In the circles of talanoa, no reader can be objective or innocent. We engage in talanoa because we are committed and obliged, but we differ in what our obligations are. Moreover, in Pasifika, we are obliged to be in talanoa because talanoa keeps us ticking.

Invitation

Over the years, a cohort of liberation and cultural critics have introduced a rainbow of invitations and keywords into the auditoriums of biblical criticism: Preferential option for the poor. In whose interest? Womanist. Mujerista. Margins. Voices. From this place. From other places. Third World. Solidarity. Resistance. Protest. Indecent. Queer. Decolonize. Indigenous. Minority. Migrant. Black. Subaltern. Buffalo. Minjung. Earth. Water. Islander. And many more. And most important to note here, there is still room for more to be added into the high-ceiling auditoriums of biblical criticism. There is room for more is the spirit of talanoa.

Under that long rainbow of keywords (above), this work is an invitation for readers to be (re)committed and (re)obliged *but* not to the traditional-, to the pālagi- or to the main-lines. Rather, the invitation here is to (re)commit and (re)oblige to normal characters and subjects like widows (such as Orpah), orphans (like Obed), dispossessed (like the redeemer), silenced (like Bathshua), ignored (like the crowd at the gate, and the women in town), and many more.

The PBS bible studies named and gave attention to some of the normal characters and subjects in the Ruth narrative, but their talanoa are bigger than the readings proposed in the chapters above. I will come back at some point and twist their talanoa further, and upend the readings offered herein, but simply note here that being committed and obliged is ongoing. On and on. Further and further.

Humility

For normal people, donors and advocates are helpful in situations where they are losing grounds. Donors and advocates provide support, alternatives and lifelines. But they can also patronize and burden people, and in extreme cases some donors and advocates take advantage of their clients. Some donors and advocates help themselves to the resources for – and of – normal people. Those ones also prey on resources and on lives.

In a way, readers function as donors and advocates for the text, and for the communities of readers. And the same temptations apply to readers – to patronize, burden and prey upon the text and communities of both experts and normal people. Hence the invitation to (re)commit and (re)oblige comes with a three-part reminder: to read justly, to read with loving care, and to read humbly.

Release

Talanoa, whose wings spread wider than Boaz's wings, permit PBS participants to introduce characters in the Ruth narrative to other biblical and native characters, and on several occasions the PBS participants gave me homework to do. One of my pieces of homework (from the migrant PBS group at Adelaide) was to introduce Ruth, after she disappeared from the narrative, to Job's wife. What might they say to each other?

Needless to say, i have not finished that homework. I have done a lot of thinking about it but at this point, like other students and learners, i have not finished my homework. For now. When i do, when i feel that i can tell (talanoa) the upending and interweaving of the stories (talanoa) of these biblical women characters, i will take my homework back for further conversation (talanoa) with the PBS communities. And i expect them to share their responses and talanoa, in which they will affirm and disagree with elements in my reading.

I share my failure here because that was one of the many instances when i lost my ground in the PBS gatherings. Job's wife was not in my plan, and i had to release my illusions of control over that particular PBS gathering because one participant wanted to hear her story in the disappearance of Ruth.

Reality check: release is never complete. In Pasifika, one can never be cut off completely from one's obligations or from one's relations. In fact, keeping one connected is the key function of kaupapa (ways, routes) and whakapapa (heritage, roots) – they keep one connected to places and peoples, to traditions and aspirations, in the past, the present, and the future.

In terms of the Ruth narrative, the list of names at the end releases the big talanoa from the narrator's telling (talanoa) and in another way the list of names connects the narrator's story (talanoa) with other biblical narratives. In this regard, 'release' does not mean a complete breaking away. This is somewhat similar to the release of Israel from Egypt in the exodus story. Israel is released from Pharaoh and Egypt and ended up being bound to YHWH and Moses in the wilderness. From there, the narrative extended. Further and further.

Release is not an end in itself. It is never complete. Along the same lines, losing ground is never complete.

For the Adelaide session in question, my plan was to learn what the participants thought Ruth would say to Orpah; but one participant's wish was to hear what Ruth might say to Job's wife. I lost my ground also because i went to learn from a group of Pasifika migrants, but one participant wanted to learn from me. And as she explained her case, her wish was not hers alone. Her community was behind her. She was their orator.

And so, our talanoa turned to Job's wife. That migrant community felt sorry for Job's wife because she did not have a name and because Job scolded her, shouted her down, in order to shut her up. She suffered the same loss as Job. She was the mother of the crushed children and co-head of the household, so she would have had to face the families of their murdered servants. Job should have seen that she too suffered for naught.

She gave Job a reasonable suggestion, given that God did not protect their upright family. She had good reasons to curse God, but Job shut her up:

> Then his wife said to him 'Do you still persist in your integrity? Curse God, and die.' But he said to her, 'You speak as any foolish woman would speak. Shall we receive the good at the hand of God, and not receive the bad?' (Job 2.9–10a, NRSV)

This gives her a good reason to curse Job as well. How would Ruth enter and upend the talanoa of Job's wife is the homework that i have not finished.

No matter in which Bible – the Hebrew Bible or the Christian Bible (see Chapter 1) – one prefers to read the Ruth narrative, it lies in the same 'covers' with the blurb of one and a half verses on Job's wife.[5] So, to ask what these two female characters might say to each other is to release them from their own biblical contexts so that they could witness to what it means to both be in 'the covers of our Bibles' (Dube, 2014). Along these lines, Ruth the Moabite widow might shed some light on the unnamed, most probably foreign, wife of Job.

Invitation

The homework that i was given is more interesting and more engaging than whatever answer or reading that i will find and offer later. This leads me to a humbling invitation to fellow interpreters: give up the desire, and obsession, of providing answers to every question or challenge.[6]

I extend this invitation particularly to readers who might be driven by the urge to find answers and resolutions to the questions and challenges that biblical texts or other readers pose. Let some of the questions and challenges stand, and talanoa may thus continue. Put another way, release and come to terms with the illusions of control (see Havea, 2003).

Humility

The above invitation is not new, and not strange. Most students of theology and hermeneutics have, at some point in their journey, reached the awareness that the questions that one formulates are as – if not more – important as the answers that one discovers. In that light, the above invitation is a humble reminder: to have the courage to let go of plans, to release control, and to humbly entertain what might at first sound like irrelevant questions. In other words, do not be afraid of losing ground.

I often wonder how the biblical narrators would, if they were to return from their resting places, react to the interpretations that centuries of readers have proposed? Might they be interested in agreeing or disagreeing? Might they chuckle, because they are not as controlling? Might they be upset, because interpreters have not gone far enough? Might they reorient and retell, because they want to go further and further?

Earth

Because the PBS participants did not want Ruth to disappear before the narrative that bears her name ends, we imagined her going into other narratives and places where she might engage and be engaged by other characters. Where else could Ruth have gone?[7]

There were many answers, mainly because Pasifika natives have creative (and sometimes dirty) imaginations, but one of the answers that was shared across the PBS groups was that she could have gone back to moana (sea) and fanua (land, earth). These two realms are interconnected – one cannot think of one without also thinking of the other; in Pasifika terms, one cannot go back to one without also going to the other. If Ruth had gone back to moana and fanua, she would have indeed stepped over the narrator's lines and passed through the Bible's covers. She would have thereby given support for Dube's assertion that a biblical story 'writes itself on the pages of the earth'.

Interjection: Climate change is part of Earth's talanoa in response to what humans have written on its pages. The climate crisis requires that we read what Earth has written as well as account for what human civilizations – which includes the Holy Bible – have razed on the pages of the earth.

To be fair, one should not expect to find the good, and not find the bad also, in what Bible stories have written on the pages of the earth. Some of the Bible stories are not life-affirming nor are they justice-affirming, and they have accordingly written death and injustice on the pages of the earth (cf. White Jnr, 1967).

In an obvious way, the PBS groups did not want the main female character to bow out to the male narrator's agenda. This is an example of normal readers looking for, and finding, hidden transcripts in the fractures of public transcripts (here: biblical narrative). The PBS bible studies demonstrated that, with some promptings, hidden transcripts can break through hegemonic lines to provide opportunities for dissension and resistance.

The PBS groups did not want Ruth to be shut off (like Job's wife), and their motivation was wanting to resist the gender discrimination behind the narrative (qua public transcript). And in wanting Ruth to return to the moana and fanua, they set stepping stones for biblical critics who are responsive to the calls of critical and cultural theories: reading for hidden transcripts is a platform for thinking and reading intersectionally (see Yee, 2020). In biblical studies, reading intersectionally requires interrogating the Bible and their interpretations (read: writings on the pages of Earth) for evidence of biases and discriminations due to race, gender and class. Gale Yee emphasized those three fields of struggle and called attention to the 'etceteras' as well.

The foregoing theoretical connections would be nonsense to and irrelevant for the PBS groups. Their main interest was focused on Ruth (character, narrative) walking on to the pages of moana and fanua which, obviously, are not 'etceteras'. Moana and fanua are vital and unavoidable.

Invitation

The invitation is thus clear: read for hidden transcripts and be open to finding moana and fanua in the fractures of intersectionality. In the context of climate change, this invitation is urgent. If we do not seek moana and fanua, we may lose their interests under the waves of capitalism.

But seeking alone is not enough. We must also find. For if we do not find moana and fanua, we lose the ground of everything that we are. However, seek not because of who or what we are, but because of the ground that we are losing.

Humility

Finding does not automatically result from seeking. We may seek but not find, so we need to work hard at it. In the context of climate change, ecological critics have encouraged shedding our default anthropocentric (human-centred, human-preferring) values and converting them into ecojustice practices instead.[8] To shed anthropocentrism requires humility on our part as readers and as seekers.

In terms of moana and fanua, how can we not find them? On islands, even the blind can find moana and fanua.

Prompts for further talanoa

The painting by Tenene Nelu (Figure 10.1), a native artist living in Funafuti (Tuvalu), is of a female Jesus. The challenges that this work presents for Christology and contextual theology have been discussed by Maina Talia (2021), and i offer here another reading of this native text.

I must first confess, however, that Jesus is not the reason why this work appeals to me. Rather, i am obliged by the etceteras in the painting and i, stepping over the agenda of the artist (which Talia presented in his essay), swab the female Jesus in the canoe with other (re)migrants to the shores of Tuvalu

Figure 10.1: Tenene Nelu, Iesu fafine *(female Jesus) (2017).*
Used with permission of the artist.

and, by extension, Pasifika and other lands. I am drawn to this
work because it depicts arrival and crossing over the pages of
the earth.

Further and further: moana and fanua are two of the pages of
the earth, and climate trauma is witness that they have been
ravaged and charred by what human civilizations have written
on them. The sky (lagi) and the underworld (lolofonua) are
two other pages of the earth, and both are deep but not endless.

The painting in Figure 10.1 is about the pages of the earth.
The setting is the meeting of moana, fanua and lagi (sky).
Lolofonua (underworld) is not visible, but everything depicted
in this work (according to this reading) relates to lolofonua.
    The waves roll gently on to fanua, and moana extends behind
the canoe towards the setting sun across the lagi. A native man
wades out (at the centre right edge of the image) towards the
canoe, but it is not clear whether he is there to push the canoe
away or to receive it. A group (at the bottom left) perform a

fātele (Tuvaluan dance) from on shore, suggesting that they are there to welcome the traveller, whose outstretched arms suggest that she was surfing the canoe on a wave.

On the surface, Nelu's work connects moana, fanua and lagi. The scenery is calm, and the atmosphere is joyous, displaying the paradisiac kinds of situation that tourists and foreigners associate with islands.

In native eyes, Nelu's work brings pain and trouble. The setting sun is going to *pulotu*, the home of native deities, thus bringing lolofonua to the surface. The cutting rays of the sun across the reddening sky forecast a very hot next day. Hot sun burns native skins as well. The black noddy birds (*gogo*) on the horizon are seen in Tuvalu as unlucky birds: if they fly pass, and cry over, a group of people at their evening meal, that is a sign that someone in the community will die in the foreseeable future. Upon death, pulotu (lolofonua) is the first stop.

As the gogo are about to pass over the canoe and the dancers, one wonders if they are bringing back food for their chicks on land. One cannot rule out the possibility, which is a common reality in these latter days, that the birds are returning with plastic rubbish to feed their chicks. This possibility is invited by the rubbish of human civilization – plastic and aluminium – that litter the point where moana and fanua meet (at the bottom right of the painting).

In the old days in Tuvalu, a person who has done wrong and brought shame was put in a canoe (*paopao*), taken out to the moana where holes are punched into the canoe and then set adrift. This ritual, known as *fakafolau*, was a life sentence. The one who was set adrift in a canoe with holes seldom found his or her way back to land.

But in Nelu's work she does.

What might she and Ruth talk about, at the meeting of moana, fanua, lagi and lolofonua?

Notes

1 In the Hebrew Bible (see Chapter 1), the books of Chronicles function like a roll call intended to mark the end of the collection.

2 To coin another play on words: the end (is in) tends and extends.

3 Canonization determined which books to include in the canon, and thus the canon was closed. But closing the canon does not mean that the processes of interpretation were also closed. In fact, closing the canon marked the opening of interpretation and the processes of scripturalization.

4 For instance, the observation that indigenous people do not relate *as owners* to and over the land has been used to justify the registering of the land for the crown and the removal of indigenous people from that land.

5 The narrative lifetime of Job's wife was one and a half verses long, which was the biblical version of the 2-minute noodles.

6 I quickly add two qualifications: this invitation is not an excuse for not doing my homework – i have failed, and my guilt is extra painful because i have failed normal people – nor should it be taken as justification for others not doing their homework.

7 On the wings of talanoa, the more fitting question is: where could Ruth *not* have gone?

8 The Earth Bible collaborators propose six ecojustice principles – Earth and all its components have intrinsic worth, are interconnected, can raise their voices, according to shared purposes, that require mutual custodianship, and resistance (see Habel, 2011, pp. 1–2) – and push for critical hermeneutics of suspicion, identification and retrieval (Habel, 2011, pp. 8–14).

11

Acclimatizing readings

A hidden story is a story that is in danger of being forgotten because that story is never told and passed on to the next generation. (Champion, 2014, p. 21)

The threshing floor (Ruth 3) and the gate (Ruth 4) were public places where characters acclimatized – that is, they informed and familiarized, as well as influenced, adjusted and negotiated with – one another. At the threshing floor, Ruth induced Boaz to be a redeemer (גאל) and he rushed off early the next morning[1] to become the kinsman (ידע) that Naomi projected (cf. 3.2). In that connection, Ruth – under Naomi's influence – acclimatized Boaz. And then at the gate the following morning, Boaz – under Ruth's influence – acclimatized the unnamed redeemer. Boaz conned the redeemer, and he backed out because he did not want to buy (קנה) Ruth also. Instead, the redeemer told Boaz to redeem (גאל) the right to redeem (גאל) for himself (cf. 4.6). At both public places, acclimatization took place in the sense that one character affected and converted another character. Here, acclimatization may be taken as a figurehead for redemption.

Acclimatization takes place in this reading as well, by telling (talanoa) Ruth 3 with Ruth 4 as parts of an intertwining big story (talanoa). In fact, acclimatization takes place in all readings (interpretations). All readings connect stories and texts, as well as bring out hidden elements in and behind stories and texts. The challenge here, then, is not just to tell hidden stories, as the Indigenous Australian Denise Champion invites, but to also tell hidden aspects of familiar and well-known stories. In this regard, acclimatization is at the heart of storytelling (Champion, 2014) and of reading and interpretation.

My choice of keyword is influenced by the climate matters that shaped the PBS bible studies, but the keyword is in itself suitable for grappling (in all contexts) with the Ruth narrative. There are ongoing attempts to learn, to know, to affect, and also to influence, to negotiate, to convert, over the course of the narrative. I referred to the threshing floor and the gate above, but traces of acclimatization are also present in the events at Moab (e.g. marriage), on the road, in the field and in the town – both within as well as behind[2] the narrative. One may thus read Ruth as a narrative that exhibits the spirit of acclimatization in both public and private places. In other words, to echo my characterization of talanoa, Ruth (book, narrative) carries acclimatization under its wings.

In this final chapter, i join the wings of the Ruth narrative with the wings of talanoa and spread them over the tasks of interpretation. How might this work, which has been intentional about negotiating the genres and practices of biblical study with those of bible study, acclimatize the tasks of biblical interpretation? What matters of concern consequently arise for labourers in the commentary business? What are the signposts to approach and/or avoid? I reflect around these questions over three linked sections: interpretation involves practices that seek to secure texts and meanings; commentary involves practices that re-open texts and multiply readings; acclimatizing readings are practices that diversify and re-wild.

Reading in security

The Ruth narrative gives the impression that the characters shared the same understanding of the plot, and also of one another (see, further, Koosed, 2011). The characters come across, including in the Masoretic Text version, as if they spoke the same language and shared the same values despite their diverse gender, age and cultural-religious conditionings. In other words, the characters are presented as if they were on the same page – the narrator's page.

Narrator's page

There are, however, movements *behind* (see Chapter 1), *within* (see Chapters 3 and 4) and *in front of* (among readers, as in the PBS bible studies) the Ruth narrative that together make the narrator's page move (shift, turn). And in the backwashes and shadows of those movements are attempts to also secure (protect) the narrator's page: these attempts to secure also take place *behind*, *within* and *in front of* the narrative. The attempts to secure meet at and cross over significant points of intersection – for instance, in the figure and legacies of David.[3] In terms of the attempts to secure, i demonstrate with the following ruminations:

Behind: The location of the Ruth narrative in between the books of Judges and Samuel, identified in Chapter 1 as a Christian project, discredits judgeship and justifies kingship. Ruth is thereby a narrative voice that calls (read: prepares the way in the wilderness) for kings to 'return' the favour of the Lord to Israel. The drive of the Christian project was towards a 'son of David' who will come later in the Christian Bible and so, behind the narrator's page, David is like 'Mr So-and-so' whose sandal will be removed and be given to the (real) Christian redeemer.

Within: The Ruth narrative secures David to the house of Judah, from where leadership came in the biblical past. Judah spoke up for and thereby saved Joseph (Gen. 37.26–27), who secured the house of Jacob/Israel in Egypt, and Judah's clan was placed at the front (east) of the camp in the wilderness (Num. 2.3–7) from where they led the march of the refugees from Egypt. At their arrival, Judah was the first to go up against the Canaanites (Judg. 1.2), the people of the land, and later against the Benjaminites (Judg. 20.18), the last in the house of Jacob. Ruth is thus a narrative voice that appoints David to lead and redeem Bethlehem (and, by extension, Israel)[4] against foreign enemies and wicked kinfolk, and consequently unites as well as reserves the seats of leadership (read: messiah) and redemption (read: saviour) for the house of David.

In front of: Within the covers of the Bible, the Ruth narrative opens a gate for any son of David to be a leader and testament (witness) to the Lord's favour and redemption. After the narrator's page ended, many sons of David came forth, stepping over their sisters (2 Sam. 13) and over the sons and daughters of Saul (1 Sam. 14 and 18), and over many pages of biblical history (1—2 Kings, 1—2 Chronicles), to compete for David's throne (see 1 Kings 1–2). In terms of the Christian project, Jesus the son of Mary was the son of David whose kingdom mattered the most, on earth as it is in heaven.

Beyond the covers of the Bible (à la Dube, 2014), Ruth is a narrative voice that inspires migrant and resident readers to vow and deliver companionship and security for minoritized bodies and communities. In the afterlife of the narrative (à la Koosed, 2011), the narrator's page has been a gathering place for all sorts of reading practices and interests.

The relation between *the movements of* and *the attempts to secure* the narrator's page are not spin-offs, one from the other, nor self-evident. Rather, they are products of reading that witness to the capacities of a narrative to convince, hand over, redeem and scripturalize. Here, as i presented in Chapter 10, scripturalization means that a narrative can extend itself as well as authorize the extensions that it makes. But the bottom line is that scripturalization and the extensions – whether in terms of movements or in terms of attempts to secure – are products of reading. In this light, what i refer to as the narrator's page is also the product of reading. The PBS bible studies presented a particular understanding of the narrator's page – the product of reading by native Pasifika people. This is both a confession as well as an invitation, for *outing* other understandings of the narrator's page.

Readers' turn

Many readers approach the narrative with the assumption that they are expected to meet the characters on the narrator's page and to understand the plot according to the narrator's terms. When they do, they receive the ticks of approval from the elders and the witnessing crowd at the gate of their reading communities. And they, so to speak, go to town in order to occupy their acquired inheritance and produce heirs who will keep and tend the narrator's plot and terms.

That the Ruth narrative is found in scriptures has acclimatized readers to interpret it in particular ways. Across the boundaries of *our many Bibles and scriptures* (to push Dube's challenge further along), the narrator – with his characters, plots and terms – and the readers are acclimatized to be *wantoks* ('one-talk[s]'): one-language, one-community, one-destiny, one-everything. This effect is an upshot of scripturalization that, in the context of this chapter, is a figure for acclimatization.

The PBS bible studies show, however, that those impressions and expectations are not as straightforward, as clear, as reasonable or as achievable. The narrator's page and its meanings are slippery. The more determined the PBS interpreters were in trying to secure (determine) the meanings of the text, the more meanings (alternatives) we found. In other words, the narrator's page shifted – stealthily, Ruth might add – under the persuasions of the PBS interpreters. And because interpretation involves ongoing translation of texts and understandings (see also Gaffney, 2009), the PBS interpreters found the narrator's page to be shifty also. The narrator's page often played hard to catch and shifted away from our attempts to secure (lock) it. These features and observations would easily apply to other communities of readers outside of Pasifika. What is true within Pasifika is also true outside of it. The narrator's page shifts under, and sometimes shifts away from, the cajoles of all interpreters.

On the PBS-constructed narrator's page, Naomi (re)turned to the plot on several occasions – when she departed from Moab, when she chased Orpah home, when she sent Ruth to the threshing floor, and when she began to nurse Obed – in and for her interests, and security. She was widowed but she was not desperate, and Ruth and the neighbourhood women participated in securing her security. So did Boaz. And with the disappearance of Ruth and Boaz towards the end of the narrative, Naomi again became the sole survivor of her family. But this time with a nursing child upon her bosom, given to her by the women, witnessed by the narrator and celebrated by the PBS interpreters. On the narrator's page, according to the PBS interpreters, Naomi was in security.

Ruth's 'disappearance' was a shifty subject for the PBS interpreters. She might have gone somewhere else, outside the narrator's plot, even beyond the pages of our scriptures, and several options were presented in the foregoing pages. And with each option, the narrator's page (was) shifted.

But with Boaz's disappearance, there were only two options for the PBS interpreters. Boaz might have died, along the lines proposed in rabbinic circles. This option, however, was not popular among the PBS interpreters. Boaz did not have to die behind the narrative. If Ruth could have lived on, so could Boaz. The more appealing option was for Ruth to disappear but leave Boaz with Obed.[5] The women gave Obed to Naomi, and the PBS interpreters expected Boaz to have come along with his son. According to the PBS interpreters, therefore, they would have formed an alternative 'family of choice' – Obed, Boaz, Naomi (compare Mona West, 2020).

On the narrator's page, Mahlon's inheritance shifted from Mr So-and-so to Boaz, to Naomi, to David. But the PBS readers turned the narrator's page away from David: Boaz is revived (redeemed) and Obed (the inheritance) brought him to become a restorer of life and a nourisher of Naomi's old age (4.15). The redeemer and the inheritance together put Naomi in security, and the PBS interpreters thereby made Naomi occupy the narrator's page.

From another slant, this PBS option allows for seeing this event as a biblical version of a 'disappearing father' – the father ends up with the child at another woman's house. This is not the final turn, of course. For as long as there are readers, the narrator's page will turn. As long as there are readers, there will be more acclimatization and the losing of ground.

In security

Not all readers are creatures of scriptures, or residents in the textualized worlds of our Bibles. If all readers were, we might be able to secure the narrator's page according to the narrator's terms.

From another slant, not all readers are open to the oralizing turns of talanoa – which involves fishing around and playing hide and seek (a favoured form of play for impoverished Pasifika children) with the narrative. By introducing insights from the oralized world of talanoa in textualized form, this work is a platform where these two readerly leanings may negotiate. It is also a platform for negotiating the drives and biases of the labourers of 'biblical study' and 'bible study' (see Chapter 1). Here also, my declarations are confessions as well as invitations.

As in talanoa, reading is not an exercise in finding and telling everything. No one knows everything and no one can tell everything about a story or text. Reading can only be particular and partial (pun intended), so there will be remainders that remain untold.[6] Sadly, the untold remainders are 'in danger of being forgotten' (Champion, 2014) when they are not told and passed on to future generations. Sadly also, some of the remainders are not even noticed, or deemed worthy of being noticed and discussed, by many tellers/readers in the current generation. This work is accordingly encouragement for readers to notice, to tell and pass on untold remainders to future generations.

Commentary business

The commentary genre has enticed a crowd of witnesses. Each commentary seeks to secure the text and at the end each also exhibits the slipperiness (un-security, unruliness, wildness) of the text. The more enduring (read: privileged and connected) among the authors update their commentaries and release new editions, revisions and expansions, and as a consequence they witness to the ongoing negotiation between *seeking to secure the text* with the *un-security of the text*. This aspect of the commentary business is also in danger of being forgotten because it is not told and passed on to future generations. My allegations here apply to commentaries on Ruth as well as to commentaries on other books of the Bible.

The commentary business continues to thrive with its products lasting for several seasons, thanks to the inputs of print and publication. The chances to forget are thus reduced, but the privilege of being remembered goes to only a few among the elites (so-called literates). There are thus two elitist traits of the commentary business relating to who are remembered, and who may remember (namely, consumers and readers who can understand the rhetoric and expectations of the commentary genre). With these two traits in mind, i talanoa around two effects of the commentary business: to remember, to forget.

Remember

Ruth has also been read as an etiological narrative that explains how a Moabite woman came to be a great-grandmother for King David. The etiological narrative is uncomplicated: Naomi brought Ruth out of Moab, and Boaz brought Ruth into the house of Judah, the house that David came to inherit. To that i add that Ruth was a deserving addition. She was determined to go all the way and she worked very hard to establish and secure a home for herself and for Naomi (two widows and (re)migrants) in Bethlehem, Judah. This involved Boaz redeeming Ruth as a bonus to the inheritance of her late husband Mahlon. Boaz is thereby remembered as the redeemer of Mahlon and the keeper of the house of Judah, the primary guardian and beneficiary of the Hebrew Bible's memory. Boaz is the one who set Ruth up in the line for leadership over Judah. The etiological narrative remembers Naomi and Boaz as primary movers in positioning Ruth along the path that leads to David, and the Christian project reduced the chances for missing this point (or: investing in a different account).

The commentary business profits from remembering characters like Ruth and the roles that supporting characters like Naomi and Boaz played in depositing her in the memory banks of Judah. The same narrative has been read according to other points of reference and interest – for example, loyalty, love, marriage, courage, womanhood, ethics, theology – but all of these exegetical labours employ the tools, and scavenge for transcripts, of memory. In these regards, the commentary business is heavily (in)vested with the fruits of memory – remembering.

In my withdrawals (pun intended) from the commentary business, i have found the insights that cultural critics offer – for example, by hyphenating the term 're-membering' – most encouraging and profitable. In my mind, re-membering stands for four events that arise in response to the plights of dis*member*ment: (1) for recalling and memorializing the dismembered (lest they are forgotten), (2) for assembling and mending the dis-membered (according to how they were), (3) for gathering and moulding the dismembered into an alternative form or body (different from how they were), and (4) for reviving and redeeming the re-membered memory or body. The first two events have been circulated widely as connotations of re-membering (see, e.g., Greene, 1991; Tengan, 2008; Dokotum, 2013), and i will briefly reflect on the last two.

Whereas the second event requires one to have an idea of how the dismembered used to be, so that one may put it back together accordingly, the third event does not require such pre-knowledge. The second event is the main currency in the commentary business, while the third event is the wind in the wings of talanoa. In the third event, the labour of re-membering is not chained to the past or to a blueprint that needed to be followed. On the other hand, the third event has room for membering an alternative form or body with the gathered elements. With respect to the commentary business, the second event is a privilege that is not available to most normal and native people. But the third event is inviting and liberating, allowing the labour of re-membering to extend into a second harvest (as in Ruth 2.23; see Chapter 6).

In the Ruth narrative, examples of the third event include Ruth not going back to her mother's house as Naomi ordered, Ruth having a dig at Naomi when she came back from gleaning in the field, Ruth pushing Boaz to become a redeemer at the threshing floor, and the women giving Obed to be a son for Naomi. These third events, among others, are discussed in the PBS bible studies. And, needless to say, the PBS bible studies are examples of the third event. In this regard, the third event is in the Ruth narrative as well as in the PBS world and worldview.

The fourth re-membering event – reviving and redeeming the re-membered – is one of the key drives of the Ruth narrative. This was also one of the drives of the PBS gatherings, for what use is talanoa on and around the Ruth narrative if in the end the narrative withers and dries up? And what use is conducting bible studies if in the end native Pasifika communities wither and dry up? These questions are not in the fine print of the commentary business, but they keep the commentary business alive. As talanoa requires gathering communities to keep talanoa (story, telling, conversation) alive and relevant, as well as give the communities food for thoughts (read: keep them fed and funded), so does the commentary business require communities of readers to keep it funded and operational, lucrative and enticing.

The labour of re-membering is at the heart of the commentary business, and the above ruminations push the envelope away from the privileges of experts (which is endorsed by the second event) into the wisdom (third event) of communities (fourth event). This work leans behind this push and thus joins other envelope- and limits-pushing communities, including queer and womanist critics (see Townes, 2016), already inside the high ceilings of the commentary business. We use different tools, but we all are labouring for re-membering.

Forget

The first (recall and memorialize) and second (assemble and mend) events of re-membering work against the loss of memory. Re-membering as a countering venture is close to the heart of the Ruth narrator: Elimelek and his sons died in Moab away from their homeland and, as far as the narrative is concerned, they were like Zelophehad – they died for their own sins, and they were not involved in any rebellion (Num. 27.3). Their names should not be forgotten, and redeeming their inheritance is one way to counter the loss of their memory. Indeed, they were redeemed and re-membered in the narrative; but with a stealthy turn, their redemption involved the third and fourth events of re-membering noted above – for the sake of someone else.

Reading Ruth as an etiological narrative for David shatters the narrator's counter against the potentials for memory loss. The re-membering of David (a layer added later to the narrative) leads to the forgetting of Elimelek and his sons (one of whom was the main subject in the exchange of the right to redeem at the gate). In this connection, three qualms arise: first, that there is intertwining of the labours of re-membering with the foul of forgetting; second, that both re-membering and forgetting are selective processes; third, that forgetting is not fully innocent or accidental. I will briefly locate these qualms in the shadows of the commentary business.

First, there is intertwining between re-membering and forgetting. Re-membering Ruth intertwines with forgetting Orpah; re-membering Naomi intertwines with forgetting the mother(s) of Ruth and Orpah; re-membering Boaz intertwines with forgetting Mr So-and-so; re-membering the house of Judah intertwines with forgetting the house of Elimelek; re-membering Obed intertwines with forgetting Mahlon; and so on. There are other factors involved in each of these referents, but my emphasis here is that there is intertwining between re-membering and forgetting. And in terms of the drive of this chapter and the frame for this work, there is intertwining between acclimatization and losing ground.

The intertwining of re-membering with forgetting is a hall-mark of the commentary business as well, in so far as the commentary genre requires authors to stay on the narrator's 'page'. It does not matter here what the narrator's page looks like or says; rather, what matters here is that faithful commentary authors re-member and forget as/what the narrator's page does.

Second, re-membering and forgetting are selective processes. Re-membering privileges and forgetting discriminates, and to borrow the rhetoric of association drawn in previous pages, what is true on the narrator's page is also true on the pages of commentaries. This will be the case for as long as commentary authors buy into the privileges and discriminations that they see and (under)write on the narrator's page.[7]

Third, and more controversial of my qualms, is the charge that forgetting is not fully innocent or accidental. I agree that there are slip-ups and blunders in the faculties of memory but given the longevity of the Bible and the long history of biblical redaction and translation, along with the increasing wealth of knowledge in the commentary business, any remnants of forgetting – especially in interpretations – are not fully innocent or accidental. In other words, in the commentary business, forgetting – and, by extension, not noticing and not seeing – are intentional and political.

Each of the PBS bible studies identified instances of forgetting (including hidings, disappearances) in the Ruth narrative – from forgetting the neighbours and helpers at the beginning of the narrative all the way to the disappearances of Ruth, Boaz and Mahlon at the end of the narrative, and many other forgotten characters and interests in between. In many of these instances, we were not sure if the narrator was innocent or not. But for us as readers, we cannot be innocent if we continue to forget (read: ignore) those. The least that we can do is to *call out* the politics of forgetting – which underwrite the losing of grounds – on the narrator's page.

Losing innocence

Re-membering and forgetting, trademarks of the commentary business, are selective but not innocent. Labourers in the commentary business are neither comprehensive nor innocent, and many would not argue against my confession despite their laborious efforts to address and explain as many – if not all – of the issues and questions that they find in the text. We know that we cannot cover all the bases, but we give it our best efforts for the sake of the commentary business.

In the case of the PBS interpreters, they were swift to acknowledge that they did not know even 5 per cent of what could be said about the Ruth narrative. But it was not spontaneous for them to see that they were not innocent in their interpretations. Their default starting position was to assume that they were innocent, as a result mainly of the pious attitudes that they were raised to adopt when they read the Bible – as people of faith they were raised (read: brainwashed) to endorse the Bible, which their communities revere as holy. But it did not take much stirring to get them to 'fess up that they did not endorse everything in the Bible and pretending to be innocent (and pious), as they learned in church, made them look naïve (a few spoke of looking like hypocrites). And as a consequence, without being introduced to the insights of Paul Ricoeur on naivetés, several PBS interpreters joked about how participating in bible study helped them 'lose their innocence' (in several Pasifika languages, the same expression has sexual overtones – 'lose their virginity'): they are not naïve but natives, and their churches benefit from making them look like naïve hypocrites.

The following five stirring points worked with the PBS interpreters, and i present them here as our offerings to labourers in the commentary business who are anxious about the dynamics of re-membering, the politics of forgetting, and the illusions of innocence. These stirring points are opportunities for acclimatization across the divide between biblical studies and bible studies.

Talanoa

First, it helped the PBS interpreters to read the Ruth narrative in the world, and with the worldview, of talanoa. The Ruth narrative is not (1) a revealed and traditioned story (talanoa) with (2) clear and resolute meanings to be harvested by readers and (story)tellers (talanoa); rather, (3) the shape, flow and meanings of the narrative are gleaned and redeemed upon the conversations (talanoa) among gathered communities. In this formulation, the commentary business stops at the second step – at reporting the findings (harvests) by experts. This work is thus an invitation for labourers in the commentary business to go all the way to the third step of talanoa – to the gleanings by and with normal people.

The Ruth narrative (and thus other scriptural texts) antici-pates the third event of talanoa – conversation, storyweaving. Readers are expected to read, to reflect, to retell and to re-mem-ber the narrative, but also to forget (something about) the narrative if there are no consequent retellings (à la Champion, 2014), conversations or storyweavings. The textual constitu-tions of scriptures reduce the chance to forget and at the same time discourage the third talanoa event of conversation and storyweaving. Textuality *protects* scriptural texts from being forgotten, as well as *inhibits* the will to converse around those texts, and to interrogate and queer them. The commentary business inherits the respect that readers give to scriptures, and profits from the protection-and-inhibition forces of textuality.

For the PBS interpreters, the third event of talanoa requires engaging, interrogating and queering the text. Thus, reading the Ruth narrative in the world, and with the mindset, of talanoa *invites* (rather than inhibits) conversation and story-weaving with abundance of time and space for interrogation and queering.

Unhouse

Second, it also helped the PBS interpreters to read with the attitudes of normal people who react to their masters with the courage to seek refuge in a foreign place (e.g. Naomi and

Elimelek and their family at Moab), to push back (e.g. Ruth on the road to Judah), to flatter (e.g. Ruth at Boaz's plantation), to manoeuvre and negotiate (e.g. Ruth at Boaz's feet), to refuse (e.g. Mr So-and-so before the elders), and to take over (e.g. the women of the town, and the patriarchal agenda). These readerly attitudes would be considered indecent by many of the minders and keepers of faith communities, because they lean more towards problematizing rather than corroborating, but the attitudes are rooted in both the Ruth narrative (within the text) as well as in Pasifika's (alter)native cultures (outside of the text). From *within* and *in front of* the Ruth narrative, these readerly attitudes can help to unhouse the master's tools.[8]

To employ these readerly attitudes, to use the traditional categories of the commentary business, is to be both exegetical (because they are found in the text) and eisegetical (because they are found outside of the text). In this connection, to put it more boldly, exegesis involves eisegesis and, similarly, eisegesis involves exegesis. It is un-Pasifika, and unreal, to assume that there is clear separation between exegesis and eisegesis. One is in and a part of the other. One cannot do one without also doing the other.

In the commentary business, the distinction between exegesis and eisegesis is one of the sharp tools in the master's toolbox. But in the world of talanoa, to imagine a distinction and to favour one (exegesis) over against the other (eisegesis) are tools for dismemberment. In this connection, the tools of the commentary business wound the bodies that it seeks to re-member. And so, in my native mind, the solution is simple: if such tools are unhoused then the commentary business can invest in more acclimatizing efforts. Moreover, there are blunt (pun intended) and engaging tools in Pasifika, such as talanoa and art, that serve the concerns and interests at the heart of the commentary business.

Rejection history

Third, it also helped the PBS interpreters to re-member that the Bible has 'histories of rejection' in Pasifika. The Bible came with the Christian mission, first established in Maohi Nui (on the island of Tahiti) by the London Missionary Society in 1797, and so it is a relatively recent (in comparison to native wisdom) arrival to Pasifika. The corroboration of the Christian mission with European colonial powers forced the Bible into Pasifika, and so the PBS communities associated the Bible with occupation, settlement and colonization.

In Pasifika, there are two histories of rejection: first, the Bible is the scripture that justified the rejection of our people and our ways; and second, some of our people rejected the Bible together with the Christian mission (cf. Murray, 1885). Mindful of these histories of rejection, the PBS interpreters found the courage to be critical of the colonialist drives within and behind (manifested, for example, in the patriarchal agenda) the Ruth narrative.

Re-membering the 'histories of rejection' invites reconsidering what is involved in one of the recent arrivals into the commentary business – the study of a text's 'history of reception' (or: reception history). The issue here is with how the term 'reception' is used. To understand 'reception' as referring only to 'acceptance' is problematic because in Pasifika 'rejection' is part of our reception of the Bible. And since there are two forms of rejection, as indicated above, the substance of the study needs to be plural – 'histories' – and hence varied.

Humour

Fourth, it also helped the PBS interpreters to interpret with a sense of (island) humour. Metaphorically speaking, interpretation is not only the flexing of one's muscles over a text but also the tickling of the text to laugh, dance and play. Tickling is one of the ways in which we make the book talk (à la Callahan, 2006) in Pasifika.

When i used the tickling metaphor with the PBS interpreters in Tonga, they reminded me that one can be tickled to the point of farting. And thus, we added, interpretation sometimes bust the text. Hence the more appropriate approach is to tickle the text so that it tricks and resists what we say about it. To interpret is to grab and excite the text, and it helps to realize that the text can slip through one's fingers.

On many occasions, the Ruth narrative escaped the PBS tickling. On those occasions we saw the (ontological) foreignness of the narrative to our native world, the limitations of our (epistemological) worldviews, as well as the (sovereign) liberty of the text to fart at our tickling.

Humility

Fifth, it also helped the PBS interpreters to interpret with humility. This temperament allowed us to identify with the characters, the narrator and the enforcers of the patriarchal agenda *as well as* push away from them. We accordingly were sympathetic to Ruth as a foreigner and a widow, but we were also troubled by her ninja moves – she was not naïve nor innocent when she cornered Boaz. In that connection we felt sorry for Boaz, but he too was not innocent – he used Ruth as a disadvantaging bonus to banter and barter with Mr So-and-so. And with Mr So-and-so, as well as with the narrator, we were both sympathetic as well as troubled.

Humility allowed us to be both warm and cold to the characters, to the plot, to the narrator and to the redeemers of the Ruth narrative. This is not about 'sitting on the fence', but about affirming that one can be on both sides of the fence. In Pasifika, humility is the temperament that encourages us to both connect and disconnect.

Invitation

These stirring points worked with the majority of PBS interpreters, but not with all. Some natives are irritated by talanoa; some natives strive to be masters; some natives prefer to accept rather than reject; some natives have no sense of humour; and some natives have no humility. There is no one-size-fits-all when it comes to natives, as it is with the labourers in the commentary business.

I presented five of the stirring points above with an invitation to the labourers of the commentary business to try them for size and become acclimatized just as the PBS interpreters were. Along with this invitation is another point of stirring: why can't readers who are stirred in these ways, including the normal people of Pasifika, be also accepted as labourers in the commentary business?

Climate control

With appropriate technology one can change – and even control – the temperature inside rooms and houses, but control seems humanly impossible when it comes to the temperature of the planet (outside). This is not to say that we humans should just give up trying. Rather, this is to say that we need to collaborate with other creatures and at least *try* to stabilize the temperature and climate of the planet. This requires us to listen to other creatures, to respect the planet's biodiversity, and to assist in re-wilding the planet. In other words, it is possible to deaccelerate climate change (one of the contexts for this work, see Chapter 1) and consequently stabilize the temperature and climate of the planet; this effort requires human labour to redeem biodiversity and re-wild the planet.

To redeem biodiversity and re-wild the planet, together, is to step back from the modern drives of civilization and development. These drives have had harmful impacts on the planet, extinguished many organisms and life forms, and made the planet less homely for all of its inhabitants. And while human beings might be able to find refuge in rooms and houses, other creatures do not have that privilege.

Truth be told, not all humans have the privilege to step into climate-controlled enclosures; the impoverished members of the human race will be left to the elements together with other species of the animal and plant kingdoms. They all are losing ground, thus making the call for acclimatization – here, through redeeming biodiversity and re-wilding the planet – critical and urgent.

Another context for this work is the relation and interflow between bible study and biblical study (see Chapter 1). On this intersection, i raise two questions that presume that there are lessons that we can learn from the hopeful goal of stabilizing climate change: How might bible study and biblical study harness each other's climate? How might the talanoa of biodiversity and re-wilding work in bible and biblical studies?

Biodiversity

Without using the term, which is technical and foreign to the world and worldviews of the PBS communities, the bible studies show awareness of biodiversity *within*, *behind* and *in front* of the Ruth narrative. For instance, attention was drawn to the two harvests within the narrative; the possibility that there were animals working behind the narrative[9] (to carry loads) was proposed; and insights from the native calendar and seasons helped make sense of the famine and the emotions around it. The earthiness of the narrative was also interpreted in the context of the ancestors and in the intersections of moana, whenua, langi (sky) and lolofonua (underworld). In these regards, the PBS bible studies respected biodiversity without naming it as such. And thus, the technical term 'biodiversity' is an appropriate label for the world and worldviews of natives.

With respect to biodiversity, the PBS bible studies present two invitations for labourers in bible and biblical studies. First, to look for and see biodiversity *within* and *behind* biblical texts. This invitation is not only to metaphorically smell the roses but to also feel the thorns, touch the dirt and notice other creatures and inanimate structures within and behind biblical texts. And second, to bring the talanoa of biodiversity *within* and *behind* biblical texts into 'a big talanoa' with the talanoa of biodiversity *in front* of those texts. This second invitation can also help motivate the commentary business to pass through the impasses of textuality (as noted above).

Re-wilding

Outside of the frames of climate change and biodiversity, but at the intersection of bible and biblical studies, 're-wilding' may also be understood as having to do with, first, reading the 'wild' within and behind the text and, second, reading so that the text becomes 'wild' (again). These connotations, to recall my musings above, invite less of trying to control (or tame) and more of tickling the text.

In the PBS bible studies, the Ruth narrative was read as, and read in, ways that it remained, wild. The wildness of the narrative was not only because of the manoeuvrings of talanoa, but wildness itself was within and behind the narrative as well. The push-backs (or negotiations) between Naomi and Ruth, between Naomi and the women, are examples of wild instances within the narrative; the relocation of the narrative and the overpowering Davidic agenda are examples of wild instances behind the narrative; and the refusal of the PBS interpreters to let Orpah walk away, or to let Ruth die, are examples of wild instances in front of the narrative.

The PBS bible studies may thus be seen as opportunities to re-wild bible and biblical studies. In this connection, re-wilding can take place with normal people shedding light (pun intended) on the reading of biblical texts. In both contexts, bible and biblical studies, normal people have something to teach about biblical texts.

Hiku

Talanoa usually ends with a *hiku* (tail) in the form of a song, a riddle, or another talanoa. The hiku serves two functions: first, similar to the tail of the moana, the hiku of a talanoa may be a 'calming place' where participants in talanoa (like the tired creatures of moana) may rest and let their wounds heal. Second, similar to the tail of a bird, the hiku of a talanoa may give it balance as it soars (away).[10] For these reasons, each chapter ends with 'Prompts for further talanoa'.

After some time, with further reflection, the hiku of a talanoa often returns to haunt, trouble and disturb. In my case, what happened at the gate is haunting. The process of redemption was sealed with the witness of the elders and the gathered crowd. In the enticing world of faith, as well as in the lucrative commentary business, witnesses confirm and conclude matters that may be contested. On that note, what else did the witnesses at the gate confirm and conclude?

> They also witnessed the commodification of a foreign woman – Ruth.
> They also witnessed the dispossession and dismemberment of a dead relative – Mahlon.
> They also witnessed the lineage of 'Elimelek' – my God is king – pushed *out of place*.

Prompts for further talanoa

out of place 3[11]

i look out
from a room that has become a working place
from a kitchen that is still open for more learning
from a dwelling that has become a crossing
from a home that feels like a prison

i look out
into silent skies, still huffing and puffing stain and pollution
touching shores still littered with the rubbish of civilization
masking the tears and fears of transmission and infection
that burden the black, the brown and the refuse of election

i look out
into ghostly streets, drained of intentions and chances
and i see parents desperate to transport their family to the
next day
and i see pests and beasts, hovering with no load to yoke
and i see masked leaders buzzing like mosquitoes
looking for lives and wealth to suck

i look out
and feel islands ravaged by the cyclones of climate denial
and beaches having a break from burning tourists
and slopes of trees, so far to even feel their breeze
and neighbours, so close yet so far

i look out
from our place, with my body and my imagination
and i feel other places, other bodies and other imaginations
that, like mine, are also out of place

i look out
because other arts, other strokes, other ways
other wisdoms, other eyes, other voices
other winds, other spirits, other waters
other bodies, other graveyards, other ancestors
other tears, other 'rears, and other others
can let me come out from
out of place

December 22
when Ma'ata Fe'aomoelotu returned to
her parents and ancestors
at lolofonua, langi, whenua, moana

Notes

1 Boaz's early morning departure brings to mind Abraham, who set off early in the morning to sacrifice his child (Gen. 22.3). This intertextual suggestion is another example of acclimatization taking place in reading.

2 For example, the influence of the patriarchal agenda and the dominating Christian project (which capitalized on the lineage of David, see Chapter 9) behind the narrative.

3 There are other political (e.g. inheritance, land), economic (e.g. redemption) and theological (e.g. providence, grace) points of intersection but i opt to tease out the more scandalous one for Christian communities.

4 The Christian project has taken this drive further, to the edges of the 'new world', under the wings of Christian empires that preached colonial expansion justified by the 'doctrine of discovery'. Put simply, colonization and coloniality are extreme manifestations of acclimatization.

5 This option was appealing because it was unusual. Instead of the father disappearing, the PBS interpreters imagined what it would mean if the mother disappeared but left the father with the child(ren), which also occurs in Pasifika.

6 Seasoned tellers of talanoa hold something back, as baits to draw their listeners into conversation (talanoa). These baits usually end up becoming the highlights of the talanoa event.

7 To an extent, the monkey saying ('monkey see, monkey do') applies to us in the commentary business: readers see, readers (under) write.

8 I'm appealing here to Audre Lorde's feel of frustration, that one cannot dismantle the master's house with the master's tools.

9 In the bible studies, 'behind' also refers to something that was presumed by the narrative but not named by the narrator.

10 The hiku of the Ruth narrative is the genealogy of David which was added to tame the narrative. The PBS reading (see Chapter 9), on the other hand, prompted the narrative to fly. Herein is another invitation to labourers in bible and biblical studies, and in the commentary business, to let the hiku of biblical texts and the hiku of interpretations soar.

11 There are two 'out of places' under whose wings this one flies: Edward Said, *Out of Place: A Memoir* (1999) and Jione Havea and Clive Pearson (eds), *Out of Place: Doing Theology on the Crosscultural Brink* (2010).

Bibliography

Althaus-Reid, Marcella, 2005, *The Queer God*, London and New York: Routledge, 2005.

Althaus-Reid, Marcella and Lisa Isherwood, 2007, 'Thinking Theology and Queer Theory', *Feminist Theology*, 15.3, pp. 302–14.

Amit, Yairah, 2001, *Reading Biblical Narratives: Literary Criticism and the Hebrew Bible*, Minneapolis, MN: Augsburg Fortress.

Anzaldúa, Gloria E., 1987, *Borderlands: La Fontera – The New Mestiza*, San Francisco, CA: Aunt Lute Books.

Avalos, Hector, 2007, *The End of Biblical Studies*, New York: Prometheus.

Bareket, Elinoar, 2017, 'Chesed: A Reciprocal Covenant', *TheTorah. com* (https://thetorah.com/article/chesed-a-reciprocal-covenant, accessed 5.5.21).

Becking, Bob, 2021, 'Review of Johanna W. H. van Wijk-Bos', in *The Land and Its Kings: 1 – 2 Kings*, Grand Rapids, MI: Eerdmans, 2020, in *Review of Biblical Literature*, vol. 2 (www.sblcentral.org/API/Reviews/13740_71473.pdf, accessed 5.5.21).

Black, Fiona C. and Jennifer L. Koosed (eds), 2019, *Reading with Feeling: Affect Theory and the Bible*, Atlanta, GA: SBL Publications.

Block, Daniel I., 2015, *Ruth*, Exegetical Commentary on the Old Testament: A Discourse Analysis of the Hebrew Bible, Grand Rapids, MI: Zondervan.

Boer, Roland, 2007, *Rescuing the Bible*, Malden: Blackwell.

Brenner, Athalya (ed.), 1993, *A Feminist Companion to Ruth*, Sheffield: Sheffield Academic.

Brenner, Athalya (ed.), 1999, *A Feminist Companion to Ruth and Esther*, Sheffield: Sheffield Academic.

Brett, Mark G., 2018, 'Redeeming Country: Indigenous Peoples under Empires and Nation States', in Jione Havea (ed.), *Religion and Power*, Lanham, MD: Lexington Books, pp. 176–82.

Callahan, Allen Dwight, 2006, *The Talking Book: African Americans and the Bible*, New Haven, CT: Yale University Press.

Champion, Denise, 2014, *Yarta Wandatha*, Salisbury (South Australia): Uniting Aboriginal and Islander Christian Congress.

Chukka, Sweety Helen, 2021, 'Reading Her Story in His Narration: Zuleika and Her Otherness in Genesis 39', in Jione Havea and Monical Jyotsna Melanchthon (eds), *Bible Blindspots: Dispersions and Othering* (forthcoming), Eugene, OR: Pickwick.

De La Torre, Miguel A., 2021, 'The Colonial Oppressiveness of a Biblical Concept: Hospitality', in Jione Havea (ed.), *Mediating Theology* (forthcoming), Leipzig: Evangelische Verlagsanstalt.

Dokotum, Okaka Opio, 2013, 'Re-Membering the Tutsi Genocide in *Hotel Rwanda* (2004): Implications for Peace and Reconciliation', *African Conflict and Peacebuilding Review*, 3.2, pp. 129–50.

Donaldson, Laura E., 1999, 'The Sign of Orpah: Reading Ruth through Native Eyes', in Athalya Brenner (ed.), *A Feminist Companion to Ruth and Esther*, Sheffield: Sheffield Academic, pp. 130–44.

Dube, Musa W., 1999, 'The Unpublished Letters of Orpah to Ruth', in Athalya Brenner (ed.), *A Feminist Companion to Ruth and Esther*, Sheffield: Sheffield Academic, pp. 145–50.

Dube, Musa W., 2014, 'Boundaries and Bridges: Journeys of a Postcolonial Feminist in Biblical Studies', *Journal of the European Society of Women in Theological Research*, vol. 22, pp. 139–56.

Elvey, Anne, 2020, 'Climate as Context', in Jione Havea (ed.), *Theological and Hermeneutical Explorations from Australia: Horizons of Contextuality*, Lanham, MD: Lexington Books, pp. 125–38.

Eskenazi, Tamara Cohn and Tikva Frymer-Kensky, 2011, *Ruth*, The JPS Bible Commentary, Philadelphia, PA: Jewish Publication Society.

Fentress-Williams, Judy, 2012, *Ruth*, Abingdon Old Testament Commentaries. Nashville, TN: Abingdon.

Fewell, Danna Nolan and David M. Gunn, 1992, *Gender, Power and Promise: The Subject of the Bible's First Story*, Nashville, TN, Abingdon.

Fewell, Danna Nolan and David Miller Gunn, 1990, *Compromising Redemption: Relating Characters in the Book of Ruth*, Louisville, KY: Westminster/John Knox.

Fewell, Danna Nolan, 2017, 'The Ones Returning: Ruth, Naomi, and Social Negotiation in the Post-Exilic Period', in Katherine E. Southwood and Martien Halvorson-Taylor (eds), *Women and Exilic Identity in the Hebrew Bible*, London: Bloomsbury, pp. 23–40.

Gaffney, Wil, 2009, 'Ruth', in Hugh R. Page Jnr et al. (eds), *The African Bible: Reading Israel's Scriptures from Africa and the African Diaspora*, Minneapolis, MN: Fortress, pp. 249–54.

Giles, Terry and William J. Doan, 2016, *The Naomi Story – The Book of Ruth: From Gender to Politics*, Eugene, OR: Cascade.

Greene, Gayle, 1991, 'Feminist Fiction and the Uses of Memory', *Signs*, 16.2, pp. 290–321.

Gunn, David M. and Danna Nolan Fewell, 1993, *Narrative in the Hebrew Bible*, Oxford: Oxford University Press.

Gunn, David M., 1980, *Fate of King Saul: An Interpretation of a Biblical Story*, Sheffield: Sheffield Academic Press.

Habel, Norman, 2011, *The Birth, the Curse and the Greening of Earth: An Ecological Reading of Genesis 1–11*, Sheffield: Sheffield Phoenix Press.

Havea, Jione, 2003, *Elusions of Control: Biblical Law on the Words of Women*, Atlanta, GA: SBL Publications.

Havea, Jione, 2010, 'The Politics of Climate Change, a Talanoa from Oceania', *International Journal of Public Theology*, 4, pp. 345–55.

Havea, Jione (ed.), 2021a, *Doing Theology in the New Normal*, London: SCM Press.

Havea, Jione (ed.), 2021b, *Mediating Theology*, Leipzig: Evangelische Verlagsanstalt.

Havea, Jione (ed.), 2021c, *Theologies from the Pacific*, New York: Palgrave.

Hereniko, Vilisoni, 2004, *Pear ta Ma 'on Maf* (The Land Has Eyes), Suva: PBS.

Jobling, David, 1998, *1 Samuel*, Collegeville, MN: Liturgical Press.

Jones III, Edward Allen, 2016, *Reading Ruth in the Restoration Period: A Call for Inclusion*, London: Bloomsbury.

Kamaara, Eunice Karanja, 2020, 'Who is Christ for Ali? Refugees in a Post-Truth Age', in Jione Havea et al. (eds), *Mission and Context*, Lanham, MD: Lexington Books, pp. 63–76.

Kates, Judith A. and Gail Twersky Reimer, 1994, *Reading Ruth: Contemporary Women Reclaim a Sacred Story*, New York: Ballantine.

Koosed, Jennifer L., 2011, *Gleaning Ruth: A Biblical Heroine and Her Afterlives*, Columbia, SC: University of South Carolina.

Korpel, Mario C. A., 2001, *The Structure of the Book of Ruth*, Assen: Van Gorcum.

Laffey, Alice L. and Mahri Leonard-Fleckman, 2017, *Ruth*, Collegeville, MN: Liturgical.

Lau, Peter H. W., 2010, *Identity and Ethics in the Book of Ruth: A Social Identity Approach*, Berlin: De Gruyter.

Lau, Peter H. W. and Gregory Goswell, 2016, *Unceasing Kindness: A Biblical Theology of Ruth*, Downers Grove, IL: InterVarsity Press.

Levy, Barry, 2016, 'What Was Esther's Relationship to Mordecai?', *TheTorah.com* (www.thetorah.com/article/what-was-esthers-relationship-to-mordechai, accessed 5.5.21).

Linafelt, Tod, 1999, *Ruth*, Berit Olam: Studies in Hebrew Narrative and Poetry, Collegeville, MN: Liturgical Press.

Ma'ilo, Mosese, 2018, 'Island Prodigals: Encircling the Void in Luke 15:11–32 with Albert Wendt', in Jione Havea (ed.), *Sea of Readings: The Bible and the South Pacific*, Atlanta, GA: SBL Publications, pp. 23–36.

McLeod, Jason, 2015, *Merdeka and the Morning Star: Civil Resistance in West Papua*, St. Lucia: University of Queensland Press.

Melanchthon, Monica Jyotsna, 2021, 'Women Masculinity: Hindu India and Second Temple Judah', in Jione Havea and Monica Jyotsna Melanchthon (eds), *Bible Blindspots: Dispersion and Othering* (forthcoming), Eugene, OR: Pickwick.

Moore, Stephen D., 2001, *God's Beauty Parlor and other Queer Spaces in and around the Bible*, Stanford: Stanford University Press.

Murray, A. W., 1885, *The Martyrs of Polynesia: Memorials of Missionaries, Native Evangelists, and Native Converts, Who Have Died by the Hand of Violence, from 1799 to 1871*. London: Elliot Stock.

Packett, C. Neville, 1971, *Guide to the Republic of Nauru*, Yorkshire: Lloyds Bank Chambers.

Pouono, Terry, 2021, '*Taulaga* in the Samoan Church: Is it Wise Giving?' in Jione Havea (ed.), *Theologies from the Pacific* (forthcoming), New York: Palgrave.

Powell, Stephanie Day, 2018, *Narrative Desire and the Book of Ruth*, London: Bloomsbury.

Reddie, Anthony G., 2019, *Theologising Brexit: A Liberationist and Postcolonial Critique*, London: Routledge.

Rogers, Garth (ed.), 1986, *The Fire has Jumped: Eyewitness accounts of the eruption and evacuation of Niuafo'ou, Tonga*, Suva: Institute of Pacific Studies, University of the South Pacific.

Sakenfeld, Katharine Doob, 1999, *Ruth*, Interpretation: A Bible Commentary for Teaching and Preaching, Louisville, KY: John Knox.

Schipper, Jeremy, 2016, *Ruth: A New Translation with Introduction and Commentary*, AB, New Haven, CT: Yale University Press.

Scott, James C., 1990, *Domination and the Arts of Resistance: Hidden Transcripts*, New Haven, CT: Yale University Press.

Sinnott, Alice M., 2020, *Ruth: An Earth Bible Commentary*, London: Bloomsbury.

Spivak, Gayatri C., 1988, 'Can the subaltern speak?' in Cary Nelson and Lawrence Grossberg (eds), *Marxism and the Interpretation of Culture*, pp. 271–313. Urbana and Chicago: University of Illinois Press.

Stone, Ken, 2001, 'Homosexuality and the Bible or Queer Reading? A Response to Martti Nissinen', *Theology & Sexuality* 14: 107–118.

Storie, Deborah, 2020, 'Mission and Violent Conflict: Seeking *Shalom*', in Jione Havea et al. (eds), *Mission and Context*, Lanham, MD: Lexington Books, pp. 165–178.

Talia, Maina, 2021, '*Kauafua fātele* for Christ'sake: A Theological Dance for the Changing Climate', in Jione Havea (ed.), *Theologies from the Pacific* (forthcoming), New York: Palgrave.

Taule'ale'ausumai, Feiloaiga, 2021, 'Pasifika Churches Trapped in the Missionary Era: A Case in Samoa', in Jione Havea (ed.), *Theologies from the Pacific* (forthcoming), New York: Palgrave.

Tengan, Ty P. Kāwika, 2008, 'Re-membering Panalā'au: Masculinities, Nation, and Empire in Hawai'i and the Pacific', *The Contemporary Pacific* 20.1: 27–53.

Tomlinson, Matt, 2020, *God Is Samoan: Dialogues between Culture and Theology in the Pacific*, Honolulu, HI: University of Hawai'i Press.

Townes, Emilie M., 2016, 'The Road We Are Traveling', in Gay L. Byron and Vanessa Lovelace (eds), *Womanist Interpretations of the Bible: Expanding the Discourse*, pp. 359–368, Atlanta, GA: SBL Publications.

Vaai, Upolu Lumā, 2021a, 'A Dirtified God: A Dirt Theology from the Pacific Dirt Communities', in Jione Havea (ed.), *Christian and Native Theologies from the Pacific* (forthcoming), New York: Palgrave.

Vaai, Upolu Lumā, 2021b, '*Lagimālie*: Covid, De-Onefication of Theologies, and Eco-Relational Wellbeing', in Jione Havea (ed.), *Doing Theology in the New Normal* (forthcoming), London: SCM Press.

Vaai, Upolu Lumā and Aisake Casimira (eds), 2017, *Relational Hermeneutics: Decolonizing our Mindsets and the Pacific Itulagi*, Suva: University of the South Pacific and Pacific Theological College.

Van Wolde, Ellen, 1997 [1993], *Ruth and Naomi*, London: SCM Press.

Venter, Pieter M., 2018, 'The Dissolving of Marriages in Ezra 9–10 and Nehemiah Revisited', *HTS Teologiese Studies/Theological Studies*, 74(40), a4854 (https://doi. org/10.4102/hts.v74i4.4854, accessed 5.5.21).

Weeramantry, C. G., 1992, *Nauru: Environmental Damage under International Trusteeship*, London: Oxford University Press.

Wendt, Albert, 1973, *Sons for the Return Home*, Auckland, NZ: Penguin.

West, Mona, 2006, 'Ruth', in Deryn Guest et al. (eds), *The Queer Bible Commentary*, London: SCM Press, pp. 190–4.

West, Mona, 2020, 'Ruth, Naomi, and Boaz as a Family of Choice', in *Sex & Bible*, kindle edition, Point of View Publishing.

White Jnr, Lynn, 1967, 'The Historical Roots of our Ecologic Crisis', *Science*, 155, pp. 1203–7.

Yee, Gale A., 2020, 'Thinking Intersectionally: Gender, Race, Class, and the Etceteras of Our Discipline', *Journal of Biblical Literature*, 139, pp. 7–26.

Yothu Yindi, 1991, 'Treaty', in *Tribal Voice* (CD).

Yothu Yindi, 2000, 'Gone is the Land', in *Garma* (CD).

Index of Biblical Women

(Outside of the Ruth narrative)

Index of Biblical Texts

(Outside of the book of Ruth)

Old Testament

New Testament